BATTLING

CORRUPTION

IN

AMERICA'S

PUBLIC

SCHOOLS

BATTLING

CORRUPTION

IN

AMERICA'S

PUBLIC

SCHOOLS

LYDIA G. SEGAL

with a foreword by James B. Jacobs

Northeastern University Press · Boston

NORTHEASTERN UNIVERSITY PRESS

Library of Congress Cataloging-in-Publication Data
Segal, Lydia G.
   Battling corruption in America's public schools / Lydia G. Segal.
      p.   cm.
Includes bibliographical references and index.
      ISBN 1–55553–584–4   (cloth : alk. paper)
      1. Public schools—Corrupt practices—Illinois—Chicago—Case studies.
2. Public schools—Corrupt practices—California—Los Angeles—Case
studies.   3. Public schools—Corrupt practices—New York (State)—New
York—Case studies.   4. Education, Urban—Illinois—Chicago—Case
studies.   5. Education, Urban—California—Los Angeles—Case studies.
6. Education, Urban—New York (State)—New York—Case studies.   I.
Title.
   LC5133.C4S44   2004
      371.01'0977'11—dc21   2003008319

Designed by Steve Kress
Composed in New Baskerville by Creative Graphics, Inc., in Allentown,
Pennsylvania.
Printed and bound by Thomson-Shore, Inc., in Dexter, Michigan. The paper is
Dexter Offset Natural, an acid-free sheet.

MANUFACTURED IN THE UNITED STATES OF AMERICA
08   07   06   05   04   5   4   3   2   1

To Tulku Rinpoche Thondup,
by whose loving presence
I am sustained

CONTENTS

The appearance of this splendid book is cause for celebration. Professor Lydia Segal has produced a work of mature scholarship, governed by her strong voice and based on her own research and theoretical analysis. It will stand for many years as the leading work on the pathology of the urban school bureaucracy.

Battling Corruption in America's Public Schools throws down the gauntlet to proponents of public school reform. If the problem of school reform were not complicated and intractable enough, Professor Segal has illuminated protracted systemic corruption rooted deep in the structure, organization, and operation of the nation's largest school systems. Even worse, she shows how this systemic corruption distorts the school systems' priorities, putting children's education last. And the situation is exacerbated by certain centrally mandated anticorruption controls that do not prevent—and perhaps generate—corruption while blocking initiative, creativity, and effective decision making at the level of the individual schools.

This book forces us to consider whether urban public school systems can be fixed. To be sure, more money will not cure the problems that Lydia Segal has exposed. As with foreign aid to many developing countries, the money never gets to the recipients for whom it is ultimately intended. Rather, it is siphoned off via corruption, waste, and abuse.

Professor Segal's recommendations for decentralization and reorganization are sensible and surely worth trying. She suggests breaking up the urban school bureaucracy by essentially turning every school into a self-sufficient charter school free from bureaucratic mandates, reshaping the school system, and privatizing various operations. Although, as she notes, the resistance to reform of urban school bureaucracies is formidable, the need for such radical structural change could hardly be more pressing.

James B. Jacobs
Warren E. Burger Professor of Law and
Director, Center for Research in Crime and Justice,
New York University School of Law

Though long passionate about public education, I became involved in it in an unusual way. After graduating from Harvard Law School, I interned in the Manhattan District Attorney's Office for Edward Stancik, then head of the Rackets Bureau there. A short time later, as tales of public school jobs in New York City being sold for sex and cash filled the airwaves, Mayor David Dinkins appointed Stancik to head a new $3-million agency, the Special Commissioner of Investigation for the New York City Schools (SCI), to investigate school fraud and make recommendations for systemic reform. When Stancik asked me to join his team, I jumped at the chance to be part of an agency that promised to clean up a system that seemed desperately to need it.

For three years, from 1991 through 1994, I led dozens of investigations as special counsel, interviewed many witnesses under oath, listened to numerous conversations secretly recorded by confidential informants, and contributed to developing the office's policies on various legal issues, ranging from sting operations to protecting confidential informants.

To hear phrases such as *sting operation* and *informant* in the context of public education and children was terribly disturbing. But at the time I joined the office, New York City was still in the throes of its twenty-six-year experiment with political community control of schools, which had invited a level of corruption that recalled the days of Tammany Hall. Allegations of different kinds of wrongdoing, particularly political patronage by local community school board members, flooded the SCI. A steady stream of employees, some motivated by years of sheer frustration in dealing with the school bureaucracy, others by the wish to get even with those who had allegedly gypped them out of their share of boodle, offered secretly to record conversations with their acolytes. These conversations opened an extraordinary window into a hidden Kafkaesque world where people with starkly contrasting motivations shared criminal labels.

On one side of this underworld were people like some local board members who transformed their school districts into patronage mills, handing out jobs and contracts to friends, lovers, and campaign workers. These board members, who referred to themselves as *godfathers* and *godmothers,* talked primarily about *making deals* and getting *pieces,* or patronage hires. Words such as *children* and *education* were not part of their daily vocabulary except insofar as they could be exploited as a source of patronage, power, or money.

On the other side were principals and administrators who furtively colluded to break the cumbersome school regulations and union contracts that prevented them from doing their jobs effectively. These people clearly cared about educating children. They risked punishment and the ire of unions by illegally paying unauthorized people to fix leaky toilets and wire classrooms for computer use so that they could be ready by the first day of class. They conspired with vendors to buy equipment prohibited by the bureaucracy, such as extralarge computer screens for their sight-impaired pupils.

SCI's findings triggered numerous largely beneficial reforms, including a state law that all but dismantled the local school boards, thus vastly reducing political patronage. However, abuses continued in some pockets of the system, and many dedicated employees remained trapped in a dysfunctional organization.

I became convinced that, for lasting reform, it was necessary to bring to light the disparate problems that the school system generated and tackle their root causes. I joined the faculty of John Jay College of Criminal Justice, City University of New York, where I teach law and public administration in its undergraduate, masters, and doctoral programs. And I determined to write a book.

With the support of the Smith Richardson and John M. Olin Foundations, I immersed myself in decades of reports and articles on the New York City public schools. I also delved into hundreds of reports on America's second- and third-largest school districts, Los Angeles and Chicago, interviewed many officials there, and published a number of articles on school management and corruption reform. Two of these articles, published in *Public Administration Review,* have been adapted in Chapters 12, 13, 14, and 16.

I had nearly finished my manuscript when I had the opportunity to join the School Design Project directed by Dr. William G. Ouchi, professor of business administration at the Anderson School of Business at the University of California at Los Angeles. The project, funded in part by the National Science Foundation, examined the effects of organizational structure in six school districts in North America: the three largest—New York City, Los Angeles, and Chicago—and the three most decentralized—Houston, Seattle, and Edmonton, Canada. My role was to study accountability and control in each district, affording me the opportunity to expand on the themes I had begun researching.

For over a year, as part of the School Design Project, I conducted dozens of in-depth interviews with central, school, and union officials, school inspectors general, and auditors. I interviewed consultants, assistant district attorneys, and members of local watchdog groups. I have incorporated some of the data and materials gathered during that year into this book. The material enriches my study of the New York City, Los Angeles, and Chicago school districts and enables me to offer hope that real reform is possible through the example of Edmonton, Canada. The material in Chapter 18, which discusses Edmonton, is part of what I gathered for the School Design Project.

This book is dedicated to calling attention to the root flaws in America's three largest school districts and providing recommendations for what to do about them. I sincerely hope that it will bring a new perspective to the debate about school reform in all large urban districts and help instigate the profound changes necessary for our children's future.

I am enormously grateful to Professor James B. Jacobs of New York University Law School for his support and encouragement since I joined the academy. His comments on my writings have always led me to push myself harder. Our conversations have energized my thinking.

I am also greatly indebted to Dr. William G. Ouchi of the Anderson School of Management at the University of California at Los Angeles for the wonderful opportunity to collaborate on his pioneering School Design Project, for kindergarten through twelfth grade, and for generously letting me use some of that data in this book. He obtained entree to the highest-level officials in all six school districts we studied, affording a rare opportunity for in-depth research.

I am thankful to the late Edward F. Stancik, Special Commissioner of Investigation for the New York City Schools, for the unique opportunity to serve in his office and learn about the largest school system in the nation. His successor, Commissioner Richard Condon, and the office's talented staff, notably Deputy Commissioner Regina Loughran, Chief Investigator Tom Comiskey, and Donald Schwally, have been very important to my research.

I owe special gratitude to Professor John Kleinig of John Jay College for his support, helpful comments on all my writings, and the insight he has shared with me over many years. Professors Diane Ravitch, Joseph Viteritti, Nathan Glazer, Frank Anechiarico, Bruce Cooper, Eli Silverman, Todd Clear, Barry Latzer, Tom Repetto, Robert McCrie, Patrick O'Hara, Daniel Vona, Steve Kline, and William Heffernan have also given me helpful suggestions and sparked many ideas over the years. Barbara Porcopalaia lent her expert skill to create clear organizational charts. Bruce Cooper, Tim DeRoche, and Carolyn Brown were invaluable in helping me analyze school budgetary information. My thanks also go to the many school officials who shared a wealth of invaluable insights about their districts, including Beverly Donohue, chief financial officer of the New York City schools; Richard Lindsay, head of school construction in Houston; Don Mullinax, school inspector general in Los Angeles; Maribeth Vander Weele, former school inspector general in Chicago; Louis Benevento, executive director of the Division of Financial Operations in New York City; James Lonergan, director of building services for the New York City schools; and numerous others whose names I have kept confidential or changed, as noted in the book, to protect their privacy.

I greatly appreciate Northeastern University Press acquisition editors William Frohlich and Sarah Rowley and former editor Scott Brassart for believing in me and offering many wise suggestions. I feel very fortunate to have had the exquisite copyediting of Gretchen Smith Mui, who made important improvements throughout the manuscript, and the expertise of production editor Emily McKeigue and associate director Jill Bahcall.

The research and writing of this book were made possible by the generous support of the Smith Richardson and John M. Olin Foundations. I also thank those foundations that sponsored the School Design Project: the National Science Foundation (Grant no. 0115559), the Frank and Kathy Baxter Family Foundation, Dr. Peter Bing, the John M. Olin Foundation, and the Thomas B. Fordham Foundation.

I am more grateful than I can express to my parents, Fred and Micheline Segal, for so many years of nurturing and encouragement. Their appreciation sweetens everything I do.

I could not have written this book without the loving presence of Tulku Thondup Rinpoche, who has given me fortitude at every step, day in and day out, for many years.

As the United States faces global competition from national economies fueled by excellent public education systems, school reform is among our
country's most pressing concerns. Experts warn that as U.S. students continue to fall increasingly behind those of other countries in core subjects
like math and science,[1] graduates will not have the skills necessary to make
a comfortable living, allowing other economies with superior school systems to outpace ours.[2] The longer our children stay in school, moreover,
the worse they do in relation to other nations. American fourth graders
came in seventh among thirty-eight countries in math and science in
1996. By eighth grade, in 1999, they came in twenty-first, behind even
small countries like the Slovak Republic.[3]

While such overall trends are distressing, the problem with American
education is in our great city schools, particularly the inner city—not in
suburban or rural schools, many of which are successes by most measures.
It is in cities such as New York, Chicago, Los Angeles, Detroit, and Philadelphia where the largest numbers of children cannot read, write, and
compute at acceptable levels and where racial gaps between whites and
blacks and Latinos are widest.[4] It is in large cities that minority boys in particular, trapped in poor schools, have the greatest chance of flunking out
and getting sucked into the downward spiral of crime and prison.[5] Public-
school pupils from large cities are also less likely to take college entrance
tests such as the SAT than pupils from the rest of their state. If they do,
they tend to score lower than state averages.[6]

It is also in many of our great cities where school buildings that in the
1920s and 1930s stood out as glorious emblems of the era's top municipal
architecture are now dilapidated, their parapets falling, their libraries
bare. Many teachers go without basic teaching supplies.[7] Parents have to
buy "crayons, soap, tissues and even toilet paper" at some schools.[8] A number of students have to stand because there are no chairs. In Los Angeles,
some school toilets do not have running water. "It is no wonder that the
kids are near rioting" and that "good teachers leave," one prominent Los
Angeles architect commented of the public school students in that city.[9]
This view was echoed by California's bipartisan Little Hoover Commission,
which has studied public schools in that state for decades.[10]

As employers lose confidence in graduates' readiness for work, the hopes of many young people for a better future are shattered. As one advertising chief executive officer summed up the graduates of New York City public schools: "It is almost impossible to hire competent clerical and/or entry-level help for administrative work from the New York City schools."[11]

The crisis has sparked a heated debate about how to revive urban public schools and about the efficacy of vast infusions of money, talent, and reforms. Experts have tried dozens of good ideas, from charter school legislation and higher standards, to technology in the classroom and alliances with business, to uniforms and vouchers. Some of the nation's best and brightest have lent a hand. A string of superintendents with impressive track records as educators, state governors, corporate lawyers, former prosecutors, and businesspeople have been hired to try to turn districts around in cities from New York and Chicago to Los Angeles and San Diego.

Meanwhile, per-pupil spending on public education has soared in the past thirty years, and big city school bureaucracies have burgeoned.[12] From 1997 through 2000, school spending in New York City went up by 30 percent, for instance, while enrollment rose only by 2 percent.[13] At the same time, the average amount spent per pupil since 1970 in that city has risen faster than the rate of increase in the U.S.'s real per capita income over that time.[14] From 1997 to 2000 alone, per-pupil spending rose by 20 percent in inflation-adjusted terms.

But despite these efforts, virtually no large city school districts have shown improvement in math and reading scores in the past five to ten years.[15] Sure, some individual schools here and there have made amazing turnarounds. Sure, the charter school movement has enhanced various schools in many cities. But as Diane Ravitch and other scholars point out, none of these successes has translated into districtwide improvement.[16] Sadly, with the exception of a few bright spots such as Houston, which has aimed to free every one of its schools from bureaucratic controls and which in the fall of 2002 was cited by the Broad Foundation as the best city school system in the United States and awarded $500,000,[17] large urban school systems appear to be largely impervious to meaningful broad-based reform.

It is telling that Mayor Rudolph Giuliani was able to improve almost every facet of New York City except its schools. He got the smut out of Times Square, the mob out of the Fulton Fish Market, and entrenched corruption out of the Jacob Javitz Center. He made it feel safe to ride subways after the notorious Bernard Goetz incident a decade earlier. Even the "Teflon Don," as John Gotti Jr., the flamboyant head of the Gambino crime family was known, was brought low under his administration.

But try as he might, Giuliani could not raise student test scores, fix tat-
tered school buildings, reduce waste, or change the way the schools delivered education. Part of the reason was that he did not have full control
over the school system. The New York City Board of Education (BOE) had
long been semiautonomous from city hall, as reflected by its move in 1939
from Manhattan, the seat of mayoral power, to Brooklyn across the East
River.[18] Although Giuliani fought for the reins to the system, the state legislature repeatedly refused to hand them over. (The state did eventually
put the mayor in command of schools in summer 2002—but only after
Giuliani's term had ended and his successor, Michael Bloomberg, a successful businessman whose education agenda was unknown and who
posed no obvious threat to the education establishment, was ensconced in
the office. Bloomberg then took the symbolic steps of moving school administrators back to Manhattan in the old Tweed Courthouse in city hall's
backyard and renaming the agency the Department of Education.)

But Giuliani's lack of control over the school system cannot fully explain why it remained the one bastion of government almost wholly impervious to his administration's urban improvement efforts. Even without
direct control, Giuliani could still exert influence on the schools. He managed, after all, to pressure two chancellors—Raymond Cortines and Rudy
Crew—to step down. After Cortines publicly trumpeted a new collective
bargaining agreement with the powerful school custodian union as a major breakthrough, Giuliani rejected it as a farce and led a renegotiation of
the contract on the school system's behalf, in an incident that undoubtedly
contributed to Cortines's departure. He also managed to force the Board
of Education to make its budget more transparent—a battle that many
previous mayors had taken on, only to be defeated by seemingly endless
stonewalling and litigation by the school system. Giuliani also helped
shepherd through the state legislature a revolutionary school-reform bill
that stripped the city's thirty-two community school boards of twenty-five
years of treasured hiring and budgetary powers. But despite all this, Giuliani could not get into the innards of the system to improve achievement,
significantly reduce waste, or fix school buildings.

CORRUPTION AND HOW EDUCATION IS DELIVERED

One impediment to reform that no one is seriously studying in the debate
over how to improve public schools is systemic fraud, waste, and abuse.
This omission is surprising because a number of school districts, particularly large urban ones, have compiled impressive records of fraud and
waste.

In New York City, decades of law enforcement investigations, city and state audits, political commission reports, grand jury reports, citizen group studies, and media exposes paint a portrait of a school system that has been afflicted by wrongs: theft, extortion, political patronage, nepotism, bribery, fraud, and even alleged murders and suicides. Investigations of other large urban school systems, including Chicago, Detroit, Los Angeles, Washington, D.C., Jersey City, and Newark, have revealed similar abuses.

But most education experts gloss over school corruption records as if they were irrelevant or at best incidental to education reform.[19] In what perhaps typifies the attitude of many scholars, one prominent expert commented that the school scandals in Chicago during the 1980s and early 1990s were "easy things to repair compared to changing the way education has been delivered."[20] He apparently never considered that one problem might be tied to the other. But the evidence suggests that corruption and the way public education is delivered are interwoven in many ways.

First, the record suggests that the consequences of fraud and waste on learning can be devastating. The most academically beleaguered school systems tend to be the ones with the longest, most serious, most systemic investigative records. Districts such as Jersey City and Newark, New Jersey, Roosevelt on Long Island, and Lawrence, Massachusetts, where chronic academic failure has prompted state takeovers, revocation of school licenses, and other drastic measures, have also been plagued by theft, fraud, waste, and mismanagement. Their records are in stark contrast to those of more academically successful urban districts such as Houston, Seattle, and Edmonton, Canada, where the incidence of waste and abuse is far lower and the severity is less.

This pattern is evident within school districts, too. In New York City, where the public school system was for many years divided into thirty-two local community school districts, local school districts most beleaguered by corruption tended to rank lowest in math and reading scores. Local districts with the highest test scores, on the other hand, had the fewest cases.

Although poor pupil performance on tests has many causes, there are many ways in which corruption and waste could plausibly harm learning. Theft and fraud deplete resources and libraries, often hitting hardest those districts that can least afford them. Payroll padding siphons millions of dollars a year from the classroom. Kickback schemes involving textbook companies have resulted in children receiving dated, discarded books. Fraud has contributed to dilapidated buildings where children sit in broken chairs under gaping holes in the ceiling and go without basic supplies like toilet paper. In Chicago, some schoolchildren had to learn in decrepit hallways and bathrooms during a decade of unbridled extortion, theft, and bribery by central school facilities administrators and contractors.[21] Meanwhile, dedicated teachers and principals become demoralized and eventually leave, draining districts of talent they desperately need.

Second, while some experts dismiss scandals as mere surface rashes on the periphery of school systems, they are driven by far deeper pathologies within. Corruption is in a sense a symptom of something else gone awry. The underlying illness, moreover, causes not just corruption in the modern sense of illegality but also corruption in the broader, classical sense of the term *corruptio,* meaning perversion of purpose.[22]

This book suggests that the root of the problem lies in the ever-tighter traditional corruption controls—the layers of bureaucratic oversight; the detailed standard operating procedures, rules, and regulations; and the over-specification of money—that schools imposed on their operations over the decades. These control mechanisms were supposed to ensure against fraud and waste. But as urban schools grew larger, they have actually eroded oversight, discouraged managers from focusing on performance, and made it so difficult to do business with districts that employees and contractors have sometimes had to seek "creative" or illicit ways to get their jobs done. The result is the worst of two worlds: Crooks who want to bilk the system can do so because the top has little handle on what is going on below, but employees who want to improve learning must sometimes break the rules.

FROM THE PROBLEM, A REMEDY

The problem suggests the remedy. Since the root of the pathology is the consuming effort by school headquarters to control virtually every detail of what happens below, the answer must be to loosen top-down controls, push decision-making authority down the chain of command, and find other ways to check employee behavior. The premise implicit in cumbersome school bureaucracies is that red tape is the price that must be paid to fight waste and corruption. However, not only do current control devices not work in large districts; better ways exist to check misbehavior that can also help the system function better.

This book advocates radically reshaping school districts to put real decision-making authority in the hands of principals and local school managers. It recommends a new balance between accountability for job performance and fiscal compliance. Although the buzz-word in education today is *accountability,* by which politicians generally mean holding principals responsible for student achievement, most principals and field managers have so little control over the way they deliver education that it is unfair to hold them wholly responsible for student achievement. How can any manager be responsible if a central office tells him or her what to do at practically every turn?

However, this book allows for a renewed emphasis on accountability for performance, not just for principals but for the entire district. But it also advocates new types of fiscal oversight and monitoring that allow officials to catch problems before they escalate and use their common sense to determine risk of abuse.

So long as such proper safeguards are in place, this book suggests, decentralization can reduce corruption and waste. Most school corruption today does not occur in schools or instruction. Most waste is embedded in central regulations, not in schools. Further, examples are provided suggesting that, when principals and managers are given authority and held properly accountable, they sometimes go to extraordinary lengths to stretch every dollar for schoolchildren—in contrast to the apathy normally found among employees whose every decision is dictated from on high.

Drawing on public administration, microeconomics, and white-collar crime theories, this book examines the root causes of what is wrong with large school districts today and makes detailed recommendations for what to do about it. It focuses primarily on the three largest school districts in the nation—New York City, the nation's biggest; Los Angeles, the second largest; and Chicago, the third largest. These districts' size facilitates the study of corruption because the larger the organization, the clearer the impact of structure.[23] But many comparisons are drawn to other urban districts, including Jersey City, Newark, and Paterson, New Jersey, as well as Detroit and the most decentralized district in North America—Edmonton, Canada.

Part I examines the patient and his symptoms. It gives readers a perspective on the sheer magnitude of America's three largest school districts, emphasizing that corruption is not about a missing box of no. 2 pencils. It then lays bare the record of fraud, waste, and abuse that has afflicted these school systems, describing its scope, nature, and severity and its toll on learning.

Part II examines the remedies administered in the past—top-down accountability controls—and whether they helped cure the problem. The striking findings are that, despite a multitude of central controls, waste and corruption persisted, with the costliest problems in central divisions where controls originate.

Part III offers a diagnosis. It develops a theory that explains why fraud, waste, and abuse have persisted after so many decades of reform attempts, exploring the root causes that provide incentives for the problem.

Parts IV and V offer the prescription. To help reformers avoid pitfalls of the past, Part IV examines two rather unsuccessful decentralization experiments in the New York City schools. One is its twenty-six-year experiment with community control of schools, which began in the heat of the civil rights movement in 1969 and ended by state legislative fiats in 1996 and 2002. The other is the decentralized managerial system of school custodians, or building superintendents, which has been creating scandals since the 1920s and is still in effect today. Part V sets forth a blueprint for how to reshape districts and decentralize discretion to lessen incentives for wrongdoing and enhance management. It includes a description of success stories from other districts and programs within districts.

It is my heartfelt hope that, by exposing some of the hidden costs of top-down controls in the three largest districts and describing how other districts have overcome these problems, this book will spur new debate in the effort to improve America's great city schools.

THE PATHOLOGY: LAYING THE RECORD BARE

CHAPTER ONE

PUBLIC EDUCATION AS BIG BUSINESS

Most people do not think of schools as corrupt or wasteful. In fact, scholars note that wrongdoing should be less likely in organizations that arc devoted to helping society than in organizations that are not.[1] However, the tale of public school corruption is one rich in ironies, unexpected juxtapositions, and disconnects between hope and reality. The lofty idealism that inspired early advocates of public education, for example, contrasts with the opportunism that motivated many to seek jobs in public schools. The optimistic utopianism of reformers to guarantee integrity and efficiency through central school bureaucracies belies the dishonesty and waste these structures actually generated. The ultimate irony is that today conscientious employees sometimes need to break the rules simply to do their jobs well.

Charity was the original impetus behind many urban school districts. In the early 1800s rich families donated huge sums of money to start free public schools to help immigrants and the poor.[2] Advocates of public education during the 1800s trusted in the basic goodness of public schools with crusader-like zeal and held an almost evangelical belief that these institutions would civilize and secure Christian values and democracy in America.[3]

Yet by the late 1800s, public schools had become a trove of power, political patronage, and profit for a number of people with less-exalted motives. In those days large city school systems were often divided into local wards or regions, each run by an elected school board of trustees with broad power over school personnel and funds.[4] Whenever trustees were voted out of office, large numbers of teachers, principals, and even school janitors could expect to be fired to make room for new staff loyal to the incoming trustees.

In some large eastern cities such as New York and Chicago, allegations of local board members selling jobs and promotions were common. In 1864, for instance, an entire ward school board in New York City was suspended together with some principals for colluding to extort payments from prospective teachers and contractors.[5] Indeed, one of the more colorful figures of the day, William Marcy Tweed, later the famed "Boss Tweed" of Tammany Hall, launched his political career from a ward school board. By the time he rose to the mayoralty some years later, he was all too familiar with the reservoir of patronage and contracts that the school system offered. Longing to get his hands on them, he convinced the legislature to abolish the independent lay school board at the top, which New York, like most public school systems, used to separate schools from partisan politics, and to replace it with a Department of Public Instruction that answered to him.[6]

In Chicago in the early 1920s, a former Board of Education chairman, vice chairman, board members, board attorney, and forty political cronies were indicted for school graft.[7] Board officials would tip off their friends about land that the school board wanted to buy so that they could quickly buy it and resell it to the board at inflated prices. Some school officials would order unnecessary equipment from favored vendors and award lucrative contracts to shell companies. They would extort kickbacks from school engineers seeking promotions.

Other paradoxes emerged in public schools as the twentieth century unfolded. In the first half of the 1900s, progressive reformers embarked on a mission to stamp out waste and dishonesty from public schools with as much moral fervor as public school advocates had pursued in establishing public schools in the previous century. With avid confidence in the new "scientific management" theories of the day—that centralized bureaucracies and professional expertise would ensure better education and more integrity—progressive reformers set about redesigning schools to make them perfect. They pushed power up from the local school boards into central bureaucracies, professionalized staff, and established top-down accountability mechanisms designed to enforce compliance with rules and regulations.

But scandals continued to erupt in the 1900s. In some cities it seemed that the more inoculations against corruption a school district received, the more resistance it built up.

THE DIMENSIONS OF URBAN PUBLIC SCHOOLS

To begin to understand all this and grasp what is at stake, it is helpful to put the sheer magnitude and complexity of urban public schools in perspective. School corruption and waste are not about a missing box of staples. Even before they grew to today's massive proportions, public schools in America's great cities had long been a big business, with large sums of money at stake and considerable opportunities for power and patronage.

Urban schools in particular grew especially rapidly starting in the 1930s, when people began flooding into cities from the countryside and the little rural schoolhouses that peppered the nation.[8] Today, 31 percent of U.S. students attend school districts with at least 25,000 pupils.[9] America's 100 largest school districts each have at least 45,000 students; 25 of these districts have over 100,000 students each.[10]

The dimensions of America's three largest school districts—New York City, Los Angeles, and Chicago—are particularly staggering. As William Ouchi's and my forthcoming book, *Making Schools Work*, notes, New York City, the largest school system in the country, has over 1.1 million students, a budget of over $13 billion, over 1,200 schools, and 140,000 employees.[11] Los Angeles is the second largest, with three-quarters of a million pupils, a $7-billion budget, 900 schools, and 80,000 employees. Chicago, the third largest, has half a million students, a $3.5-billion budget, 600 schools, and 45,000 employees.[12]

The operating budgets of the New York City and Chicago school districts are each bigger than the entire amount most states spend on education.[13] Their capital budgets are in the billions (see table 1). The size of the New York City school operating budget alone would rank seventh in the nation if it were a state.[14] This system owns more square footage than any agency in the nation after the U.S. Department of Defense and the U.S. Post Office.[15] It receives 45,000 work orders a year that range from requests to "build a new floor" to requests to "fix the toilet."[16] With 74 percent of its students eligible for free or reduced lunches under federal law, it is the second-largest food provider in the country after the U.S. Army. It delivers over 850,000 meals a day during the school year[17] and 300,000 a day in the summer at a cost of over $250 million a year.[18]

Individual schools in urban districts also tend to be large today. Elementary and secondary schools in America's one hundred largest districts have an average of 708 students each. Eleven of these one hundred districts have schools with an average enrollment of 1,000 students.[19]

Urban high schools, which came into existence as unique, colossal enterprises in the early 1900s, now seat thousands of pupils and cost tens of

TABLE 1. Operating and capital budgets of the three largest school districts (2000–2001)

	Operating Budget in Billions	Capital Budget in Billions
New York City	$13.236	$1.277
Los Angeles	$6.966	$2.293
Chicago	$3.575	$0.569

SOURCE: William Ouchi, Bruce Cooper, Lydia Segal, Tim DeRoche, Carolyn Brown, and Elizabeth Galvin, "The Organization of Primary and Secondary School Systems" (unpublished paper).

millions of dollars to operate. The average public high school in Los Angeles enrolls 3,239 students; in Chicago, 1,370; in New York City, 1,683.[20] As one veteran principal described it, running a high school today is "like running a medium sized corporation."[21] His school, Edward R. Murrow High School in Brooklyn, part of the New York City system, has 3,600 pupils, 450 staff, and an $18.7-million operating budget. And that is still smaller than some other high schools, such as Brooklyn Technical High School, with 4,079 students and an operating budget of $20 million. These costs, moreover, do not include items such as electricity, gas, heat, employee pensions, and litigation costs that are paid by the city or the central school system.

THE VARIETY AND COMPLEXITY OF SCHOOL DISTRICT SERVICES

The sheer variety of tasks and categories of people involved in running a school district also gives perspective on the breadth of the terrain potentially affected by abuse. As society's expectations of schools and court mandates multiplied in the last century, schools became, as one former president of New York City's central school board noted, "a one-stop shop where parents drop kids off and ask the school to raise them."[22]

Social workers, nurses, dentists, neighborhood workers, substance abuse prevention specialists, and truancy officers tend to students' mental, physical, and social health. Psychiatrists, physical therapists, and other specialists care for special education children. Bus drivers, bus "matrons," bus inspectors, and other specialists work on transportation. Procurement officers screen vendors, negotiate prices, draw up contracts, and oversee purchasing procedures. Lawyers with different specialties draw up, review, and negotiate collective bargaining agreements and defend schools in employee grievances and arbitration proceedings. Lunchroom workers, nutritionists, and food buyers purchase, evaluate, store, and deliver lunches and breakfasts to children below the federal poverty line. Education experts must constantly develop and administer tests to personnel such as lab technicians, lab specialists, and secretaries, whose jobs regularly require updated licenses. Experts in construction, architecture, engineering, leasing, hazardous waste removal, and real estate law tend to school buildings, many with complex heating and air conditioning systems, elevators, and swimming pools. Because of violence and vandalism, school systems must provide security and navigate often tricky relationships with city police.

The largest school districts may even need demographers to help them plan school construction. Building planners in the New York City school system, for example, hire demographers to help them anticipate how the city's ever-changing vibrant neighborhoods will respond to what is happening around the globe. A hurricane in Haiti usually translates into an enrollment surge in District 17; a political shakeup in Eastern Europe means more students in Districts 21 and 22. Why? Because today Haitian immigrants tend to flock to Brooklyn's District 17; Eastern Europeans, to Brooklyn's Districts 21 and 22. Similarly they need to know that Asian immigrants today tend to congregate in District 25 in Flushing, Queens, now known as the "new Chinatown," and Poles in District 14.[23]

Last, as some of the most political local institutions, urban school districts, particularly in tensely multiethnic cities such as New York, Los Angeles, and Chicago, need public relations personnel and lobbyists. In New York City, at least before Mayor Michael Bloomberg took over in the summer of 2002, the top executive had a fleet of assistants and spokespeople to help manage his relationship with the central school board, the mayor, and other city and state politicians.[24]

Schools also need staff to manage the fiercely competitive interests of local constituents. School leaders in overcrowded cities need assistance in handling demands by different groups for new schools and seats. Even a proposition as seemingly simple as moving pupils from overcrowded neighborhoods to areas with plenty of room can be fraught with political peril if not skillfully handled. In New York City, for example, executives would likely need assistance to manage the demands of districts like District 28 in Queens. The upscale end of that oblong district, Rego Park, is mostly white and 120 percent utilized. But the other end, Jamaica, is mostly poor and black and 30 percent empty.[25] As chancellors have found, busing children from Rego Park to Jamaica or vice versa, no matter how logical, is simply not politically feasible.

THE FINANCIAL VALUE OF PUBLIC SCHOOL CONTRACTS AND JOBS

With all their responsibilities and requirements, large school districts offer many opportunities for lucre and power. Consider the size of contracts at stake. The Los Angeles Unified School District (LAUSD) pays about $80 million a year to just six bus companies to transport pupils.[26] In the late 1990s it poured $160 million into a single high school, the Belmont Learning Center—and that was just to complete part of it.[27] The New York City school system spends $2 billion a year on supplies, over $60 million on textbooks, $40 million on leases, $300 million on private preschool vendors, and, in 2000, $18 million to train parent-led school leadership teams.[28] A contract to remove asbestos at a single school easily goes for half a million dollars. News articles suggest that one New York construction contractor raked in nearly $1 billion in school construction contracts from 1959 through the early 1990s.[29] The Facilities Division pays one architectural firm $4 million to survey and rate the condition of every school building it owns once a year simply to enable it to prioritize renovation projects.

With so much money flowing through the schools, the amount they can potentially lose to fraud or questionable billing is significant. In New York City, the FBI charged that the construction company had submitted $4.5 million in inflated school construction bills over five years. In the LAUSD, investigators charged that a single vendor hired to provide special education services had billed nearly $1.5 million in questionable costs.[30] In Chicago, a single private provider of off-site special education instruction allegedly received $115,000 by falsifying attendance records.[31]

Cost overruns due to racketeering and mismanagement can also be enormous. Change orders to build a single school, Fiorello H. La Guardia High School near Lincoln Center in Manhattan, which prosecutors found to be ensnared in a web of corruption and mismanagement, came to over $50 million.[32]

Simple, honest mistakes can be dear, as well, particularly if a district is mismanaged. In what was apparently an oversight, for instance, the LAUSD paid one company $14.3 million for a three-year telephone contract for nothing. Officials paid the money without having a contract in place.[33] In the Chicago public schools before Chief Executive Officer Paul

Vallas and his team started cleaning up that system in 1996–97, auditors found that the Bureau of Payroll Services had mistakenly overpaid employees $348,000 in 1991 alone.[34] The Benefits Program, meanwhile, was allegedly paying 3,000 ineligible dependents, some of whom had been dead for years.[35]

Although the vast majority of people who work in and with schools are dedicated and honest, those who are unscrupulous stand to rake in thousands of dollars. Some undercover operations have shown vendors kicking back between 10 to 15 percent on procurement, construction, and repair contracts in New York City.[36] On a $750,000 contract, that comes to $75,000 to $112,500. Among the few who have chosen to be dishonest, upper-echelon officers have collected between $150,000 and $200,000 to approve phony bills; mid- to lower-level administrators, between $2,500 to $5,000 per contract; and low-level inspectors from $10 to $1,000. Crooked inspectors have been caught taking up to a thousand dollars from vendors to look the other way on violations.[37]

PERSONAL STRESS: MURDERS AND SUICIDES

The most dramatic indication of how high the stakes are in the largest city schools is accounts of people allegedly driven to murder or suicide over school contracts or tawdry investigations. Take school construction and maintenance. As the investigative reporter Eddie Dunne recounts, Dan Conlin, president of Local 891, the powerful New York City school custodians union, was shot dead in August 1987 during a ferocious round of collective bargaining negotiations with the board of education in which private contractors stood to gain or lose millions of dollars.[38] Two hit men aided by two accomplices pumped five bullets into Conlin's head as he was driving to his Brooklyn headquarters. The two gunmen were sentenced to eighteen years to life; one accomplice, a juvenile, had his record sealed; and the other accomplice died shortly after his arrest.

Although the person who masterminded the killing remains at large, police evidence pointed strongly to a window contractor who stood to lose hundreds of thousands of dollars if Conlin's wishes prevailed. At the time he was murdered, Conlin was challenging a board of education plan to allow central administrators to contract out a number of school maintenance projects without input from custodians, the school building superintendents. Conlin wanted custodians to be in charge of letting those contracts. A 1994 investigation sheds light on what the fuss may have been about: those who controlled the contracting process were taking kickbacks from vendors. The window contractor was among those busted.

All the vendors who had obtained contracts through the central office without custodial input would likely have felt threatened by Conlin's bid for control, but the window contractor had reason to be particularly fearful. The central office had given him five contracts to replace school windows, one of which was for $448,000. A tense dispute occurred between the contractor and the custodian at the first school where he was awarded a window replacement contract. The dispute put him in danger of defaulting, a precarious position because contractors who defaulted on their first contracts with the school system were not allowed to bid on school projects again. Conlin, eager to blacklist the contractor, spent a good part of July checking on his progress and scrutinizing his work. Although prosecutors never charged the window contractor—they did not believe that the evidence against him was sufficient—the investigation unearthed no other person with as strong a link to the murder.

Consider, too, three other murders involving school supplies at the multimillion dollar, five-story New York City school warehouse in Queens. In January 1989 John Thomas, a custodian who worked there, was shot twice in the head near the warehouse. His body was unearthed in the garage used by the warehouse. At the same time, two other warehouse custodians, a man and a woman, mysteriously disappeared. Police believe they were burned in the large incinerator in the warehouse boiler room.[39] A short time later, hundreds of videocassette recorders and televisions were discovered stolen from the warehouse.

Police never solved the murders. Although the charred remains of two people found six years later in upstate New York were thought to be those of the male and the female custodian, the bodies were too badly charred to identify. Nevertheless, investigators believe that the murder and disappearances of the custodians were linked to the theft of the electronic equipment from the warehouse. Investigators branded the theft an inside job. They speculated that the three victims knew about the equipment and other fraud at the warehouse, which was widely known to be hemorrhaging supplies, and that an interested party had their bodies burned in the warehouse boiler room furnace.[40]

Suicides are another indication of the high stakes in education. Over the past fifteen years in New York City, at least two school officials killed themselves as prosecutors began to close in on and pressure them to testify about wrongdoing. In January 1993 the body of Alfredo Mathew Jr., superintendent of District 12 in the South Bronx, was found in a locked motel room in Albany, where he was attending a conference. His head was covered in two plastic bags bound around the neck with duct tape.

At the time of his death, Mathew, a veteran school administrator, had landed the plum job of superintendent of Community School District 12 in the Bronx, a $102,900-a-year post with control over millions of dollars of school jobs and funds. The central office had hoped Mathew would clean up corruption in the district—his predecessor and two local school board members had been led away in handcuffs on a variety of corruption charges in 1990.[41] But once in office, Mathew allegedly used the district as his personal job and piggy bank. Probes in 1991 and 1992 suggested that he had diverted school funds for his personal expenses, such as life insurance premiums, meals, and gasoline.[42]

Mathew's suicide note, however, blamed two other investigations that were closing in on him. One, by the Special Commissioner of Investigation, revealed that he had transformed the school district into an enterprise for political patronage where jobs were doled out to friends, relatives, mistresses, and politically connected people while merit was "thrown out the window."[43] The other probe, led by the U.S. Attorney's Office for the Southern District of New York, suggested that Mathew had masterminded a conspiracy to steal $185,000 from two antipoverty agencies he chaired in the Bronx. According to the criminal complaint filed, instead of spending the money to help destitute children and the elderly, Mathew and his cronies spent it on restaurants, home furniture, flowers, toys, airline flights, clothing, and tickets to Yankee games.[44]

Another school official, Anthony Losacco, apparently also committed suicide when law enforcement officers closed in on school-related wrongs. A witness in an investigation into alleged fraud in Community School District 4 in Manhattan, he was found with a gunshot wound to the head on the day before he was to meet with prosecutors to testify before a grand jury in 1988.[45] Although a mere teacher's aide, he was believed to have had firsthand knowledge about a secret slush fund and missing money. Losacco had been distraught about testifying and had warned prosecutors that he had been threatened with physical harm if he testified.

A SOURCE OF POLITICAL PATRONAGE

Public schools can also provide patronage. At various points in urban public school history, mayors and other politicians have battled for control over school jobs, sometimes going so far as to abolish the independent lay central school boards set up to keep partisan politics away. At other times, though, politicians used the lay boards themselves as patronage banks. In Chicago, the seventeen-member central lay school board that existed before a 1995 state law replaced it with a smaller board was allegedly riddled with patronage. To get on that old board, candidates had to go through the highly political process of getting nominated by the School Board Nominating Commission, composed of local school council members. Then they had to get approved by the city council, which allowed aldermen to lobby the mayor to put their relatives on the board.[46] Early in the century, in 1917, the mayor of New York City appointed to the central board a person whose only qualification was that he was the mayor's personal physician.[47] He chaired the important Committee on Buildings and Sites despite having no experience in construction.

Although civil service curbs patronage in a large part of public school workforces in various cities today, in their effort to appease certain segments of society some districts periodically experiment with reforms that open up swaths of jobs to patronage. Examples are New York City's community school boards that were intended to promote community hiring and Atlanta's experiment with requiring the board of education to boost minority hiring.[48]

CHARTING CORRUPTION, WASTE, AND ABUSE

In the 1990s, in the wake of highly publicized school scandals, America's three largest school districts were each forced, for the first time in their histories, to accept oversight from independent, permanent law-enforcement-like offices whose primary purpose was to root out fraud, waste, and abuse. These offices, known generally as inspectors general, did not report to school management. They were staffed by professional auditors and investigators and given broad law enforcement authority such as subpoena power.[1]

New York City, the first to establish an independent school inspector general, did so in 1990, when it created the $3-million-a-year Special Commissioner of Investigation (SCI) for the New York City School System. (The office has lost some of its independence, however, since the mayoral takeover of schools in the summer of 2002.[2]) Chicago was the second district to have a school inspector general, when the state legislature created the Office of Inspector General in 1993. After some reforms, this $2.5-million office now reports to the central lay school board.[3] Los Angeles got an independent inspector general in 1999, when the $6.3-million Office of Inspector General was created, reporting to the elected lay central school board.

These inspectors general all marked an enormous change—politically, psychologically, and with respect to accountability—for their districts, which had been accustomed to rubber-stamping internal auditors and investigators who had little ability or incentive to unearth serious problems. Today, each school inspector general issues comprehensive annual or biennial reports detailing its findings and recommendations for disciplinary action, prosecution, and systemic reform.[4]

As a result of these reports, scholars today have an extraordinarily rich and comprehensive source of data about the types of problems that the three largest districts generate. While it must be remembered that audits and investigations are not convictions, inspector general reports, particularly when taken together with grand jury reports, indictments, plea-bargain agreements, criminal complaints, media exposes, court settlements, and convictions, provide a detailed and likely reliable description of the variegated symptoms that affect the districts.

The white-collar crime literature suggests numerous possible ways to categorize corruption in organizations, such as by severity of the crime (e.g., felonies vs. misdemeanors vs. violations), type of crime (e.g., theft, forgery, patronage, and so forth), or operational function (e.g., the kinds of wrongs found in procurement, hiring, payroll, and so forth), among others. But with respect to public schools, several other, unique categorizations suggest themselves.

MOTIVE

People who engage in school corruption appear to fall into two categories: those who are out to milk the district and those who commit fraud in order to get their jobs done better. While there is some overlap,[5] as some people who start out engaging in fraud for worthy causes can end up bilking the system for selfish reasons, these two kinds of culprits should be distinguished.

The presence of employees out to swindle their district indicates a deep pathology akin to a disease like cancer, where the patient's own cells attack him. The presence of employees who break rules to get their jobs done connotes a less serious condition akin to, say, boils, where the body is actually trying to protect itself by eliminating toxins through the skin. Something is wrong in both cases. But the response in the second betrays a healthier organism. So, for example, when officials of the Los Angeles Unified School District (LAUSD) ignored cumbersome competitive bidding rules in order to purchase over 300 portable classrooms amid frantic efforts to create space for a class size reduction program,[6] their conduct should not be lumped together with officials who avoided competitive bidding to give a favored company a sweetheart deal.

LEGAL VS. ILLEGAL: SEAMLESS CONNECTIONS

The second important feature that jumps out from the data is the limitation of using traditional demarcations between legal and illegal conduct to describe the problem. Much of what is wrong with the three largest districts is not criminal or illegal. Rather, it is abusive and grossly wasteful. *Abuse* is conduct that deliberately or recklessly advances a group's or individual's personal interests at the expense of the agency's primary formal goals.[7] *Gross waste* is the obvious overpaying for items that are necessary or the paying for items that are obviously unnecessary.[8] Gross waste betrays an indifference or reckless blindness to the agency's best interests.[9] Unlike corruption, abuse and gross waste are not illegal. But they can be just as or more harmful to the agency's mission. And because the people who engage in abuse do so knowingly, abuse is morally wrong. In fact, abuse should and probably would be illegal if it were not sanitized by collective bargaining agreements, arbitration decisions, district policy and practice, and poorly drafted laws.

In America's three largest school systems, abuse is often found hand-in-hand with corruption and waste. All three thrive under mismanagement, and each feeds the other. When management is not watching out for the agency's best interests, it is more likely to agree to abusive, wasteful collective bargaining provisions and facilitate corruption, because crooks think they can get away with it. When employees see school managers repeatedly putting other people's interests before children's welfare, that behavior sends the message that children are not important and that saving money does not matter.

ABUSE IN THE NEW YORK CITY CUSTODIAL CONTRACT

Consider the example of *temporary care* assignments in the collective bargaining contract between the New York City school system and school custodians, the building superintendents who clean and repair schools.[10] Although a few of the abuses in temporary care are being phased out, thanks to the valiant efforts of James Lonergan, director of Building Services, it is illuminating because it shows how an interest group can conspicuously and deliberately injure a school system for years and yet still be totally within the law.

Temporary care assignments were originally devised for schools that were suddenly left without a custodian, whether because of death or illness. In such cases, another custodian from another school would take on the responsibility for overseeing the building on a temporary basis.

Under the union contract, the Board of Education (BOE), now called the Department of Education, has to pay temporary care custodians a full second salary for caring for the orphaned building, even though custodians are not required to put in any overtime to do so and do not need to maintain a physical presence in the second building for any length of time.[11] As auditors noted, it is physically impossible for custodians to work full time on two buildings at once.[12] Paying custodians two full-time salaries, moreover, contradicts the assumption in the rest of custodians' contract: that caring for one building is a full-time job requiring full-time attention.

In fact, since temporary care assignments are plum jobs handed out on the basis of seniority, there is no guarantee that a custodian's regular school building and his temporary care building will even be geographically close. A custodian from Washington Heights on Manhattan's northernmost tip could easily be put in charge of a second school in Lower Manhattan, on the island's southern tip—a commute of nearly one hour each way by subway. As one school official whose district has had to endure such problems told the *New York Times* about these custodians, "Sometimes they come, sometimes they don't come."[13] Without supervision, cleaning crews have little incentive to do a good job. Floors might not get mopped. Leaks might not be fixed.

Custodians have abused even this abusive contractual provision. Temporary care was intended as a stopgap measure to last about eight weeks until a new candidate could be hired and processed. But custodians can drag out their temporary care assignments for years because the contract does not prohibit it. For custodians this prospect was a bonanza. For a custodian making $127,000 a year, every month on temporary care can boost his income by about $11,000.

Custodians further manipulated temporary care assignments by restricting the number of people qualified to get them. Temporary care often becomes available in the largest schools where the pay is better, because that is where the oldest, most senior custodians work. Until recently, under an archaic provision in the custodian contract, custodians needed a stationary engineer's license to run large schools (over 82,000 square feet).[14]

But twenty-five senior custodians basically held the keys to who got a license. To get a stationary engineer's license, a custodian needed either five years' experience working with a high-pressure boiler outside the New York City school system or a one-year night apprenticeship with a New York City school custodian who had a high-pressure boiler. But since only about twenty-five schools in the city had high-pressure boilers and since custodians decided who could apprentice with them, they could help keep the supply of qualified custodians low, a situation that translated into more temporary care for them.

The irony was that stationary engineers' licenses were largely unnecessary. These licenses were technically required to run high-pressure boilers, which used to be common in the city's large schools. But as of 2001, fewer than 25 of 1,100 New York City school buildings had high-pressure boilers.[15]

Finally in 2001, after about ten years of negotiation with the custodians union, the school system managed to rescind the requirement for a stationary engineer's license for custodians to run large schools. As of 2003, all that will be required is a refrigeration license, which can be obtained in one year. While this will not eliminate temporary care, it will make it harder for senior custodians to hoard all the best assignments.

OVERTIME ABUSE IN THE LAUSD

The transition from abuse to corruption can be practically seamless. The example of overtime in the LAUSD suggests how built-in abuse encourages and leads to corruption.

On paper, the LAUSD requires employees to explain why they need overtime and to get permission beforehand to ensure that the money is necessary to achieving district goals. But a comprehensive 2001 audit by the Office of the Inspector General suggested that the LAUSD inherently sanctioned the widespread abuse of overtime as a gravy train for personnel in the way it was organized.

The central Budget Services and Financial Planning Division was supposed to monitor the overall overtime that every school and division spends. But under the LAUSD chain of command, if a division went over budget, Budget Services had no authority to do anything about it. So division officials who went over budget simply submitted their overtime expenses to Budget Services and noted the variance from their original budgets. They did not bother to explain why they overspent because they did not have to.[16] Even divisions that were not allocated any overtime budget incurred overtime expenses without providing any explanation.

The upshot? Employees throughout the central bureaucracy billed increasingly more overtime every year from 1998 to 2000 and went increasingly over budget.[17] By 1999–2000, total LAUSD overtime was 228 percent over budget! Some divisions billed almost three times as much overtime as they were budgeted. Moreover, the rate by which employees were exceeding budgeted overtime rose faster from 1998 to 2000 than the number of classified employees and students did.

Needless to say, with no one at the top apparently in charge of overtime, a number of managers throughout the LAUSD also neglected overtime supervision. As a 1999 audit and other investigations show, many employees took excessive overtime without any evidence that a supervisor had approved it, in some cases resulting in fraud.[18]

ABUSE OF CHICAGO'S PLAYGROUNDS AND STADIUMS

Another example of abuse by administrators leading to corruption was the Chicago Public Schools (CPS) Department of Playgrounds and Stadiums before Chief Executive Officer Paul Vallas and his management team revamped it at a savings of about $19 million.[19] Top department administrators had turned practically the entire program into an ocean of sinecure jobs and overtime. They got the CPS to pay for one fieldhouse per playground, each staffed by three full-time attendants. This was blatant abuse because most playgrounds had no fieldhouse, as auditors discovered. But it was legal, since it was in the contract.

But management's message inherent in the abuse led to rampant corruption in the field. Few attendants bothered to show up at all; they basically took their paychecks and ran. When auditors visited those few playgrounds that had fieldhouses, they rarely saw more than one, at the most two attendants. At one school the only attendant on-site was fast asleep at his desk in the fieldhouse. At another school a lone attendant was locking up at 5:00 p.m., even though the CPS was paying to keep playgrounds open until 9:00 p.m. In fact, leaving work early was systemic among those attendants who showed up. Auditors found that most school playgrounds were closed in the afternoons when they were supposed to be open. Children were sometimes seen trying to climb inside.

The same abuse pervaded Chicago's school stadiums. Whenever auditors made unannounced visits, staff were either nowhere to be seen or doing nothing "that could be construed as work-related."[20]

WHERE CORRUPTION OCCURS

The third identifying characteristic that bubbles up from the data on school corruption is where it occurs in the districts. The highest incidence of corruption occurs among central, district, and school noninstructional personnel. To the extent that it occurs in schools, most of it is limited to personnel such as cafeteria workers and custodial staff, who report to the central or regional office, not directly to the principal.[21] Total losses due to school cases appear to be a fraction of the losses due to central cases based on publicized reports by school inspectors general in all three districts.

Take the Los Angeles school system. In fiscal 2001, of the inspector general investigations and audits where a fiscal loss could be determined, school-based fraud and waste totalled about $48,000. Central fraud and waste, however, totalled $21,550,920. This means that school-based losses were about 0.2 percent of the central losses in Los Angeles that year, as measured by officially published school investigations and audits. Even if this finding is tempered with the caveat that publicized reports of wrong-doing necessarily offer a distorted picture of actual wrongdoing since wrongdoing is generally secret and hard to detect, the figures are dramatic enough to warrant the suggestion that the districts' biggest corruption and waste problems are in the central office.

Also notable is where corruption occurs in the central office. In all three districts, systemic fraud (although not waste and abuse, which seem to be spread around) hardly ever occurs in instruction. Instead it far more frequently affects noncore areas, such as transportation, construction, adult education, building maintenance, and so forth.

INTENSITY OF CORRUPTION

Fourth, it is useful to diagnose school corruption, waste, and abuse on the basis of intensity: Are they opportunistic and occasional or systemic and chronic? Some sporadic, opportunistic fraud and waste is almost inevitable in any large organization.[22] But systemic patterns suggest a deeper, constitutional problem.

What is striking about the New York City, Los Angeles, and pre-1997 Chicago school districts is how systemic and persistent corruption, waste, and abuse have been in certain noncore areas. The intensity of the problem is such that, as the following examples show, investigators unearthed the same kinds of schemes year after year, sometimes for decades.

SCHOOL SUPPLIES

Take school supplies, a multimillion dollar industry in many large urban school districts today. New York City, Los Angeles, and pre-1997 Chicago have all had recurrent problems in this area: theft, poor record keeping that stymies auditors, and overpayment for goods.

In New York City, school employees used to call the Bureau of Supplies the "Bureau of Surprise" because they never knew what they were going to get when they opened their boxes. The main warehouse was dubbed the "The Sieve." There were widespread complaints that if goods arrived at all, they would be inferior in quality to, less in quantity than, or completely different from what had been ordered.

But the point is that none of this was new. The Bureau of Supplies had been abusing the system since 1909, when the city's Charter Commission recommended scrapping the bureau altogether and handing its functions over to a new, citywide purchasing agency.[23] As early as 1917, investigators branded the bureau's records as "inaccurate, unreliable and misleading" and prone to theft. To cover up, managers would cook the books.[24] Investigations in 1936,[25] 1942,[26] 1977,[27] 1980, and 1984 all uncovered similar problems. The main difference was the amounts lost. In 1977 auditors could not account for $500,000 worth of supplies[28]; by 1982 they could not account for $7.6 million.[29]

Waste in the warehouse was chronic, too. In 1984 auditors found a stash of $4.5 million worth of unused textbooks for which the New York City school system had overpaid and then failed to return to the publisher for credit.[30] Also lying around was a forty-eight-year supply of eight-cent post cards. Apparently, when the postage rate rose to nine cents, the eight-cent cards were just left there.[31]

Not until the 1995–96 school year, nearly eighty years after the Bureau of Supplies' first major scandal, did the BOE finally shut down the warehouse, but it took television cameras catching workers walking off with boxes of supplies. The highly publicized videotapes showed that the main warehouse had dozens of points of access. Trucks that were supposed to distribute goods to schools were seen driving off with loads of school equipment to sell to private stores. These truckers fueled a thriving black market of school merchandise that could commonly be found for sale on the streets of New York within days after it left the warehouse.[32]

In Chicago, Paul Vallas dealt with longstanding abuses in school warehouses by shutting them down and distributing to the schools whatever they contained. So when he and his deputies discovered about $250,000 in equipment, including 24,000 pieces of furniture sitting apparently forgotten in one warehouse, they distributed them to schools.[33]

CHRONIC OVERPAYMENT FOR GOODS

Another example of an intense, systemic problem was gross overexpenditure on necessary goods and services. This problem tended to emerge in the same areas of school districts, suggesting a subculture with a high degree of indifference to the schools' best interests. In pre-1997 Chicago, for instance, school division heads of areas such as procurement, facilities, and lunches did not seem to notice or care that their departments were hemorrhaging money. A 1993 external investigation suggested that the CPS was overpaying for hundreds of hardware items. It was reportedly shelling out $75 for electrical blank plates that normally retailed for 80 cents and $198 for boiler pressure release valves that retailed for $30.[34] An investigation of the food department suggested indifference there, too. One major food supplier was charging the district top dollar for quality fruits and vegetables but delivering cheaper, inferior ones. School officials apparently did not notice.[35]

Overpayments were common in the New York City school system in these areas, too, some going back to the 1920s.[36] In 1942 the Bureau of School Lunches was paying 250 percent more for vegetables than the rest of the city, even with the same contract specifications.[37] The Bureau of Supplies was paying 20 percent more for printing supplies than it needed to. About forty years later the BOE was buying 12,000 gallons of bleach for $1.08 a gallon, when the local supermarket sold a gallon for less than 70 cents. It was spending $119 for ten-speed bikes, when local department stores sold similar models for $79.99.[38] It was paying millions of dollars above official list prices for textbooks it could easily have purchased at 20 percent and 40 percent discounts at well-known retail stores.[39] A local school board leased office space for $5 million when similar space was available in existing school buildings at no cost.[40] During New York City's fiscal crisis in the 1970s, when the city was being forced to borrow money at very high rates, the BOE let over $2 million sit for over two years in checking accounts that were not earning interest.[41]

ABUSE IN THE NEW YORK CITY SCHOOL BUS PROGRAM

Sometimes recurring problems, instead of being solved, become legalized. School transportation in New York City is currently the most expensive school bus program in the nation, where charges of expensive monopolies for select bus companies go back to 1935. At that time the central school board's Committee on Finance and Budget found that one very expensive bus company had a virtual monopoly on school bus contracts.[42]

Seven years later, however, this same bus company still had a monopoly. No one could explain to investigators why it was the only bidder on school bus contracts. Although it unearthed no crime, a probe revealed the unsettling fact that the bus company appeared to be surviving off the school system; BOE contracts represented 97 percent of its gross business. Even more bizarre, the bus company paid salaries to the federal commissioner of jurors for the Eastern District of New York, his wife, and his son, even though the wife had no apparent job except to give "over-all advice"[43] and the son no longer worked at the company.

Thirty-six years later, in 1978, audits showed that the BOE still "discouraged competition" and did "all within its power to protect" one company in the award of nearly half a billion dollars' worth of bus contracts a year. The company that had most of the contracts was the most expensive. It had also overbilled the BOE by $1.4 million over six years.[44] But the central school transportation office kept competition at bay by refusing to give bidders the bus routes, thus making it virtually impossible for them to enter bids. The BOE promised to conduct a comprehensive study of the problem, but a follow-up audit in 1983, five years later, found that nothing had really changed.[45]

After years of being dogged by auditors and investigators, the school transportation division eventually adopted a formal policy that exempted bus contracts from competitive bidding altogether. It secured a waiver from the state that allowed it to extend school bus contracts rather than require bidding. In effect, the school system sanitized the lack of competition and insulated the two companies that dominated the school busing market, one of which controlled about 80 percent of the system's 3,800 bus routes, from legal attack.

Ironically, attempts by mayors to undo the abuse sometimes resulted in its being embedded even more deeply into school protocol. When Mayor Ed Koch pushed the school system to open its bus routes to more competition in 1979, a three-month bus strike followed. To end the strike, the school board agreed to a provision requiring any new company that won a school bus contract to hire existing drivers and bus personnel on the basis of seniority and at the same salary, essentially giving these employees the lifetime job guarantees of civil servants.

The point is that the new provision officially undercut any realistic chance for vigorous competition. The school system now not only had no obligation to solicit bids—it could continue to grant existing companies contract extensions indefinitely—but it also had no incentive to solicit bids to save money. The high labor costs that the new provision imposed made it virtually impossible for outside bus companies to underbid existing ones. So although the number of companies with school bus contracts eventually rose to 78, a number of the new companies were reportedly subsidiaries that had overlapping ownership and shared garages and offices with the preexisting few that still dominated the market.[46]

Today, hundreds of thousands of dollars of waste are built into the policy. Not only is there no meaningful competition for contracts, but the city school system also pays bus drivers a full day's work even if they only work a couple of hours a day. And the department has been criticized for not monitoring the drivers to determine whether they are shortchanging the district.[47]

THE LAUSD TRANSLATION UNIT

Fraud can sometimes reach such a pitch of intensity in small, unattended pockets of school districts that it turns these tiny units into enterprises wholly dedicated to profiteering. Consider the LAUSD's $5-million-plus Translation Unit, which provides translation and interpretation services for the district. A 2001 inspector general investigation suggested a unit seriously affected by nepotism.[48] The unit's upper-echelon officers had allegedly transformed it into a job bank for their extended family and friends. At least one relative of a top official reportedly got a job in the unit even though he did not live in the United States.

Nepotism made it easy for family and friends to bilk the unit. Some family members allegedly never showed up for work. Others did not put in the hours they were paid for. A number were working other jobs while on the unit payroll.[49] But because family members were supervising other family members, they signed forms, authorized checks, and covered for one another. Two sisters of one top official, with the help of other family members, allegedly falsified invoices and got paid for work they never did.

THE LAUSD DIVISION OF ADULT AND CAREER EDUCATION

The same acute level of corruption appeared to affect the LAUSD Division of Adult and Career Education (DACE), as two 2000 investigations suggested.[50] Senior and midlevel DACE officials allegedly used the division to enrich themselves and their colleagues—nineteen people in all—by giving one another fictitious overtime. They allegedly ripped off hundreds of thousands of dollars by pretending to work overtime at phony teaching jobs at schools under the division.

Fraud reportedly filtered through many layers within the division as upper-echelon officials enlisted subordinates to help perpetrate the fraud. Senior administrators and an upper-lever officer in the technology unit arranged for the fictitious assignments. Personnel in the division's Fiscal Services unit identified appropriate funding sources from which the bogus workers could get paid. Personnel in the Office Personnel unit prepared the "request for personnel actions" forms and got the appropriate class codes, job titles, and work hours for the fake assignments. Principals created phony overtime teaching work and countersigned fake time cards and payroll reports.

Some of the people who received the overtime were executives and administrators who were not even eligible for it because of their positions. Others were certificated employees who vastly exceeded their overtime allowances.[51]

WHERE THE MONEY GOES

The data on corruption in the three largest school districts paint of a picture of an Alice-in-Wonderland world of inverted ideals where a few con artists have cooked up every imaginable way to profit from the system. A few school employees and vendors have devised scams to get their hands on the money flowing through these school districts.

EMPLOYEE AND VENDOR SCAMS

Some officials at various levels in the hierarchy have systematically colluded with colleagues to extort payments from vendors desperate for lucrative contracts. In 1989 twenty-six inspectors and administrators, some high in the chain of command in the BOE Bureau of Maintenance (now the Division of School Facilities), were convicted for methodically extorting tens of thousands of dollars from school construction contractors for nearly a decade.[1]

The Bureau of Maintenance had a long history of corruption. As one criminal case revealed, before 1977 officials would extort kickbacks from contractors on an ad hoc basis.[2] But the city's fiscal crisis in the mid-1970s opened more opportunities for profiteering by increasing the number of emergency oral contracts permitted. These contracts dispensed with most competitive bidding rules. So from 1977 to around 1987 officials in charge of school construction in different parts of the city established a schoolwide schedule of payoffs, which they called "the System."[3] Under it contractors had to kick back 2 percent of routine original contracts, 5 to 10 percent of change orders, and 10 percent of emergency contracts. Every month officials would meet in restaurants to divide the spoils. Borough office area managers and assistant area managers would each get 10 percent, general inspectors and inspectors 40 percent.

Officials made sure that cooperative contractors had their payment vouchers and bills processed promptly and steered emergency jobs to them. But if contractors were uncooperative, facilities officials would drive them out of business. They would "lose" their invoices, withhold or delay their payment approvals, and not pay them for work they had done. And they would make sure these contractors never got any other BOE work again.

The plight of contractors who resisted the System is exemplified by the case of Gary Novick, who learned about the System when he started working for the BOE in 1979. At first he strongly resisted payment demands. But after officials kept "losing" his invoices, he paid kickbacks seven to nine times between 1980 and 1983. Officials still forced him out because, he believes, he had not been sufficiently gung ho.

The problem seems to continue to some degree to this day. In December 2001, eleven school custodians were charged with rigging contracts for window washing at a number of schools in return for 10 percent cash kickbacks. Some custodians pocketed as much as $62,000. School windows, needless to say, were never washed.[4] About two years later, in February 2003, police arrested eighteen other custodians along with yet another window cleaning contractor on charges of bribery and bid rigging. The state attorney general announced that the custodians had a deal with the contractor that netted them between 10 to 50 percent of the value of each window cleaning contract, a deal that had been in effect for at least four years.[5]

Officials have devised various other ruses to profit from vendors eager for contracts. Some get vendors to hire family members, for instance. Shortly after the former superintendent of Community School District 9 in the South Bronx informed a contractor to whom he had given over $1 million in business about his wife's stellar credentials, the contractor hired her as a consultant.[6]

Officials can also get vendors to hire *them* on the side, in violation of conflict of interest rules. The central BOE officer in charge of testing in the 1970s, for instance, allegedly took $400,000 from a publishing company to co-author the citywide reading tests that the BOE used.[7] After a cheating scandal, auditors advised the BOE to solicit bids from publishers who did not work with the school official. But the official refused, insisting that the test had been chosen by an objective committee, on which he merely served as an advisor.

Not all vendors are victims. Some pour a great deal of energy into figuring out how to cement contracts and entwine school officials' interests with their own. Consider the complex relationship between Vidata International and the BOE as reported in the press.

A training company, Vidata first landed its $2-million, four-year contract with the BOE in 1970 through a central board member who had consulted for it. The board member maneuvered to avoid competitive bidding and a signed written contract.[8] An investigation later revealed that the company paid him $10,000.

Before long Vidata had enmeshed the interests of many BOE officials with its own in various ways. It allegedly introduced school officials to prostitutes (who claimed that they were just interested in dating BOE men) and showered employees low and high with gifts of cash and gadgets such as electric lawn mowers, hedge cutters, electric drills, and digital clock radios.[9]

Vidata also retained a top officer in the BOE's Audio-Visual Bureau as a paid consultant.[10] It paid other school employees second salaries to serve as instructors in its training program, even arranging to hire them with the help of the appropriate unions.[11] As Vidata's owner explained it, "We just wanted to be nice, that's all there was to it."[12]

Similar complex conflicts of interest developed when the BOE illegally awarded nearly $2 million worth of work to Computer Specifics Corporation, a computer firm formed by a former BOE employee.[13] That company also hired various BOE employees.

The problem of officials seeking enrichment from contractors appears to continue to this day, although it appears to be less common in New York City than it was. In 2000, for instance, one central board member allegedly stood to make a windfall when an internet computer company he had a stake in—he was the company chairman and had a large number of stock options in it—was bidding for a lucrative BOE contract. His colleagues on the board had waived conflict of interest rules. But when the press got wind of the story and SCI launched an investigation, the board put the bidding on hold. Some months after SCI Commissioner Edward Stancik's death in March 2002, investigators closed the case.[14]

Employees and vendors also bilk the school system directly in various ways. Investigations going back a century suggest that the most common way is outright theft. Stolen goods range from computers and food to pencils and precious stone lions at school entrances.

Thievery can also include diverting money and resources. A 1995 audit, for instance, suggested that central officials were using a slush fund to bankroll chauffeured limousines, patronage jobs for top personnel, and office furniture.[15] Officials made it impossible for auditors to follow the money. They retained no receipts, made checks out to companies without any supporting documentation, paid consultants without consultant approval forms or time sheets, and authorized payments verbally instead of in writing.

Some employees also steal by billing the BOE for work not done. These scams take many forms. Sometimes officials bill for no-show family members, as did a community school district that paid the wife of a school administrator thousands of dollars in consulting fees even though she never did any work for the district. The consulting fees went to pad her husband's salary.[16] Vendors may bill for no-shows, too, as did a training company that charged for fifteen nonexistent teachers.[17]

Most frequent, however, is billing for phony overtime. It is sometimes found among middle-upper management. The director of continuing education in Brooklyn's District 23 was indicted for illegally billing over $69,000 of regular work hours as overtime.[18] But more often it is found at lower levels. A comprehensive 1984 audit of over 18,000 educators showed that their overtime, known as "per session," came to $42 million a year. This figure did not include millions in overtime for thousands of custodians, custodial helpers, and other BOE staff. Many employees billed for hours they never put in.[19] Others billed for hours they could not document. At least one person worked full-time on overtime to circumvent the regular hiring process.[20] As a result of this audit, the BOE put caps on overtime by educators.

The problem of phony overtime, however, continues to this day. In 1996 the city comptroller unearthed vast abuses in overtime of school custodial employees.[21]

Phony overtime, no-shows, "low-shows," and similar scams also affected the LAUSD and CPS particularly before 1997–98, when a new management team restructured a number of areas of the CPS and privatized parts of the workforce such as custodial helpers. In the LAUSD, overtime abuse seems to be taken for granted by officials from high up in central management down to lower-level employees. Although some low-level employees have forged their boss's signatures on overtime forms,[22] in a number of cases supervisors and officials in middle and upper management have deliberately assigned overtime to their friends knowing that they would never show up or would not work the hours for which they would be paid.[23]

Phony overtime has been a problem in Chicago, too. Numerous investigations and audits show that various categories of employees made a business out of overtime, carefully scheduling work on weekends when no one was around to check them or simply putting in for fake hours for years on end, costing the system millions of dollars a year.[24] In 1995 the CPS allocated $6.6 million for overtime for its plant operations unit alone, which it considered a "treasure trove."[25]

THE TOLL ON EDUCATION

There is a substantial literature, inspired by the work of Robert K. Merton, that argues that corruption often serves a useful societal purpose.[1] Nevertheless, the general consensus today seems to be that the long-term effect of corruption on public agencies is negative because it undermines equal opportunity and due process, conditions on which the American political ethos is predicated.[2] The evidence supports this contention in the context of urban schools, where crimes like bid rigging and bribery transform what was intended to be a meritocratic equal playing field between vendors to backroom deals that award contracts on the basis of how much a vendor can enrich an administrator, not how much value his firm can contribute to pupils.

Even more serious, corruption appears to hurt learning directly. Although many causes contribute to poor pupil scholastic performance and it is hard to single out any single factor for blame, a cursory look at some of America's academically beleaguered districts suggests a correlation between widespread, systemic corruption on the one hand and substandard pupil performance on the other.

CORRELATION TO ACADEMIC FAILURES

In New York City those community school districts with the most serious and highest incidence of corruption cases ranked lowest in citywide tests.[3] Districts ranking lowest in math and reading scores spent the most per capita on administrators, who until 1996–97 provided local school boards with political patronage, but the least on teachers, who never did.[4] Even after accounting for differences in family income, pupil mobility, students' proficiency in English, and teacher experience, elementary school students in districts where investigators had identified wrongdoing scored nearly four points lower on reading and math tests than students in other districts.[5]

The correlation is borne out in other urban school districts, too. The most academically beleaguered districts tend to be the ones with the longest, most severe, and systemic criminal records.

In Massachusetts, the Lawrence school district has one of the most flagrant investigative records in the state. Administrators spent money meant for disadvantaged children in the classroom on perks for themselves, including $400,000 on laptop computers, $3,000 on a dinner, and flower deliveries.[6] As administrative staff and salaries grew 11 percent over two years, the district spent less on textbooks, library books, and teacher development. The students, meanwhile, ranked near the bottom of the state in test scores, and dropout rates soared.[7]

In New Jersey, corruption and gross mismanagement clearly correlate with poor student performance. The three school districts that the New Jersey state education department took over—Jersey City, Paterson, and Newark—had the highest rates of systemic corruption and among the lowest test scores and highest dropout rates in the state.[8]

In Jersey City, the first urban school district to be taken over by a state, a New Jersey State Education Department investigation documented pervasive political patronage, cronyism, union pressure, and theft, along with soaring dropout rates, low attendance, and failing academic performance.[9] In a lengthy report, state investigators described a school district where jobs were systematically doled out on the basis of political patronage, union pressure, and cronyism.[10] City hall dominated school personnel decisions ranging from who got tenure and raises to who got to be a substitute. A former mayor laid off dozens of teachers who did not support his political campaign. School board members, controlled by city hall, funneled lucrative contracts to favored contractors. A gym teacher became his school's personnel chief after his union supported the incumbent mayor's reelection. The mayor's sister and stepdaughter were school board members.[11]

Needless to say, investigators found oversight in the Jersey City school district a charade.[12] The school board did not oversee the superintendent or upper-echelon administrators, the superintendent did not oversee the deputies, the deputies did not hold their subordinates accountable—and so on down the school hierarchy. Meanwhile, only 25.9 percent of Jersey City's ninth graders passed standard proficiency exams. The district's problems finally triggered a state takeover in 1989.

In Newark a state investigation uncovered one school system but two separate worlds: one, the world of central school headquarters with its exotic retreats, new cars, free meals, and abundant supplies for school board members and administrators[13]; the other, the world of chronically failing students, low attendance rates, empty school libraries, meager supplies, and decrepit buildings. Although the school system's spending per pupil was among the highest in the state, at the time of its takeover by the state, only about a quarter of eleventh graders passed the high school proficiency test.

Profit, power, and patronage took precedence over children and learning at practically every turn. The state report, more than one thousand pages, portrays the nine-member Newark school board as more interested in exotic vacations, cars, and restaurants and getting jobs for friends and family than in fixing schools. While central school officials sat in plush offices, children sat in badly decayed school buildings, a number of which were hazardous. Piles of debris covered some school yards. Walls were riddled with holes. The district leased an unsafe, rat-infested factory building as a school at $175,000 a year, even though inspection reports had long been advising the district to vacate it.[14]

Newark school officials also laundered kickbacks from contractors by requiring them to contribute $1,000 to the so-called Executive Superintendent's Scholarship Fund. If contractors did not contribute, they could not do business with the school system.[15] To increase their profiteering potential by increasing their supply of tax dollars, officials created phantom students and fraudulently overreported enrollment. Accurate attendance reporting was "careless or non-existent."[16]

Conflicts of interest, falsification of reports, willful violation of election and competitive bidding laws, misused federal funds and control over cash, and a huge backlog of capital projects were other common problems cited throughout the district.[17] The district's problems led to a court-ordered state takeover in 1995.

In Paterson, children also placed near the bottom of the state on standardized tests as school officials indulged in extensive abuses, fiscal wrongdoing, theft, and fraud. Management would approve change orders for work included in original bid specifications, for instance, giving a windfall to contractors.[18]

Of course, a correlation between corruption and subpar student performance does not necessarily mean that the relationship is causal. In some cases, the same factors that aggravate schools' vulnerability to corruption may also reduce pupil achievement. Studies link parents' involvement in their children's education to the children's academic success, for example.[19] At the same time, involved parents often serve as an additional pair of eyes to notice suspicious problems in schools and hold administrators accountable. So an absence of involved parents may simultaneously depress pupil performance and facilitate corruption.

In other cases, however, corruption appears to harm student performance directly. Although proving a cause-and-effect relationship is difficult—so many factors contribute to academic failure, and isolating the effects of corruption is complicated—there are many plausible reasons why corruption might hurt learning.

FUNDS DIVERTED FROM THE CLASSROOM

One reason is that corruption and abuse can drain resources away from the classroom. When legislators decide how much money to allocate to schools, they operate on the assumption that if they pour in a certain amount, each child will receive a certain amount. When politicians speak about school funding in terms of "dollars per child," the implication is that a certain number of dollars is needed to pay for certain programs, goods, and services that all ultimately help children. Federal, state, and city budgetary formulas are based on this kind of input-output assumption.

Although there is debate about whether increasing school expenditures makes a difference to student scores,[20] there is broader agreement that what counts is how much money makes it to classroom instruction.[21] The model on which the New York City school system has reported its yearly budgets since 1994, based on the School District Budget Model formulated by Coopers and Lybrand, ties most of the money flowing into the Board of Education to classroom instruction.[22] New York City's budget figures suggest that it spends 88.9 percent of its budget on schools—a relatively high number compared to other urban school districts.

In fact, however, corruption and abuse siphon money away before it ever reaches the classroom. Theft depletes resources and libraries, while fraud has led to dilapidated buildings where children sit in broken chairs under gaping holes in the ceiling and go without supplies like toilet paper. Payroll padding siphons off money. New York City auditors have estimated that payroll padding diverts tens of millions of dollars every year from the classroom to bloated administrations. Other studies place the yearly losses in the hundreds of millions a year. In Newark, the costs of payroll padding was in the hundreds of thousands of dollars. Corrupt and abusive schemes turn expensive programs away from helping children. Also in Newark, state auditors found that, although the district received millions of dollars as a result of its high enrollment of failing, poor, and special education students, it diverted millions of dollars from the classroom. One employee was paid a salary of $54,000 to run a do-nothing "aerospace project" from a space in Newark Airport that the district leased for $18,000 a year.[23]

Money to schools is also siphoned off by contractors chosen through bid splitting, bid rigging, and kickback schemes. Such contractors can more easily cheat on billing because of their covert, perfidious relationships with management: neither party has an incentive to blow the whistle since both have dirty hands. When New York City school administrators split $42 million into amounts of $10,000 or less that they could then hand out to preselected companies, the companies, whose products were already overpriced, were able to charge even more.[24] They charged $25.87 per thousand napkins, for instance, instead of $8.75 per thousand as available in local stores.

Even "good" corruption—corruption intended to move legitimate business through red tape—siphons money away. Many contractors factor in the cost of interest lost because of bureaucratic delays and possible payoffs in their initial bids. If not, they usually pass them back to school districts through expensive change orders later on, as cases in the LAUSD and New York City schools show.[25]

Critics might argue that although corruption, waste, and abuse hurt taxpayers, they do not hurt children because school districts can always get more money if programs are not achieving desired results—that is, if children are not learning. The monopoly status of public schools facilitates their getting more money, and court decisions to require more school funding tend to be based primarily on student academic performance, but there is a limit to how much legislators can realistically tax the public. So although a little corruption and waste can probably be offset by additional funding, once corruption and waste become rampant and systemic they are likely to surpass what tax revenues can bring in, thus cutting into children's classroom resources.

LOWER-QUALITY GOODS AND SERVICES

Corruption may not only block money from getting to the classroom. Corruption also makes it possible that what does get to the classroom is of inferior quality and less helpful to learning.

Consider how bribery and kickback schemes can hurt the quality of instructional goods and services. One 1989 investigation showed that a school board member forced his district to switch reading textbooks three times in five years as he kept shopping around for increasingly bigger kickbacks from different publishers, one of whom gave him at least $50,000.

The students, deprived of the continuity needed to build a reading vo-cabulary, saw their reading scores plunge during that period.

Kickbacks and bribery also hurt student learning in New York City's District 29 in southeast Queens. In 1996 and 1997 the superintendent there rigged a $6-million technology contract to a computer company af-filiated with the developer who owned the building that housed the school board offices. The superintendent diverted money to pay the de-veloper bogus "consulting" fees.[26] In return, the developer and computer company gave the superintendent hundreds of thousands of dollars' worth of jewelry, vacations to Europe, shopping sprees, and special deals on two-family homes on which the developer did not require her to make mortgage payments. The superintendent soon sold the homes, making tens of thousands of dollars in profits.[27]

The computer company, meanwhile, gave students archaic, inferior, sometimes nonfunctional computers.[28] One official succinctly described them as "substandard."[29] Without decent computers, which teachers had been counting on, students saw their math scores decline. By the fall of 2001, District 29, which in 1990 had some of the city's best schools and was ranked eighth overall in the city, had fallen to the bottom of Queens districts in math, with most eighth graders flunking math. Overall, the dis-trict sank to fourteenth in the city.[30]

Kickback schemes can also affect the physical condition of children's classrooms and school buildings. When construction and repair contracts are rigged, the work is often shoddy or not done at all.[31] Neglected build-ings not only create safety hazards but also harm learning in several ways. They send a message to children that they are not worth debris-free class-rooms, working air conditioners, or a functional gym, which may dampen their motivation. As important, deteriorating schools are less attractive to the kind of quality teachers whom Ronald Ferguson has shown lead to im-provements in average student test scores.[32] All this may partly explain the correlation widely found between substandard school buildings and poor test scores.[33] One study, for instance, found that pupils who learned in schools that were in poor condition scored 6 percent below children who learned in fair conditions and 11 percent below those who learned in ex-cellent conditions.[34]

LOW-QUALITY HIRES

Political patronage and nepotism can also hurt learning by making merit irrelevant and increasing the risk that low-quality people will be hired. Investigative reports and secretly recorded conversations illustrate how irrelevant merit becomes. One school board member who was being se-cretly recorded summed up the way some New York City school boards used to pick principals and other school staff: "You could have been Al-bert Einstein and it wouldn't have made a difference."[35] When the super-intendent questioned the qualifications of this board member's candi-date, the board member blew up: "Unqualified? Qualified? Bullshit. That's my recommendation."[36] "If we recommend somebody," another board member chimed in, the district had to hire that person so long as "they're not illiterate or deformed or something the matter with them." Similar contempt for merit was caught on secret audiotapes in other parts of the school system. When another Brooklyn board member lobbied his colleagues to promote a clearly unqualified person as principal, his only pitch was, "Why can't you vote for him? He's my son-in-law!"[37]

It is easy to find cases where patronage employees trumped more qualified candidates—New Jersey State Education Department auditors found such cases in Jersey City,[38] for example. It is also easy to find exam-ples of patronage hires who have been disasters. After the board member quoted earlier succeeded in appointing his son-in-law school principal, for instance, state inspectors found his school in a state of chaos and "educa-tional dysfunction."[39] The school had no music, gym, or art classes. There were so few textbooks that children could not take them home to study. Students fought in class, and some poured coffee into inspectors' brief-cases. But the principal was nowhere to be found. Meanwhile, nearly all third graders read below grade level.

In New York City, two principals who were appointed in backroom po-litical deals were dubbed "educationally corrupt" by former Chancellor Raymond Cortines. One of them had created an environment where chil-dren would roam the halls aimlessly and no learning would take place.[40] The other principal was known for her "hygiene problems"[41] and had poor leadership skills.

Patronage can also reduce the caliber of staff indirectly—by gradually encouraging the departure of top-quality teachers who become demoral-ized and depressed by the unfair system that they see around them.[42]

"GOOD" CORRUPTION

What about corruption perpetrated to help children and get school busi-ness done? Merton, other scholars, and even Supreme Court justices (such as Justice Antonin Scalia dissenting in *Rutan v. Republican Party of Illinois*)[43] have extolled the virtues of political patronage as a way to inte-grate minorities into mainstream society. Political patronage in some school districts provided jobs to many inner-city minorities. Chapters 10 and 11 will discuss the kind of corruption in which officials circumvent red tape to benefit the district's mission. As Robert Klitgaard put it, "If the prevailing system is bad, then corruption may be good."[44]

However, even this kind of "good" corruption can take a toll on education. It perpetuates a dysfunctional system by concealing how bad it is. It also sustains the myth of accountability in public schools that some scholars have described. In addition, there is something inherently antithetical between the goal of public schools, which is to teach children to be fully participating citizens in a democracy, and at the same time accepting that schools lie and cheat to accomplish this mission. Such misconduct, if embraced by schools, will doubtless seep into the culture that surrounds schoolchildren. Finally, "good" corruption can easily turn sour and subvert the district's goals.

Part III will present examples in which school officials and vendors illegally circumvent red tape for "noble" purposes that clearly improve the delivery of education, at least in the short term. But there is virtually no evidence that black political patronage in schools helped black children learn.[45] In fact, the evidence presented here suggests that patronage may have harmed learning.

HOW WIDESPREAD?

It is very difficult to study corruption, waste, and abuse empirically. Corruption is by nature clandestine. The parties involved have incentives to hide it. If upper-level school officials find out about it, they will usually be reluctant to tell researchers about it. So researchers need to rely on cases that are uncovered by the media, investigators, and law enforcement officials. But even these may never come to the public's attention. Cases can be sealed by court order or closed for political and other reasons that have nothing to do with their merits. Law enforcement may not have the resources necessary to pursue leads or substantiate a case, particularly if it is not big and splashy. Even if prosecutors pursue a case, many crimes are hard to prove. In a number of cases, school officials who took money from subordinates or from prospective job candidates repaid the money after they were investigated. Although they could have been disciplined for conflict of interest violations, these officials were not prosecuted for bribery or extortion because they claimed that the money was given to them as a campaign contribution or a loan. One New York City principal solicited $6,000 from a teacher who was seeking a promotion. The principal's father, who was a board member on the local school board, subsequently voted for her promotion. When the payment was exposed, the parties claimed the money was a loan, which the principal then repaid. No criminal charges were filed.[46]

In addition, fraud cases may be dismissed or not brought to trial because of technicalities relating to the statute of limitations or lack of a speedy trial or a prosecutor's failure to cite jurisdiction. Further, even if a corruption case makes it to the public's attention, the full extent of the problem may not. Defendants frequently cop pleas to lesser charges. Parties to fraud may receive immunity and make deals with law enforcement that conceal the true extent of their and others' involvement in wrongdoing.

On the other side of the coin, there is also a possibility that the extent of corruption may be overstated in the media. Much of the press, after all, thrives on scandal. And reporting a scandal does not require proof beyond a reasonable doubt that a crime has been committed.

Nonetheless, as far as the media goes, the shortcoming regarding empirical research of school corruption and abuse is likely to be that the problem is underreported, not overreported. Proof beyond a reasonable doubt, after all, is necessary only when a criminal conviction is at stake, not when establishing facts in civil cases or reporting accurately to the public. Further, cases reported in the media are likely to be only a fraction of what actually happens, for all the reasons described earlier.

On the basis of official investigations completed by school inspector general offices, publicly released audit reports, and criminal arrests, the problem seems significant. In New York City, the Special Commissioner of Investigation arrested about 200 people from the time the office was up and running in 1991 to July 2002. This does not include the 140 people arrested and the $23 million recovered by the New York City School Construction Authority, which until 2003 oversaw school construction and had its own inspector general just for construction.

The LAUSD inspector general referred three cases for prosecution, thirty for disciplinary action, and eleven for debarment or sanction in fiscal 2002.[47] It identified about $149 million in waste in 2002, $80 million in 2001, and $159 million in 2000—and these amounts do not include millions of dollars of questioned costs.[48]

The CPS inspector general, in its first year of operation in 1994–95, referred twelve cases for prosecution and dozens for disciplinary action, and uncovered $19.2 million in waste.[49] In 1996–97 the inspector general identified $22 million in waste and referred seven cases for prosecution.[50]

Some years ago these public cases were probably the tip of the iceberg. When one woman explained to a board official, who was secretly recording the conversation for investigators, how she knew to offer him $10,000 to get a principalship, she replied: "Nobody said it. But you know, . . . I've been around a long time, and I know a lot of board people . . . across the city."[51] When school construction contractors were paying off school officials in one of the biggest undercover investigations in the 1990s, every one of them "perceived bribery as a normal part of doing business with the board," as the School Construction Authority inspector general, Thomas Thacher II, observed.[52] No one "showed the slightest hesitation or compunction about offering bribes." In Chicago the school inspector general declared that reported cases are "not anomalies but are a microcosmic representation of the system at large."[53]

But today, after inspectors general, especially in New York City and Chicago, have been at their jobs for so many years, it may be that much of the iceberg has been broken up. Unfortunately, however, because the size of the iceberg is uncertain, we cannot know for sure.

Waste is even harder to measure. Although inspectors general and auditors in all three of America's largest districts have found thousands of dollars in waste, most waste is built into a district's structure, regulatory procedures, policies, and collective bargaining contracts.[54] This kind of built-in waste takes a toll day in, day out over many areas of the school system. Moreover, the indirect consequences of the built-in structures that give rise to waste—such as managerial paralysis, alienated vendors, and minimal vendor competition—are hard to quantify.

PART II

THE REMEDIES TRIED: THE FRENZIED SEARCH FOR ACCOUNTABILITY

THE QUEST FOR ACCOUNTABILITY

The problem with schools today is not the lack of oversight and accountability mechanisms but an overabundance of the wrong kind, along with the flawed top-down structures they dictated. This chapter explores these accountability mechanisms and what they were intended to do.

Our understanding of corruption and what we do to control it is inextricably bound to our understanding of human behavior and what motivates it. Whatever theory we hold of human behavior determines what incentives we choose to encourage or discourage such conduct.

Although a variety of theories of human behavior are implicit in the social science literature, this book is premised on the postulate, shared by many scholars, including rational choice and agency theorists, that human beings are resourceful, self-interested, and capable of making rational choices about their conduct. Being self-interested does not mean that people are egotistical or evil. It simply means that they choose whatever course of conduct they believe will bring them the greatest satisfaction and happiness.[1] This could mean stealing and cheating, but it could also mean being altruistic.

Criminologists who subscribe to theories such as rational choice, routine activity, and deterrence additionally emphasize that when people have the opportunity to commit a crime, they weigh the downside—such as the risk of getting caught and punished and being stigmatized by society—against the upside—such as their potential gains and the ease of engaging in crime—before deciding what to do.[2] So, given human self-interest, if no one is watching, the crime is easy to commit, and the potential gains are high, crime may well ensue.[3]

All of this theory is pertinent to corruption and corruption control in complex organizations. If human behavior is inherently self-interested, it follows that controlling employee conduct will be a perennial concern in every organization. As agency theorists explain, any time one person, the principal, hires another, the agent, there will be a problem of control because the agent's interests will not always coincide with the principal's.[4] In pursuing his or her own interests, the agent may neglect or even subvert the organization's goals.

The most common way organizations guard against subversive or remiss employees is to separate supervision from implementation.[5] This separation is the beginning of oversight mechanisms that spring from the profound understanding that people are self-interested and rational.

COMPLIANCE AND PERFORMANCE ACCOUNTABILITY

Saying that oversight is necessary to guard against fraud and waste is only the beginning, however. There are many ways to set up an oversight relationship and many models of supervision. Under one model, principals attempt to control their agents by scripting out in advance how they must do their work through detailed, uniform procedural rules and regulations; the supervisors' role is to ensure that employees follow mandated procedures. The premise is that the less discretion employees have, the fewer the opportunities for deviance, waste, or abuse. This model of oversight is often called compliance accountability or accountability for inputs because the focus is on ensuring compliance with inputs or procedure.[6]

Common ways to ensure compliance accountability include issuing rules, regulations, or standard operating procedures; earmarking funds for specific purposes; and establishing layers of supervisors to watch others. Bureaucracies were in large part conceived to promote compliance.

Compliance accountability may be contrasted with a different model of accountability under which principals control agents by ensuring that they deliver results that accord with the principals' goals. The focus is on the quality of goods and services produced, not on the rules or procedures to produce them.[7] Employees have wide berth in deciding how to do their work. Supervisors mostly check that they get the job done to the satisfaction of constituents and agency goals. Since the focus here is on job performance—*outputs*—this kind of accountability is often called accountability for performance or outputs. Common ways to ensure performance accountability include establishing goals and standards, determining whether employees meet them, and imposing positive or negative consequences accordingly.[8]

Traditionally, there has been an implicit trade-off between compliance and performance accountability. One key purpose of compliance accountability is to limit the opportunities employees have to rip off their organization. But dictating procedures and decisions from on high in advance of knowing what problems will arise in the field is an inherently clunky way to ensure that the organization's goals are met. The bigger and more complex the organization and the more varied and changing its constituents' needs, moreover, the more inefficient compliance accountability becomes. When constituents' needs are as varied and changeable as are public school children's in big, diverse cities, school districts are likely to encounter new problems requiring solutions that do not comport with protocol. But because compliance accountability does not allow much deviation from protocol, it invariably sacrifices some degree of performance in the name of fighting corruption, waste, and abuse. However, this sacrifice is often in vain because tight compliance accountability actually provides incentives for fraud, waste, and abuse in agencies of a certain size and shape.

In its strictest form, compliance accountability is incompatible with performance accountability. The greater the number of decisions that are determined at the top and that field managers merely implement, the more unfair it is to hold them accountable for results. How can a manager fairly be held responsible for the quality of goods and services if he or she has no significant control over how they are delivered?[9]

But compliance accountability is a necessity in the public sector. Because goods and services reach thousands or millions of people and because the money public officials handle comes from all taxpayers, the government has a fiduciary duty to ensure that money is spent properly and in accordance with the legal health, safety, and constitutional rights of all citizens. Further, Americans have long relied heavily on process and procedure to ensure fundamental fairness and equity in the allocation and expenditure of taxpayer dollars and to promote diversity. As Dennis Thompson suggests, Americans put a premium on having a diversity of goods and services, sometimes making the process more important than substance.[10] That is why government institutions, schools included, are likely always to be hemmed in by some procedural rules and why performance accountability is unlikely completely to replace compliance accountability.

A SPECTRUM OF COMPLIANCE ACCOUNTABILITY MECHANISMS

Procedural rules beg many questions. How many procedural rules are needed? How detailed should they be? When and how often do supervisors check employees for compliance—before they begin work? after every step along the way? at the end once they have finished? And how intrusive is the checking? Should supervisors stop business at every step of the checking process or monitor it continuously, stopping business only if they find something amiss?

These are important questions because compliance accountability can be thought of as a spectrum, with the strictest compliance controls at one end and the most liberal at the other. In its stricter forms, compliance accountability scripts out in advance in great detail exactly what employees must do and how they must do it. It earmarks money in advance, for example, and requires it to be spent only on set goods and services. This approach can be dubbed the *top-down control* version of compliance accountability. The more indulgent versions of compliance accountability, on the other hand, may require employees to comply with a few, loosely worded laws and rules that leave some room for discretion.

The intrusiveness of supervisors in enforcing compliance can also span a spectrum. On the strict end of the spectrum, employees may be required to seek permission from supervisors before embarking on work. A common example is overtime: people cannot get it unless they get approval first. Or supervisors may stop business at various points along the way to make sure the rules are being followed. Typical examples are the requirements that various supervisors sign and review forms after every major step of a purchase of services. At the more liberal end of the spectrum, supervisors may merely be required to conduct a post factum audit to verify compliance with relevant laws and procedures—after business is done. This last form of enforcement gives employees more freedom to respond to pressing problems quickly and deal with possible consequences later. Post factum audits are risky if an organization has a culture of corruption. But technology (combined with the right structure) can today make it possible for supervisors to monitor school business more closely and continuously, without being intrusive and without delaying the steps of the process. The point is that even within compliance accountability, it is possible to give managers a reasonable amount of discretion.

ACCOUNTABILITY IN THE THREE LARGEST DISTRICTS

Traditionally, America's three largest school districts, like most urban districts in the nation, favored compliance over performance accountability. And they usually opted for the most stringent forms of compliance accountability—mandating detailed standard operating procedures, often requiring employees to obtain approval before starting work, requiring supervisors to check employees along the way, and sometimes even requiring a post factum audit in addition to all of the other checks. In paying contractors who do maintenance work, for example, aside from all the checks that are in place through the process, engineering audits are often required after the work is completed to make doubly sure change orders are in order. The engineering audits entail a meticulous review of all relevant plans, specifications, drawings, and contract documents.

Although most organizations have a mix of activities—some centrally controlled, others locally controlled—what is striking about America's three largest school districts is that the majority of activities is centrally controlled. In their quest to curb fraud, waste, and abuse, the three districts, with a few notable areas of exception in New York City and Chicago, have been overwhelmingly concerned with inputs and controlling operations from headquarters.

The upshot has been to greatly limit the discretion of principals and field and middle managers through a plethora of detailed central rules, regulations, policies, standard operating procedures, and fiscal formulae. As a director at the Chicago Public Schools (CPS) Department of Procurement and Contracts put it when he described school purchasing there, "In the private sector you can buy anything, so long as it isn't illegal. But in [public school systems], you can only buy what is authorized. That's a big difference."[11]

The central offices in all three districts hold the purse strings and make most of the budgeting decisions that affect classrooms by earmarking money in advance for narrow purposes. Generally, money earmarked for one purpose cannot be used for another.

The central offices also control functions such as school maintenance and purchasing, requiring schools to follow detailed standard operating procedures. To repair or renovate buildings—even to replace a fluorescent light bulb—there are multiple checks, requiring multiple reviews of work orders, sending them to a central office, and then waiting for lengthy periods until someone reviews and, hopefully, dispatches a central worker to handle the problem. Schools cannot fix the problem themselves or hire whomever they wish to do so.

Central offices in the three districts also limit the choice of vendors from whom and types of goods managers can buy. With few exceptions, managers cannot make purchases unless they are preapproved goods from preapproved vendors. If sums go over certain amounts, permission to proceed is necessary. At the CPS, for instance, if a manager wants to buy something biddable over $10,000 or nonbiddable over $25,000, he or she must get board approval beforehand.

The central office in the Los Angeles Unified School District (LAUSD) also strongly influences curriculum and textbook choices. Even though

New York City allows principals leeway in picking textbooks, purchasing rules and pressures from the central office limit discretion. Central officials determine what classroom bulletin boards should look like, regardless of what teachers believe works best for their students. If the bulletin boards do not conform to the central office's wishes, the teachers run the risk of receiving negative evaluations.[12]

COMPLIANCE AND ADMINISTRATIVE PYRAMIDS

Compliance goals dictated the administrative shape of the three districts. In each district, the top executive—called the chancellor in New York City, chief executive officer in the Chicago Public Schools, and superintendent in the Los Angeles Unified School District—presides over a multilayered pyramidal bureaucracy because that seemed best suited to enhance top-down control. Although major changes are under way in New York City's school system, its pyramidal shape remains. (See diagrams 1, 2, 3, and 4.)

DIAGRAM 1. Organizational chart of the New York City Board of Education prior to July 2002

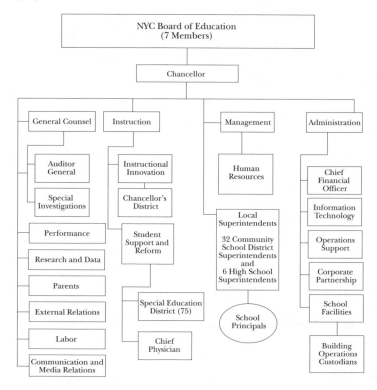

DIAGRAM 2. Organizational chart of the New York City Department of Education proposed as of January 2003

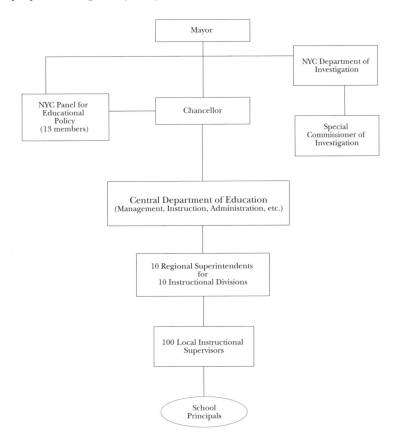

This does not mean the three districts have exactly the same design. Indeed, each district is broken down geographically into a different number of subunits that operate somewhat differently from city to city. Their governance is also different. Mayors have virtually controlled the CPS since 1995[13] and the school system since the summer of 2002,[14] but the mayor does not control the LAUSD. And some districts decentralized certain functions that the others did not. For example, the CPS somewhat decentralized school maintenance, but the other two districts did not. Nevertheless, the districts share a similar top-down frame.

As society's expectations of public schools expanded during the twentieth century, their responsibilities burgeoned. Before the mid-1970s, for instance, schools did not have to teach disabled children, who were "medi-

DIAGRAM 3.　Organizational chart of the Los Angeles Unified School District

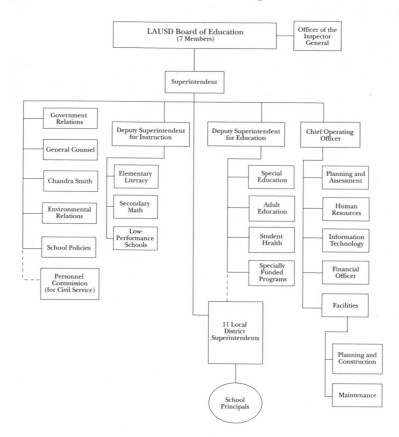

cally exempt." As late as World War II, most children in districts such as New York City and Boston left school in the eighth grade for jobs in the docks or elsewhere. And in the early 1900s, staff had virtually no employment rights. Teachers who became pregnant were summarily dismissed. Today, we take it for granted that schools must teach *all* children, honor elaborate due process procedures for staff, and meet a daunting array of other demands, many of which used to be considered the responsibility of family, community, and religious organizations.[15]

Although many other agencies also took on added responsibilities during the last century, schools were uniquely obliged to do so because they are supposed to reflect a democratic society's expectations. As the education historian Diane Ravitch has noted, "The school is the principal public institution, beyond the government itself, intentionally designed to influence the values, habits and behavior of the rising generation."[16] So as activists, labor unions, and other school interest groups foisted a diverse

DIAGRAM 4. Organizational chart of the Chicago Public School System

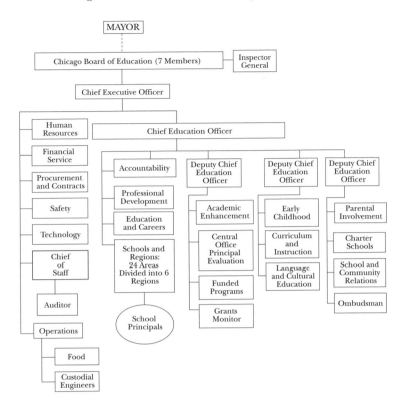

and elaborate array of obligations on schools during the 1900s, school districts had to diversify.

As schools diversified, each mission, from construction and budgeting to payroll and personnel, grew staggeringly complex. In the areas of payroll and personnel, now known as Human Resources, as new programs were added, districts had to hire more classes of employees, negotiate with a wider variety of vendors, and bargain with more unions. Each union, moreover, came to encompass many locals, each with its entitlements. The New York City school system, for instance, negotiates with twenty thousand vendors and about forty locals, which roll up into about eight major unions. New York's District Council 37, for example, has different locals representing substance abuse specialists, clerical aides, skilled carpenters, and many others. Districts have to apply the proper grievance procedures, regulations, and entitlements to each local. The payroll department must issue paychecks on different pay cycles, give increases at different intervals, allow different numbers of vacation and sick days, allow different benefits, and provide different advancement prerogatives to different classes of employees in each local. Officials must keep track of which entitlements are mandatory, applying to all members of a local, and which are custom, applying to certain groups of members.

The LAUSD, for instance, has thirteen major collective bargaining units, each negotiating its own pay scale. It has seven major types of employees on varying payment schedules, eighty earning codes, a multitude of status and time-reporting codes, and different ways to process paychecks for each employee group. Certificated employees can be placed on up to sixteen different assignments, three calendars, five tracks, four bases, nine salary tables, and four salary payment options. Moreover, as in any large district, payroll and time-keeping formulae require constant updating to keep up with new union agreements and ever-new entitlement distinctions created among employees in the same local and usually based on their date of hire. Calculations can be so convoluted that even experts get them wrong. The LAUSD processes about 195,000 adjustments and 48,000 exceptions a year because of errors.[17] School auditors there and in the CPS blamed complexity for repeated payroll errors.[18] Administrators were not always able to keep track of every class of employee's special payroll entitlements.

But despite their increased complexity and diversification, the three districts kept their overall pyramidal shapes. They spun off new central departments for every new specialty area, from bilingual and vocational education to early childhood, each under a different head.

To tackle complex tasks, districts broke them up, delegated each piece to the appropriate specialists, and had the specialists report their recommendations to supervisors so that the top level of administrators would stay in charge. This approach to solving problems, linked in the literature to "local rationality," was supposed to ensure accountability and effectiveness because experts could be trusted to take charge as professionals and yet also be held in check by the chain of command.

By the 1960s, most urban public school districts had central bureaus for virtually every function, from curriculum to transportation to supplies. Every bureau head controlled everything in that jurisdiction, from the central office down to the classroom. In New York City, the director of the Bureau of Curriculum would publish bulletins specifying the curricula teachers had to follow in every subject. In Chicago, headquarters so completely controlled functions such as teacher recruitment, selection, and placement that principals generally discovered who their new teachers were going to be only on the first day of class. One upper-level administrator at the CPS, a former principal, recalled that as recently as the 1980s a principal's first encounter with a new recruit would typically occur in the hallway and go something like, "Hi. Who are you?"[19]

Chicago today has about ninety central divisions and units, known as "downtown."[20] The LAUSD has over forty, referred to as "450 North Grand," scattered in various office buildings in Los Angeles.[21] New York City has about fifty-four divisions and units, known as "central," "downtown," or "110 Livingston" (before the building was sold in the fall of 2002). But the New York City school headquarters are still scattered in various high-rises in downtown Brooklyn and Queens as well as the old Tweed Courthouse in Manhattan, where some central staff moved in the fall of 2002 as part of the system's transformation into a mayoral agency. Part of the Division of School Facilities is slated to merge with the School Construction Authority, an office that had been created in 1990 when school capital functions were removed from the school system in the wake of school construction scandals.

Divisions, in turn, carved their various specialties into compartments and subcompartments, the idea being that each unit would report to the one above it all the way up to the superintendent, chief executive officer, or chancellor. The School Division of Human Resources, for instance, has about forty subunits in Los Angeles, ten in Chicago, and seventeen in New York City.

In addition to vertical reporting lines, the three largest school districts also created horizontal administrative layers as they grew in size. Each district carved schools into geographic and specialty areas, creating a field office for each area. The idea was to enhance oversight by having field offices closer to schools overseeing them.

The LAUSD created eleven regions or districts, Local Districts A through K, each led by a district superintendent in charge of its elementary, middle, and high schools. With 722,727 students, that is an average of nearly 66,000 students per district. The CPS sculpted itself into six regions, each headed by a region education officer responsible for overseeing about ninety schools.[22] With 435,470 students, that is an average of about 73,000 students per region.

Until the reorganization begun in 2003, New York City had forty-two local districts,[23] each headed by a superintendent. Thirty-two of these districts were geographically demarcated community school districts that oversaw most of the city's elementary and middle schools.[24] Six other districts oversaw high schools.[25] Five of these high school districts corresponded to the city's five boroughs: Districts 71, 72, 73, 76, and 77. The sixth, District 79, oversaw the city's alternative high schools for students at risk. In addition, two districts, not geographically demarcated, contained New York City's worst performing elementary and middle schools and high schools (Districts 74 and 85). Another, District 84, was devoted to charter schools, also scattered around the city; yet another, District 75, to severely handicapped special education students, also from around the city. (Beginning in 2003, these districts will be reconfigured into ten instructional divisions, each with about 100,000 students; see diagram 2.)

So far, field offices have been designed rather like their central offices. Their organizational charts look a lot like those of the central system, with staffs divided into specialty units ranging from food services to special education to finance to student mental health. But their shape should not be suprising given their limited authority. As one of the LAUSD's eleven local district superintendents noted, local districts have so many central programs to administer that they essentially spend their time following orders from on high.[26] When the district superintendents meet once a month, most of their discussion is about central projects. When they are back in their field offices, much of their time goes to figuring out how to implement central mandates, many of which micromanage their schools. The district superintendent noted that the central office had allocated 1.25 coaches to one of the district's schools and 0.75 coaches to another; did this mean she could have one coach per school? With so little autonomy, regional offices often have little choice but to mirror the central office's top-down shape and style.

CHAPTER SIX

THE CENTRALIZATION MESS

How can these highly centralized, compartmentalized school systems be explained? After all, America's three biggest school systems started out small and uncomplicated. In 1854 the Manhattan Board of Education, for example, had only 1,200 teachers (compared to 80,000 today)[1] and was run by a handful of executives and standing committees composed of elected commissioners from the twenty-two wards,[2] including the Executive Committee on Normal Schools, Executive Committee on Evening Schools, and a Finance Committee that had all of four members.[3] The central board hired experienced professionals only for those few areas that clearly required expertise. In 1854, for instance, it appointed a superintendent of repairs of school buildings.[4] Many factors fueled the byzantine compartmentalization and top-down structure that marks today's largest districts.

A REACTION TO SCANDALS

One of the most overlooked reasons for centralization is the knee-jerk reaction of schools, as of most agencies, to tighten control at the top and pile on new layers of compliance accountability in the wake of major public scrapes with the criminal law.[5]

In New York City, the pattern of scandal followed by centralization and regulation goes back to the Civil War, when Manhattan schools were divided into wards, each run by a locally elected school board. Accountability was rudimentary. Compliance accountability was of the post factum variety. At the end of every school year the heads of each ward board had to make an "accounting" to the city of such basics as what it had spent its money on and how many children it had enrolled. Principals had flexibility; higher-ups did not run their schools.

But in 1864, after an entire ward school board was suspended for forming a ring to extort teachers and contractors in exchange for jobs, reformers began to hand some of the ward school boards' actual hiring powers to the central office to reduce corruption. So although the central office was relatively weak and small,[6] it was beginning to accumulate decision-making authority as part of the drive for integrity. The premise even at this early stage was that if local officers had less discretion, they would have less opportunity for waste, fraud, and abuse.

A BELIEF IN SCIENTIFIC MANAGEMENT

The momentum toward centralization in large American cities accelerated dramatically during the Progressive era—the early twentieth century—when reformers sought to release government from the grip of powerful local political machines that had turned many government agencies, including public schools, into patronage troughs.[7] Administrative progressives saw the influence of local politics on schools and other agencies as the source of many of their ills: bribery, extortion, political patronage, favoritism, and waste. To reduce the grip of political sachems, they embraced the scientific management models that had taken root in the blossoming industrial sector and worked to centralize, certify, professionalize, regulate, and restrict employee discretion.[8] The belief was that the emerging corps of professionals in central school offices would be above politics, even-handed, and inherently less vulnerable to corruption and abuse.

Progressives believed that clean, efficient management depended on accurate and continuous flows of information from the field to the superintendent, much as heads of industries monitored goods as they went from the factory floor through mass processing to markets.[9] Reformers championed the Weberian model of bureaucracy as key to achieving this free flow of information. The vision was that each rung of the school hierarchy would monitor the rung below, distill what was going on, and report up the chain of command all the way to the superintendent. By the same token, the superintendent would issue policy mandates and rules that would cascade down the rungs unobstructed for implementation in the field.

Efficiency was another business ideal that education experts wanted to emulate in their search to reduce waste. A few experts even tried to push for schools to use corporate-style budgeting and subject every expense to a "cost-benefit justification."[10]

Although schools did not adopt every scientific management practice advocated, they adopted a number over time. The history of the three districts shows a relentless march, punctuated by brief, discreet experiments with community control and other forms of decentralization, toward centralization in relation to both school structure (as new central departments were added to the bureaucracy) and rules and regulations. To be sure, there are pockets of decentralization today—the New York City schools, for example, have recently begun to let elementary and middle school principals have some say over small portions of their budgets and are hoping to expand that portion over time—but by and large America's largest districts remain centralized.

Notwithstanding scientific management practices, tales of school fraud and waste still made headlines. The locus of the graft was now different—central and regional school bureaucracies rather than ward school boards were now the main source of trouble—but urban schools still had to deal with the ensuing bad press. They did so by invariably tightening the reins in central headquarters.[11]

In the New York City school system, the central office would issue new rules to safeguard taxpayer money and prevent fraud. At first, most central rules consisted of haphazard collections of memoranda scattered among the various bureaus. Their contents reflected the personalities of bureau chiefs and whatever problems they happened to face. Nitpicky bureau chiefs would have rules for virtually everything; disorganized bureau chiefs would have hardly any.[12]

By 1974 the New York City school system started issuing formal Standard Operating Procedure Manuals (SOPMs). At first they were basic blueprints on how to do business in the system: how to buy things, how to hire consultants, how to solicit bids, and so forth. Gradually they evolved into today's voluminous, wide-reaching SOPMs that map out virtually every step of every procedure to reduce waste and fraud.

To prevent cheating and save money, SOPMs in the New York City schools, LAUSD, and CPS require reimbursement forms to be signed and approved by multiple layers of supervisors and meticulously backed by documentation. If there is any chance that an item could be used for personal purposes, the SOPM requires the employee to attach a written explanation, which also must be approved by various supervisors. Forms with errors are disallowed. Similar checks are required to process vendors' invoices.

RATCHETED-UP STATE AND FEDERAL REGULATIONS

State and federal lawmakers also made more decisions centrally before releasing money in response to concerns that their aid to disadvantaged children was supplanting, not supplementing, local spending. So with Title 1, one of the programs launched under the federal government's Elementary and Secondary Education Act (1965) to help disadvantaged children, being poor was not enough to qualify; many districts also required the child to be enrolled in a school where there was a high concentration—65 percent or more—of poor children. The rules prohibited expenditure on anything but specific programs and required the majority of funds to be spent within certain timetables. To ensure that the money went to them alone, disadvantaged children had to be pulled out of class for special instruction (some of these rules were recently relaxed[13]).

A typical example of how state regulation was ratcheted up in response to graft was the New York State Urban Education Program. The program started in the early 1970s, when the state pumped about $40 million into the New York City school system to encourage community-based programs. Like many government initiatives during that era, the program was born of racial segregation battles in schools and was intended in part to appease minorities.

At first, program rules were scarce and loose, and few conditions were attached to the money. Hiring standards were relaxed; coordinators merely needed a certificate of competency. They had free rein in creating projects that they wanted funded and barely needed to show how they related to academics. Program money could thus be used to pay for neighborhood liaisons and neighborhood community workers and for projects such as community newsletters and afterschool programs.

With few rules and practically no accountability for performance or compliance, the program quickly degenerated into patronage and thievery. The state launched an investigation. The program's finances proved to be a mess. A $17,000 school printing press, for example, had found its way to an island in the Caribbean. In 1974 the chancellor suspended some community school board members for fiscal improprieties. Some program officials went to jail.

The state reacted by attaching numerous conditions to the money. Today, the program, now known as Pupils with Compensatory Education Needs (PCEN), is one of the most highly regulated state school programs, with money earmarked for children whose reading skills are below average that must be spent by year's end, or it goes back to the state. Unless a school was a Title 1 school, children who received PCEN services had to be separated from classmates to ensure that the money went to them and no one else.

COLLECTIVE BARGAINING AGREEMENTS, LEGISLATION, AND CONSENT DECREES

Compartmentalization and top-down structure can be partly understood as an effort to achieve social justice. In the early 1900s, following national progressive ideals, schools developed a broad variety of social services, bringing structural diversification. The LAUSD, for instance, created a health department in 1912, a subsidized lunch program in 1914, and various services for immigrant children during that period.[14]

Then, with the first stirrings of the civil rights movement in the 1950s, a multitude of ethnic, racial, and other advocacy groups used the courts, with increasing frequency and success, particularly since the landmark *Brown v. Board of Education* (1954). They have sought redress to complaints ranging from insufficient money for school construction to paltry services for the disabled to the underrepresentation of minorities and women among school janitors. Their lawsuits, sometimes backed by publicized street protests, forced school districts to grant an assortment of entitlements through judicial consent decrees, legislation, and rules and regulations—and an array of new central units to oversee their implementation.

Labor unions demanded increasing rules on employment conditions and entitlements. Municipalities, states, and the federal government issued a torrent of legislation to protect children's health and safety, ranging from building and seismic codes to asbestos abatement laws. State and city lawmakers, hoping to get credit for specific school programs and please taxpayers, imposed numerous conditions on how even small school grants had to be spent and insisted on provisions to make sure none of the money went to waste.

But school systems often have gone even further than what was demanded. The New York City Board of Education, for example, goes beyond the municipal building code by insisting that electrical wiring in new schools be encased in metal tubes. And the New York City School Construction Authority, according to a study commissioned by former chancellor Harold Levy and chaired by Peter Lehrer, a construction consultant, was far more restrictive in dealing with contractors than comparable school construction agencies in other cities, including Chicago's school construction division. Moreover, its bidding rules were far more restrictive than those of other New York State building agencies, such as the New York Dormitory Authority.[15]

An overabundance of control can also be found in instructional areas. The federal government allows school districts to roll over to the following year as much as 15 percent of the Title 1 funds that they receive but do not spend within the year. The rest, if unspent, must be returned to the government. The New York City Department of Education, however, not wanting to take as much of a chance lest the money be wasted, allows schools to roll over only 10 percent of these funds.

During this period the New York City BOE made many concessions to unions behind closed doors that went far beyond guaranteeing workers a fair and decent workplace, particularly before Watergate, when the media probed the public sector less aggressively than it does today. Some of the most egregious examples include agreements to let custodians keep school jeeps after five years of use, give them unlimited sick days, and pay for their income tax return preparation.[16]

THE INEFFICACY OF TOP-DOWN CONTROLS

The whole point of adopting scientific management practices and compliance accountability was to stanch corruption, waste, and abuse. But investigative records of the three largest school districts suggest that they could not cure the problem.[17] Although the top administrators make most of the decisions in New York City, Chicago, and Los Angeles, the central office's control of waste and abuse often appears to be more show than reality. Crooks keep finding ways around them.

The New York City BOE's detailed rules on competitive bidding, for example, require officers to collect bids from at least three vendors and then pick the lowest responsible one. The procedures, designed to fight corruption and cut costs, became tighter after every major scandal. The rules also grow tighter as the dollar value of the goods or services rises.[18]

To buy goods valued at between $5,001 and $10,000 today, it is enough for officials to have three vendors fax in their bids. But for contracts over $10,001, officials must formally solicit three written, sealed bids and read them aloud at scheduled public openings.[19] For services over $25,000, officials must prepare Requests for Proposals (RFPs). For amounts over $25,000, they must additionally register the contract with the city comptroller.

Officials have found ways to thwart competitive bidding ever since the rules started developing in the late 1930s and early 1940s. In those days school officials wanting to hire out merely had to write to invite different companies to submit bids. A 1942 investigation of the Bureau of School Supplies revealed that officials would rig bids by making sure that all the other companies they wrote to except the favored firm could not comply with what the BOE was looking for.[20]

The rules became far stricter. But officials could still rig bids by tailoring bid specifications toward a preselected vendor. For ten years, from 1965 to 1974, the BOE paid a publisher $6.4 million to create citywide tests. As reported in newspapers, at first central officials avoided soliciting bids by invoking the sole-source exception to competitive bidding, which is allowed when only one company can provide the needed service. In this case, though, there were plenty of other qualified publishers. After auditors saw through the ruse and asked the BOE to solicit competitive bids, officials simply rewrote the bid specifications to put their longtime publisher in an "advantageous position."[21]

As new checks were instituted, people found new ways to circumvent them. When the BOE started requiring three faxed bids for goods of certain prices in the 1970s, some officials began to photocopy companies' letterheads and company officials' signatures onto blank sheets and filled in whatever they wanted the bids to read. Informants said that creating fake faxed bids was "easy." A 1983 audit of District 4 describes how they did it.[22]

When the BOE required that sealed bids over $10,000 be read aloud at public meetings, officials found ways around that, too. To ensure that their eleven favored companies got $6 million dollars' worth of school repair work in Brooklyn and Queens, two top School Construction Authority project managers would unseal and read aloud all the other bids, saving the preselected contractors' for last. Unsealing the last bid, the managers would ignore the price that was written and read in whatever price would make the favored contractors the lowest bidders.[23] In return, the contractors gave one of the managers a Rolex watch, a BMW, and over $100,000 in cash; the other pocketed $3,000 in bribes.

To avoid rules requiring three sealed bids, other officials colluded with contractors to split bids into multiple orders of $10,000 or $15,000 and less. Auditors found this practice to be widespread. Of particular note were comprehensive audits in the mid-1980s[24] and mid-1970s.[25] In the Division of Food Services, administrators were so determined to hire their preselected vendors that they broke up over $42 million worth of purchase orders into over 4,200 separate transactions so that none would exceed $10,000.[26]

Officials even found ways around a rule imposed in the 1970s that contracts over $25,000 be registered with the city comptroller. When the comptroller refused to register one company's contract for $1.4 million in the mid-1970s, officials secretly hired the firm anyway. Amazingly, they paid the entire contract in increments of $250 and billed them to petty cash or "imprest" accounts, which do not require any documentation for amounts up to $250.[27]

Similar patterns appear in the LAUSD and pre-1997 Chicago. The California Public Contract Code imposes increasingly strict competitive bidding procedures as the cost of a project rises. Like their New York City counterparts, some LAUSD officials and vendors found ways around the procedures. In 1999 school officials reportedly had a deal with two painting contractors: the officials would give the painters lucrative school painting contracts, and the painters would give the officials expensive goodies such as boats, cars, cash, and a new marble floor for one of their homes.[28] To ensure that their preselected paint companies got the contracts, the officials directed them to split their bids into multiple small contracts of $15,000 or less. That way officials could solicit bids by telephone instead of going through the more formal, complex written procedures for larger contracts. LAUSD officials also had the contractors fabricate higher bids from other paint companies to make it appear that they had selected the cheapest vendors.[29]

The problem is found in some other areas of the Los Angeles system, including procurement contracts. One company split a single $125,195 contract into nine bids of less than $15,000 for work at the same school. Not even bothering to disguise its bid splitting, the company submitted all nine bids on the same day.[30]

Ruses to circumvent increasingly stringent competitive bidding and procedural rules have also been uncovered in the Chicago schools. Schemes have ranged from sole sourcing to bid splitting to manipulating bid specifications on contract proposals to favor preselected contractors.[31] In 1995 the Chicago Better Government Association found that school officials had inserted narrow procurement specifications regarding chrome chairs to steer contracts to low-quality vendors.[32]

THE DIAGNOSIS: GETTING TO THE ROOT CAUSES

CHAPTER SEVEN

TOWARD A THEORY OF SCHOOL WASTE
AND FRAUD

How do we explain the continuation of waste and abuse in the New York City, pre-1997 Chicago, and Los Angeles schools, particularly after decades of increasingly tight top-down accountability controls? Sociologists, economists, white-collar crime scholars, and organization theorists have offered a broad array of theories to explain the existence of systemic deviance in organizations.[1] The theories generally focus on one of three levels of explanation: the individual and how character traits and choices affect his or her likelihood to offend; the organization's external environment and how factors such as community values and industry norms influence crime commission; or the situational factors within the organization and how structural opportunities and incentives may induce misbehavior. A number of these theories are useful in explaining parts of the problem in schools. Theories that emphasize the cultural and sociopolitical contexts of organizations, for example, can contribute greatly to our understanding of why districts in cities such as New York City and Chicago may have longer, more serious corruption records than districts in cities such as Seattle and Edmonton, Canada, where school fraud is rare and, when it does occur, petty.

Scholars have noted that there are significant differences in what is deemed acceptable not just between different countries but even between different regions within the United States.[2] These differences are shaped by traditions and local mores that seep into local organizations and help shape their cultures, making some more prone to misconduct than others. New York and Chicago both have long traditions of political patronage and backroom wheeling and dealing. Edmonton, on the other hand, a relatively young pioneer town, and Seattle, which was officially founded around the time that New York was deep in the clutches of Tammany Hall, do not have such traditions.

Moreover, societal cultural norms are dynamically interrelated with organizational structure because the values of the larger community affect expectations regarding collective bargaining, external and internal oversight and surveillance, and governance and accountability mechanisms—all of which help shape the systemic opportunities and incentives in the workplace.

But theories about culture and the sociopolitical context of organizations offer only partial explanations of school corruption. They cannot, for instance, adequately explain why districts such as Chicago and Houston managed to reduce corruption and waste after implementing structural reforms, all while the cultural and social environment of the cities they were located in remained largely the same.

Nor can theories about culture completely explain why districts in Chicago, New York, and Los Angeles, which have different cultures and histories, display such similar patterns of waste and abuse. From the mid-1800s through the 1920s, when New York City and Chicago had large, diverse immigrant groups, Los Angeles was tiny—it had a mere 4,400 residents in 1860[3]—and was populated mostly by midwestern farmers and southerners. These differences shaped the kinds of misconduct that historically afflicted these cities. In New York and Chicago, corruption was rooted in neighborhoods and wards, where immigrant groups fueled powerful political machines. Los Angeles, on the other hand, has never had a tradition of vibrant political machines or systemic patronage concentrated in neighborhoods. Scandals were generated mostly among that city's elite power brokers, which included bankers, developers, and city department heads. Yet the same types of exploitation and ingrained corruption are found in the same central, noncore areas of each city's system.

However, organizational structure theory, which focuses on incentives and oppotunities within organizations, and rational choice, which focuses on how individuals make choices about crime and how factors in their external environment such as the prospect of punishment affect those choices, can explain changes in corruption records in Chicago and Houston and why certain deviant subcultures became so engrained in certain pockets of school districts such as New York and the Los Angeles Unified School District (LAUSD). Organizational structure and rational choice can also explain common patterns of fraud and abuse found in the three largest districts, which share similar structural vulnerabilities and incentives for misbehavior.

Although no two districts are totally identical in structure, the largest districts share an array of similar features that include shape, complexity, level of diversification, size, segmentation, specialization, and centralization. Despite a rich literature describing how organizational environments and internal processes affect deviance, few scholars have deeply examined the array of features above for their causal effect on corruption. But this book draws on the microeconomics, white-collar crime, and public administration literatures to knit together organizational and rational choice theories to provide a plausible explanation for the way structure encourages—sometimes necessitates—fraud, waste, and abuse in America's three largest public school systems.

This is not to say that other theories about culture do not help shed light on the problem; they do. But they do not necessarily trump the effects of types of organization on corruption. If people's culture and social environment discourage fraud, they will probably have internalized feelings of guilt and fear the social reprobation that accompanies revelations of wrongdoing in their communities, making fraud less attractive to them than it would be to people whose culture condones it. But if we accept that all people are rational and seek to maximize their happiness, then people whose communities predispose them against crime will simply need opportunities for fraud that are that much more tempting and easier to engage in before they seriously consider misbehaving. By the same token, if people are culturally predisposed to fraud, they may engage in it even if the opportunities and temptations are relatively few and small.

The bottom line is that, aside from those rare employees who are so pure that nothing can tempt them or so crooked that nothing can deter them, a dysfunctional organization that offers multiple tangible opportunities for fraud and makes it easy to engage in and get away with is more likely to foster corruption than one that does not, regardless of culture. Culture, while a powerful force, is mutable. Unlike destitute street criminals, white-collar criminals generally have a stake in society and their professional positions. Unless they can not assess reality, even those with a culture and history of fraud are likely to cut back if they know they are going to be caught, punished, and lose their jobs and prospects. So, while culture can in some cases mute the effects of organization on corruption, it usually cannot eradicate them.

Traditionally, most experts—with notable exceptions such as Allan N. Kornblum[4] and Solomon Gross[5] on police corruption and Frank Anechiarico and James B. Jacobs[6] on corruption in general—have attributed fraud and waste to insufficient oversight and weak internal controls.[7] By the same token, scholars like Marshall B. Clinard, Peter C. Yeager, and Edward Gross have found that decentralization and semi-independent organizational structures within large corporations promote fraud.[8] The time-honored wisdom has been that if an organization is affected by systemic fraud, it is not doing enough to oversee operations.

But schools have been tightening oversight for decades. And, although it is always hard to compare the incidence of fraud and abuse from one decade to another even in the same school district, the record shows that people have kept misbehaving. So what is wrong?

INEFFECTIVE OVERSIGHT

First, traditional wisdom is not totally wrong. Ineffective oversight is in fact part of the problem. So are unchecked semi-independent fiefdoms within large organizations. If we accept the premise of rational, self-interested human behavior, then inadequate oversight will contribute to fraud and abuse, but not for the reasons that most people think. When experts talk about inadequate oversight, they normally mean that the organization should beef up compliance accountability of the most rigid type, add more layers of supervisors, and tighten centralization—along the lines of the scientific management ideals in vogue during the first half of the 1900s.

But while too few compliance and central control devices may have been a legitimate concern in schools during the nineteenth and early twentieth centuries, today the problem is an overabundance of these devices, which now prevent the detection of corruption and encourage waste and mismanagement. Today the oversight machinery itself impedes oversight of large school districts, and the districts' clinging to control at the top levels paves the way for unchecked semi-independent fiefdoms within them. The root of the problem, however, is not necessarily semi-independence but the fact that the semi-independent units operate unchecked. And that, this book argues, is due mostly to overcentralization: the wrong shape for the wrong size of agency.

As microeconomists have established, an organization's size—the number of employees and budget—is the basic force that should drive all else about how it is structured and managed.[9] A top-down pyramidal organization, whose chief operating parts consist of functional divisions (such as payroll, supplies, and so forth), may make sense for small enterprises where running everything from headquarters is manageable. In fact, most small enterprises are shaped like this. Oliver Williamson calls these concerns *unitary form, functional organization,* or *U-Form.*[10] But as Williamson and others stress, as size increases, management practices must change to ensure effective operation and oversight. Strict forms of top-down compliance accountability must make way for a combination of different kinds of compliance.[11] A pyramidal structure carved into functional parts must yield to an organization whose individual components can be semi-self-sufficient entities that are held accountable for performance.

INFORMATION OVERLOAD

U-Form organizations ought to change shape if they grow beyond about three thousand employees because it is around this point, so economists predict, that top-down central controls become increasingly ineffective.[12] First, a chief executive can only handle so much information because of the inherent limits of the human mind, a notion known as "bounded rationality."[13] Many experts believe that the three largest school districts, particularly New York and Los Angeles, have become simply too big to oversee and manage from the top. As one California commission that has extensively studied that state's public schools declared about the LAUSD, it is "too large to serve its students."[14] And as Bernard Mecklowitz, former New York City chancellor, conceded to a city commission investigating school fiscal improprieties about fifteen years ago, "This system is massive, and we miss some."[15]

But the problem is not just a question of size. As the same California commission said about the LAUSD's enormous facilities program, "Size does not necessarily preclude success in the real estate business."[16] In fact, the literature suggests that the correlation between size and criminal conduct is equivocal. Scholars such as Robert Lane have found that firm size had contradictory effects on criminality depending on the industry and type of violation involved. He found "no clear relationship between size and violations."[17] Other scholars reached similar conclusions.[18]

Instead, the breakdown in oversight at the top of an organization is also a question of its degree of diversification and complexity, which together vastly accelerate the point at which the limits of the human mind are reached. Although size usually goes hand in hand with diversification and complexity,[19] they are conceptually distinct. Size generally refers to the magnitude of an organization's budget and staff, diversification to the number of tasks and missions, and complexity to the degree of technical, specialized knowledge required.

The Ford Motor Company can make millions of dollars' worth of cars a year efficiently because that is all it does. But urban school districts offer hundreds of services from curriculum development to construction, each run by a central division that reports to the chief executive, who is supposed to oversee and direct the major operational decisions in every area. In a big city school district, each operation is like running a large, complex corporation.

Take school construction. The LAUSD is currently trying to build over $5 billion worth of schools in five years. No school district in the United States has ever built this much this fast. It would challenge even experienced private real estate developers. So it is hard to envision how the LAUSD superintendent, whose primary job is to see that children learn, could possibly oversee and get realistically involved in major construction decisions, along with all his other missions.

School missions are also very intricate and technical. Experts are needed to "translate" information for nonexperts as it goes up the hierarchy, adding to the paperwork flooding to the top executives. Education historian David Tyack notes that during the Progressive era some reformers tried to alleviate the load on school superintendents by adding intermediate layers of supervisors of specialists, thus containing the number of administrators reporting to the top.[20] But this was at best a temporary stopgap that lost its effectiveness once districts expanded again.

In fact, by 1961 one state study found that the New York City school chancellor and his deputies could barely stay on top of operations. Upper-echelon executives, the study said, were so swamped that they did not have time to deal with much of the paperwork that crossed their desks.[21] Even lower-level regional executives such as district superintendents, who were supposed to implement policy from the central divisions, were "overwhelmed by reports and conferences."[22] And all this was when the school district was a fraction of its size today.

As a command-and-control organization grows, its structure forces executives to pick and choose where to pour their energy. As James Q. Wilson has pointed out, because there "are limits to the number of different jobs managers can manage . . . the cost of trying to do everything is that few things are done well."[23] Superintendents are thus likely to pick one or two core bureaus that deal directly with academic instruction for the regular student body. Unfortunately, while noncore programs might sound like just a few marginal areas of a school system, they constitute the bulk of school divisions today. In a city like New York, where 74 percent of public school children are from impoverished neighborhoods and students are of over 190 nationalities,[24] dozens of divisions, from drug prevention to school safety, are not immediately about academics. Even programs such as vocational and special education, which deal with instruction, may suffer the same lack of attention as noncore areas.

Because most top-down school districts do not hold central divisions accountable for performance and because the top administrators cannot realistically oversee every corner of the district for compliance, the result is that many noncore areas will be able to operate virtually unchecked, essentially free from both performance and compliance accountability.[25] That would explain why corruption in America's three largest districts is concentrated mostly in noncore areas and why some of these subdivisions have been able to transform themselves into fiefdoms dedicated to profiteering. The problem is not a lack of top-down oversight but an overreliance on it.

INACCURATE INFORMATION

Oversight in oversized command-and-control agencies suffers not just because the top administrators have too much information but also because they have inaccurate information. As economists have established, when U-Form organizations grow, they add new layers of hierarchy.[26] This causes "radial control loss": information traveling up and down the hierarchy gets lost or distorted as people at different rungs screen, select, compile, and condense it.[27] In extreme cases, executives may become so isolated from what happens in the field that they operate in a virtually imaginary world. At the same time, employees in the field do not receive accurate policy direction from the top.

INHERENT OPAQUENESS

As schools grew and became increasingly complex and compartmentalized, they also became inherently opaque, further weakening oversight and adding to inaccurate information. As Richard Hall points out, whenever subunits in an organization have a high level of expertise, they tend to see things their own way, leading to distortions in communication and problems in upward reporting.[28] Each area of a large school district today has its own regulatory language, unique terms, phrases, legal jargon, codes, and symbols. It is common to find administrators devoting entire careers to becoming experts in one narrow area.

The upshot? People who work down the hall from one another sometimes do not understand one another because they speak different languages. More important, top executives—even if they had the time—cannot realistically "see into" most divisions and subdivisions.

Consider the expertise barriers inherent in a single school function such as payroll. The New York City Department of Education issues so many different paychecks to so many different categories of employees who are on different pay cycles and receive different entitlements and pension plans that it has to have six separate payroll systems, not including payrolls for school custodians and their staff.[29] Each payroll uses its own data-processing technology and its own codes and symbols. The payroll language is so specialized that staff who work in different divisions sometimes input information inconsistently into the main computer system.[30]

Or take the DOE's five budget systems. Each has its own computer codes. Each operational area of the school system, from electricity to maintenance, has its own budget code. Employees in different divisions sometimes use different codes to refer to the same budget locations. For example, community school district employees use LCMs (location codes) to refer to the system's smallest financial units, whether a warehouse or a school. But many central administrators and school board members have other codes for these units.

Adding to the complexity, a 1996 New York State law introduced yet another budget code: BDS. So now district employees have had to figure out how to translate BDSs into LCMs. Some central divisions, such as the Division of Instruction, adopted BDSs. But others, such as the Division of School Facilities, use LCMs. Yet others use other codes.

Different divisions and databases even have different names for schools. Take Roberto Clemente School in Community School District 9 in the Bronx. The DOE's Automate the Schools (ATS) computer program refers to this school as 19K013. The Division of Assessment and Accountability refers to it as 319013. The Student Information Services database refers to it as 10K013. The Division of Transportation, Division of School Facilities, and other divisions in turn each have their own codes for the school. The New York State Department of Education, meanwhile, has yet another code for it.

The code problem is likely to get worse when the DOE opens up the twenty new alternative high schools now planned. Only four of these are to be in new buildings; the rest are schools within schools. So certain central divisions will probably not even register the existence of these new schools as independent schools on their computer systems.

Compartmentalization and opacity of information increase the risk of inaccurate information flowing up the hierarchy and so weaken oversight. But they can also impede the flow of information sideways, from one division to another, and downward, from the center to the field. All of this can have real consequences for day-to-day school operations. If a school security officer calls up the Division of School Facilities to inform it of an emergency—for example, a flood that just broke out in a bathroom in a certain school—the facilities division has to spend time figuring out just what school he is referring to before it can dispatch anyone to the site.

That is why some central divisions such as the Division of School Facilities hire an officer to decode what other divisions' symbols mean.

An illustration of how opacity and compartmentalization of information choke the flow of data downward to the field is the barrier between the New York City school fiscal and performance systems. The two do not reflect the same organization of schools and programs that actually exist in the field. So a school building that houses three independent instructional programs might get three sets of student data but only one school-based budget report.[31] The result is that school-based planners must make plans for the year without knowing how much money their school can spend.

An illustration of just how opaque even the most basic school information can be, not just to the top level and other central divisions but also to the outside world, occurred a few years ago in the LAUSD. Part of the opacity may have been intentional, but part of it was due to different compartments within the LAUSD doing calculations in different ways for different purposes.

The matter started in the summer of 2000, when the LAUSD superintendent pledged to give decision-making authority to eleven newly created local regions and cut hundreds of positions from the central bureaucracy for a savings of $46,102,464 and a reduction of 298 jobs. After the superintendent claimed that he had implemented the plan, the elected school board convened a Los Angeles civil grand jury to verify.

Auditors from Harvey Rose Accountancy working with the grand jury found the LAUSD's budget system to be almost impenetrable. The system did not distinguish between administrative and school positions in many cost centers. It could not provide the number of budgeted positions that were open in an individual position classification or cost center.[32]

To verify total savings from the multidistrict reorganization plan, Harvey Rose auditors sought payroll documents and budgeted appropriations to assess the LAUSD's costs. But data based on budget appropriations did not match data based on payroll. The payroll system accepted positions that were not authorized in the adopted budget or that exceeded the total number of positions authorized in the position classification for the organizational unit.[33] LAUSD payroll documents also included nonschool employees.

The private auditors finally had to enlist a third central unit at the LAUSD, the Independent Analysis Unit, to help integrate data from the payroll and budgeting divisions. With this unit they found that, contrary to the superintendent's claims, the reorganization plan did not net as many savings as asserted and actually increased the number of school employees overall by about 136.[34]

When a school system's compartments are too opaque to see into, the superintendent is forced to rely on division chiefs for information about what is going on. With few people (except law enforcement agencies and auditors) truly able to review what central divisions are up to, it is not hard to see how they could degenerate into fiefdoms for profiteering. As Susan Rose-Ackerman[35] and other scholars tell us, independent, unreviewable fiefdoms within a central bureaucracy offer many possibilities for wrongdoing. Just as information is easy to hide, so are fraud, waste, and abuse. In a number of instances, upper-level division officials have refused, apparently deliberately, to give out information to people trying to keep an eye on them.

An illuminating example is the huge Belmont Learning Center in Los Angeles, the single most expensive school construction project in California history. After sinking about $200 million into the project, the LAUSD had to halt construction when it came to light that the half-built school was sitting atop an oil field emanating toxic explosive gases. Although no one was prosecuted, facilities officials, it turned out, had abandoned accounting procedures and fiscal controls and not disclosed the environmental hazards and their true costs.[36]

What was notable, however, was how easily the specialized units in charge of the costly project got away with concealing what they were doing, notwithstanding the enormous sums at stake. While construction is always tough to oversee because of its technical nature, administrators made it even tougher. First, LAUSD staff and outside consultants misled school board members with respect to fact and law,[37] so central school board members essentially had little idea what they were looking at when they signed off on the construction plans. Second, "turf rivalry"[38] and a "culture of deny, defend and deflect"[39] meant that once certain fiefdoms within the school system got control over the project, they took advantage of the lack of oversight and their isolation from other divisions to engage in conduct that raised troubling questions about conflicts of interest, reckless mismanagement, and gross waste. Referring to the district's segmentation, one state commission blamed "the organizational structure [that] divides responsibility in ways that thwart accountability."[40]

CHAPTER EIGHT

WATCHING THE PENNIES BUT MISSING THE MILLIONS

In their crusade to rescue urban public schools from waste, abuse, and corrupt local political entanglements, reformers set up compliance oversight structures to save taxpayer money, prevent fraud, promote efficiency, and protect workers from abusive conduct. But these measures carried significant costs. The concern with compliance came at the expense of caring about performance. As an upper-echelon Los Angeles Unified School District executive observed after his first few months on the job, "the LAUSD is full of good people with no idea about what the results should be. . . . [They are] focused on process, not focused on results. They're running, but they won't step over the finish line."[1]

Once a school district reaches a certain size and level of diversification, not only does its top-down structure impede oversight. Its entire oversight machinery becomes a source of the very waste, abuse, and mismanagement it was intended to curb and provides incentives for new kinds of corruption.

THE COST OF WASTE

School antiwaste mechanisms ignored large pools of existing waste and generated incentives for additional waste. To save money, districts mandated compliance with elaborate procedures before they paid any money out. Layers of supervisors scrutinized invoices and reimbursement requests by vendors and employees. Tasks were broken into multiple parts so each tiny part would be given the full attention of a supervising specialist. But while oversight focused on rooting out errors in certain areas and at certain junctures within the bureaucratic process, there was no mechanism to question the waste built into the bureaucratic process itself and oversight system as a whole. While clusters of employees were assigned to pore over paperwork to save a few dollars in petty cash reimbursement requests and vendor invoices, no one seriously asked whether the millions of dollars schools invested in their myriad operations were wisely spent or whether they achieved worthy goals.

Does this mean that no school oversight structures are worthwhile, that school top-down regulations never save money, prevent corruption, or protect workers from abusive conduct? Not at all. First, there was enough swindling of large urban public schools in the 1800s and early 1900s to warrant some degree of top-down oversight. Second, while some rules might not be worthwhile, others might.

But the point is that after decades of accumulating top-down controls, most large urban districts today have no idea which ones, if any, are working as intended. Most districts have no clue whether their oversight structures cost more than they benefit. They do not seriously search for alternative, cheaper, more effective oversight mechanisms. Once rules are on the books, they tend to stay there.

The irony is that administrative progressives had once urged urban schools to adopt performance budgeting and cost-benefit justification[2] along with other scientific management practices, including top-down compliance and centralization, that were popular in industry in the first part of the 1900s. Performance budgeting and cost-benefit justification would have obligated districts to question their expenditures and their way of doing business. Districts would have had to set and prioritize goals and subject every expense to a cost-benefit analysis to determine if it added more than it cost and if it helped fulfill goals, much as modern successful businesses do.

Although the corporate sector largely shifted away from strict top-down compliance and centralization when these practices were no longer appropriate[3] and embraced cost-benefit justification and performance budgeting when it became clear that these practices were crucial to effectiveness, urban school districts stayed stuck in the past. They clung to centralization but never seriously adopted cost-benefit justification, a problem that scholars such as Frank Anechiarico and James Jacobs have pinpointed in other areas of government.[4] As Aaron Wildavsky noted about thirty years ago, government budgeting has traditionally been based on history, with increases or cuts applied across the board rather than on client needs or outcomes.[5] Today, however, innovative agencies are transforming that sclerotic process through performance-based budgeting, which shifts the focus from what the agency spends to what it accomplishes.

Performance budgeting is mostly a pipe dream in America's largest districts, however. One upper-echelon budgeting official in the LAUSD made clear just how quaint the notion was: "When [the money] comes in, we don't re-examine where to spend it. We budget incrementally. We take the previous year's budget, drop out the one-time expenditures, . . . add on the additional needs [such as more classrooms or higher utility costs]. We build those on top of the previous year's budget. We don't do a zero-based budget."[6] Although the official conceded that someone must have decided what funds to allocate where at some point, he surmised that the decision must have been made "long ago. We don't look at that now." As the LAUSD inspector general concluded in its 2001 annual report, that district does virtually nothing to tie budgeting to performance to ensure that funds are spent in the most efficient and cost-effective manner.[7]

DIFFICULTIES IN ANALYZING OVERSIGHT MECHANISMS

This is not to suggest that determining whether school oversight machinery is worthwhile is simple. Some people might object philosophically to the very premise underlying such an exercise. Implicit in determining whether oversight mechanisms are worthwhile is the supposition that there is an "optimal level of corruption," as Robert Klitgaard calls it.[8] Klitgaard, who takes an economist's perspective, charts the marginal social cost of corruption against the quantity of corruption to show that the optimal amount of corruption is not zero.[9] Similar reasoning would show that the optimal level of waste and abuse is also not zero.

But some people may believe that government should never tolerate *any* level of waste or corruption because public officials, entrusted with taxpayer money, have a fiduciary duty to act in the public's best interests and scrupulously abide by the law, just as trustees have a legal duty to act lawfully and represent the best interests of their wards. All agencies, these critics would argue, should spend whatever it takes within their budgets to fight waste and wrongdoing.[10]

The problem with this view is, among other things, that the law does not require trustees to save every penny of trust income if doing so would substantially harm their wards' best interests. Schools have many, often competing goals. Pursuing the ideal of a corruption-free, waste-free school district as an absolute moral imperative would be prohibitively expensive to taxpayers and come at the expense of attaining other worthy district goals. Just as the gist of trustees' duties under the law is to act in their wards' best interests, so too should districts prioritize competing goals in children's best interests. Most people would probably say that goals such as providing high-quality academic instruction and creating a safe learning environment are more important than, and may be jeopardized by, insisting on a corruption- and waste-free system.

Furthermore, not all school corruption and waste have the same effect on district goals. Some types of corruption harm education; others help it.[11] How much money should be thrown at the problem should thus take into consideration how serious the risk is to the district's core goals and how much money fighting the problem would take away from other worthy educational goals. In short, schools should not spend millions to save pennies.

But agreeing that the optimal level of corruption and waste is not zero still leaves the thorny task of figuring out whether school oversight devices are worthwhile. It is not enough to add all the money recouped through oversight devices and subtract the total cost of implementing them; there are many other costs and benefits of oversight devices that are hard to quantify in dollars and cents. Some of the costs of current oversight devices include managerial paralysis, difficulty devising solutions to help children with unique needs, low worker morale, and a loss of a sense of mission and perspective among employees. How does one translate these costs into money?

It is similarly hard to assign a dollar value to some of the possible benefits of oversight devices, such as general deterrence (the value of all the money that would have been stolen by people who would have misbehaved had they not believed that they would have been caught by oversight devices), public trust (the value of having the public believe that districts are strictly accountable for every dollar), and preserving the district's reputation (the value of not having to do damage control related to scandals reported in the press). Moreover, the deterrent value of oversight devices needs to be reduced by the cost of the incentives they provide for corruption. And the value of public trust that might come from strict accountability rules needs to be reduced by the cost of the cynicism bred by district ineffectiveness.

Because much of the established education bureaucracy appears to take for granted the benefits of existing oversight mechanisms, let us explore some of their costs, ranging from financial costs to corruption incentives to *corruptio*, the subversion of districts' missions.

THE UNINTENDED CONSEQUENCES OF STATE SCHOOL LAWS

Some of the costs of top-down rules are the unintended consequences of goals and policies. The problem exists not just at the district level but also at the state and federal levels. Consider the unintended consequences of the following two state laws on educational goals.

CALIFORNIA'S FIELD ACT

California's Field Act (1935), a state law intended to make public schools earthquake-proof, is a textbook example of a law that probably does more harm than good. In their race to outdo one another in protecting school-children from sitting in earthquake-vulnerable buildings, state politicians inserted so many construction requirements into the law that school building requirements far exceed what is required of any other public construction in the state. For example, the Field Act allows students to study in buildings only if inspectors were present continuously from the beginning of the buildings' construction to the end. The law thus, in effect, prohibits the LAUSD from leasing or buying existing empty buildings or floors in buildings for classroom use, no matter how safe engineers deem them.

The costs of the Field Act must be considered in the context of the LAUSD's school overcrowding crisis. Los Angeles has one of the fastest-growing student enrollment rates in California. Some classrooms have twice as many children as desks.[12] Lunch in a number of schools has to be served in shifts starting at 10:30 a.m. Experts from a school construction oversight committee estimate that from 2002 through 2007 the LAUSD will need about $11 billion worth of land acquisition, design, and engineering to supply seats for new pupils entering the system.[13]

But partly because of the Field Act's restrictions on the LAUSD's ability to lease and build schools, over 14 percent of LAUSD children endure hours of busing across the city in search of empty seats. As of 1999, about 15,000 children were bused each day because there was no room at their home school. Another 10,000 "voluntarily" left overcrowded neighborhood schools as part of open enrollment or desegregation efforts. The 15,000 children involuntarily riding buses score significantly lower on tests than those who stay in their neighborhood schools.[14] As experts have noted, these are usually children who qualify for free and reduced lunch, who come from single-parent homes, and who suffer from a variety of disorders such as Attention Deficit Disorder. By the time these children arrive at school, some of them have been on the bus for long periods; they are hungry and wildly overstimulated. Precious hours that could be spent learning must instead be wasted calming them down. Meanwhile, parents in densely populated neighborhoods who want their children close to home camp on sidewalks for days to get to the head of lines for student school applications.

THE NEW YORK STATE TEXTBOOK LAW

Another example of a state school law whose costs appear to exceed its benefits and whose unintended consequences may undermine its official purpose is the New York State Textbook Law (NYSTL), which allocates about $500 a year to every New York City teacher to buy textbooks. To guard against teachers diverting the money for inappropriate books or books for personal use, the NYSTL pays only for preapproved titles from preapproved vendors. The money must be spent by fixed deadlines or be returned.

But the rules are so restrictive that the program cannot meet a number of teachers' academic needs. Teachers cannot telephone vendors and ask for their regular catalogues; they have to request their NYSTL-approved catalogues. But, as teachers complain, these catalogues are cumbersome and filled with useless books. Books in NYSTL catalogues are also costly compared to books at discount outlets. Even if teachers find a book they like in an NYSTL catalogue, they cannot negotiate with the vendor for a discount. Nor can they use NYSTL money to buy the same book at a bargain price at Amazon.com, for example.

Ann Berger, an eighteen-year veteran teacher in a top elementary public school in Manhattan, summarized the unintended problems of the NYSTL: "If you really wanted to find the stuff you want, and get stuff that adds up to the right amount of money, it would take you twenty hours. Who has that kind of time to spend on this?"[15]

One cost of the law? Berger says that she and most of her colleagues get so exasperated with the restrictions that, as the spending deadline approaches, they routinely "blow the money," putting in "dummy orders" on books they do not need. The NYSTL is a typical example of an anticorruption, antiwaste law whose constraints are inordinately stringent, given the relatively minor risk they are intended to guard against. As Berger incredulously asks, "What books are there out there that they think they can't approve? It isn't like we're going to order the 'Happy Hooker,' or something!"

COMPARTMENTALIZATION'S UNINTENDED CONSEQUENCES

Another often overlooked cost of top-down, U-Form oversight is the cost of compartmentalization, a problem described by management guru William Edwards Deming, the champion of *total quality management*.[16] When school districts carved themselves into divisions and subdivisions and broke tasks down into multiple parts, each for different specialists, the hope was to enhance effectiveness and supervision. But the inadvertent effect was to isolate divisions, "segment" thinking, as Moss Kanter has described,[17] and strain interdivision cooperation. The problem, aggravated by the specialization and different codes and regulatory languages in modern urban districts, came at the expense of the overall district mission and overall savings.

LEAKY ROOFS AND WINDOWS

In some New York City schools in the early 1990s, as principals complained, plaster was crumbling and paint was peeling from classroom walls. The culprit was water damage from adjoining leaky roofs and windows.[18] But roofs, windows, painting, and plastering each came under the purview of separate units in the Division of School Facilities, which had four separate databases to track repairs. So separate work orders had to be made out to each unit. Unfortunately, the units did not coordinate their work. So classroom walls were repeatedly plastered and painted by some units only to be repeatedly ruined by water damage from leaking roofs and windows, for which other units were responsible.

RENOVATION OF AN OVERCROWDED LOS ANGELES SCHOOL

One example that illuminates some of the reasons for lack of cooperation among divisions concerns the renovation of an overcrowded school in Los Angeles's densely populated Cahuenga neighborhood. A renowned architect who served on a mayoral advisory committee for school construction[19] recounted how, during his tenure on the committee, the school was so jammed that the playground had to be covered with temporary classrooms. So Facilities Division officials hired a contractor to build a new, larger school on the site. In the meantime, the LAUSD bused the children, most of whom came from poor, single-parent homes, to a temporary school miles away.

The contractor promised to have the new school ready by the first day of classes in early September. But during the summer he announced that he could not finish the school until the middle of October unless he worked his people overtime. A delay would have major implications. If the school was not ready by the first day of classes, students would have to be bused for a whole additional year, since district policy was not to relocate students and teachers once the academic year had begun.

As a member of the advisory committee, the architect suggested to

Facilities Division administrators that they pay the contractor overtime to get the school built on time. Overtime would cost the LAUSD about $100,000. But busing children for an additional year would cost about $300,000, not to mention the aggravation to pupils.

But the Facilities Division had no interest in coordinating with the Transportation Division even if it would save the LAUSD money, the architect said. Why? First, their budgets flowed from different funding sources and were totally separate (capital and operating budgets in schools do not generally intermingle). Second, Facilities Division administrators had no wish to take $100,000 from their budget to save the Transportation Division $300,000 (or the LAUSD $200,000). There was nothing in it for them. In fact, if they spent the extra $100,000, they would look "like they had gone over budget." Needless to say, the architect's proposal was relegated to the dustbin.

BUSING SPECIAL EDUCATION STUDENTS FAR FROM HOME

Compartmentalization also has costs in terms of strangling reforms and keeping them off the table. New York City's rules for special education require that disabled children be placed in programs according to functional and age groupings. So the DOE spends over $2,000 per year to bus each disabled child to a program, usually far from home. Reformers such as Norm Fruchter have long proposed using the transportation money to start special education programs in students' home districts. For every five hundred disabled students per district who would no longer need busing, the DOE could save over $1 million.[20] But the idea can go nowhere because the Divisions of Special Education and Transportation get their money from different sources and have no incentive to help each other.

NO TO SMARTCARDS

The principal of George Westinghouse Vocational High School wanted to save class time that would otherwise be spent taking attendance and cut back on teachers' paperwork. So he tried to get the security division to modify the "smartcards," which his students used under the new security system to enter the building, to also collect information about student attendance.[21] But the idea went nowhere. Attendance was an administrative function, smartcards a security function. Each came under the jurisdiction of a different central division, neither of which worked with the other. The sad part is that today many principals are conditioned to not even try to solve problems by drawing on different divisions and resources in creative ways. As one principal said about such ideas, "I won't even go there."[22]

OVERSIGHT COST AND THE VALUE OF WORK OVERSEEN

Another way to gauge the myopia of oversight structures in the three largest school districts is to consider the sheer cost of oversight in relation to what is overseen. In some cases districts pay half as much money to watch other people work than they do on the work itself. In 2000 the Los Angeles school inspector general uncovered the fact that the LAUSD was spending over half as much overseeing construction and renovation projects as it was spending on the work itself. The district signed a contract by which it essentially paid one worker $100 an hour to put in a toilet and another worker $50 an hour to watch him.[23] In a few cases the district paid supervisors as much as 80 percent of the construction costs they were overseeing.[24]

OVERSIGHT COST AND THE MONEY RECOUPED

Another way to gauge the effectiveness of oversight mechanisms is to compare the cost of implementing oversight to how much it recoups. America's largest districts often spend thousands of times more to find errors than the errors are worth. Their oversight machinery treats every potential error and fraud the same way without regard for the amount of money that might be recouped. The LAUSD inspector general, for instance, found that the price the district paid for oversight was sometimes thousands of times greater than that of errors. In fact, when Don Mullinax took over as inspector general he found that the former Internal Audit Branch would routinely pour thousands of dollars on audits to hunt down sums as small as $25.

THE $4 BATTERY PACK

One of the most graphic illustrations of this lack of perspective is the case of the reimbursement for the $4 battery pack in the New York City schools. The case shows how absurdly expensive the DOE's elaborate checks on employee petty cash reimbursements are and the system's myopic insistence on enforcing all the rules no matter how inappropriate.

The reimbursement procedure begins with the employee's filling out a reimbursement request form with the appropriate paperwork attached. The employee's immediate boss must review and sign it. It then goes to the central office, where low-level staff in the Business Department key in the information. Then the department business manager there reviews and signs it. From there, the paperwork goes to two of the DOE's senior-most officials for review and signature: first the director of the Division of Financial Operations, then the school system's chief financial officer. Finally, the paperwork goes to Chase Manhattan Bank, where it is booked.

All told, when all the bureaucratic steps and personnel are included, the DOE spends about $125 to process an average petty cash reimbursement, according to a high-level official in the Division of Financial Operations and a veteran of the New York City school system, here referred to as Mr. Rossi.[25]

In the mid-1990s, a high-level school district officer who coordinated a large program submitted a form requesting reimbursement for a $4 battery pack.[26] Unfortunately, the district officer did not include an explanation for why he needed the batteries. The Standard Operating Procedures Manual (SOPM) requires such explanations whenever items could be for personal use. So a clerk in the Division of Financial Operations rejected his request.

The rejection triggered a rash of discussions and meetings among low- and mid-level management. Because the district officer was so important, a meeting was called that included the clerk, his unit director, and several upper level officers in the Division of Financial Operations. In this meeting some officials still did not get it. The unit director defended the clerk, pointing out that he was following rules designed to protect taxpayers. But he seemed oblivious to the fact that the average middle manager at headquarters made $75 an hour. Upper-level managers made even more. So with all the personnel hours involved—the high-level meetings and steps up to the cutting of the check—Mr. Rossi estimated that the school system spent well over $500 to settle a $4 claim.

Officials followed rules unthinkingly, Mr. Rossi explained, because "that is the way things have always been done."[27] The district "had a culture of no conversation among staff."[28] It has to be scripted out for them.

OVERSIGHT COST AND HUMAN CAPITAL

The focus on top-down compliance also has large costs in relation to human capital: talent, initiative, and thoughtfulness are stifled as rule compliance substitutes for reflective decision making. Apart from exceptional managers such as Mr. Rossi and others, the three largest school districts do not encourage—indeed, usually do not permit—cost-benefit decision making. As scholars have observed, in input-driven systems, following rules can become an end in itself, rather than the means to accountability. So school supervisors may work hard, meticulously following rules that yield minor savings, only to let vast sums slip away because no rule draws their attention to them and worrying about them is not their job.

A window into this mindset is provided by an LAUSD investigation that exposed how the Facilities Division wasted millions of dollars in the late 1990s. In 1997 the Facilities Division was found to have spent millions of dollars more on a $2.4 billion school construction bond project than it had projected.[29] Investigators concluded that one of the primary reasons for the overexpenditure was that the Facilities Division had given contractors shoddy, vague architectural designs—no rules mandated the quality of the designs. So as the LAUSD would clarify its architectural designs, the scope of work would change, and contractors billed for millions of dollars in change orders.[30]

But what is most revealing is that, as far as the Facilities Division was concerned, it was toiling away to save taxpayer money. How? By scrutinizing virtually every invoice contractors submitted and disallowing or rejecting expenses that failed to comply with the rules, no matter how minor the transgression. One contractor related how the LAUSD refused to pay him for work done on a school vacation day. Because that day was not a day off for his company, he showed up with his laborers, did the work, and submitted an invoice with documents certified and signed by each employee—to no avail.[31] Another contractor described how the LAUSD rejected his expenses because he filed them late, even though his reason was that the Facilities Division had not approved his work authorization in time, a common complaint among the contractors.[32]

These cases drive home the point that relying on regulatory safeguards for accountability can result in backward management. Officials put all their energy into collecting a few thousand dollars in disallowances once work is underway while wasting millions through poor planning at the beginning.

OVERSIGHT COST AND LOST BUSINESS COMPETITION

The exacting focus on compliance also has serious financial implications for school districts in relation to lost business competition. The irony is that so many bureaucratic procedures, from competitive bidding to advertising requirements, were conceived precisely to augment competition and thus hopefully reduce prices. But as one contractor working on an LAUSD construction project summed up, working for that district meant "losing money" because of the "disallowances and cost of [borrowing] money."[33] One contractor did $800,000 worth of work for the LAUSD before receiving a check.[34]

Cumbersome regulations cause some large urban school districts to take months, sometimes years, to pay contractors. In New York City, vendors who do work during the summer do not generally see a check until the fall or late summer at the earliest. In the LAUSD, it can take two years to process a bill.[35] Requisition forms must be reviewed and signed by many people and processed through various units of various departments. Each requisition order consists of three copies of different colors, each to be sent to different offices. Six to seven department units process payments, depending on the type of vendor and services involved.

The combination of time-consuming rules with a central office that questions every transgression means vendors' invoices may be held up for months. A signature might be missing, a date might not match, or back-up documentation might be insufficient. Or, as required by some districts, the colored requisition orders might not show a three-way match.

In 2001 auditors estimated that the LAUSD had about ten thousand open purchase orders and unpaid invoices totaling over $33.5 million stuffed into filing cabinets in the Accounts Payable Division. Over two thousand of these purchase orders, worth nearly $8 million, were three years old.[36] Preferred vendors, those who did the most business with the district in terms of dollars, were treated the worst.[37] Delays fed themselves: vendors' repeated inquiries about delinquent payments and school employees' queries about how to buy things forced Accounts Payable staff to spend 30 to 50 percent of their time on the telephone responding to angry customers, inside and outside the school system.[38]

Some desperate vendors offered the LAUSD cash discounts to pay their bills on time. But the district's anticorruption procedures provided no opportunity to flag their bills. So officials treated these vendors the same way as they treated everyone else. As a result, the district lost $398,526 in discounts over a six-month period during the 2000–2001 school year.[39]

Contractors further must pay for the personnel to deal with the steady stream of rejected "invoices [that] continually trickle back for minor changes."[40] One project manager working for the LAUSD estimated that a full third of his costs went into paperwork and reports for the district.[41] Smaller companies must borrow money to keep going.[42]

Large school districts often also take so long to review and sign work authorizations that project managers incur expenses before authorizations are signed, when necessary items become available.[43] The problem is that vendors cannot submit the invoices at the time they incur the expenses because they have not been authorized yet. But if they are forced to wait too long for the authorizations to arrive, officials may reject their invoices as being too old.

The upshot is that many companies cannot afford to compete for business with large urban school districts because they do not have the reserves needed to incur major expenses without offsetting revenues. Small and minority-owned businesses are often those hardest hit.[44]

Even if contractors can afford to do school business, they may choose not to because of the aggravations involved. One renowned Louisiana architect who works with small school districts and local communities across the country said that he did not renew his contract with the LAUSD in large part because it did not pay his bills on time and questioned practically every expense.[45] Similar examples have been reported in New York City.

Some vendors are obliged to halt their services in midcontract. Unfortunately, the ones who suffer most for this—teachers, principals, and managers—can do nothing about it. One Los Angeles principal could not get chairs for her students because the LAUSD had not paid its bills to Home Depot, which accordingly halted deliveries.[46] Over ten years later, the LAUSD's new inspector general could not get workstations for his new office. Home Depot had again stopped delivering because it had not been paid in one year.[47]

So it is no surprise that despite multimillion dollar school contracts, only about five companies bid on school maintenance jobs in New York City. Only a handful bid on transportation contracts in Los Angeles. The problem goes back a long way. In 1974, for instance, when comprehensive SOPMs were first drafted in the New York City schools, the deputy chancellor noted that business owners were reluctant to do business with Community School District 9 because it was slow in processing payments.[48] And in 1917, when rules in public schools were still mostly haphazard collections of policies scattered among central divisions, a report on the New York City school system found that its policies "restricted" competition for school business. Even then, school rules were more restrictive than some city hall policies.[49]

OVERSIGHT COST AND ADVERSARIAL RELATIONSHIPS WITH VENDORS

The "gotcha" mentality fostered by rule compliance has another often overlooked cost: it makes it hard to build relationships with contractors that are based on trust and focus on performance. As the president of a neighborhood association in Los Angeles who had tried for years to work with the LAUSD to build a school in his overcrowded area noted, the system's structure is adversarial. It gives contractors incentives to "stick it" to the district, "as they would to any difficult client."[50] The result? Vendors may underperform, overcharge, demand expensive change orders, and inflate bills.

In New York City, the State Moreland Commission, established by Gov-

ernor George Pataki in 1999 to investigate corruption in state government, found that contractors routinely inflated construction costs by
20 percent.[51] (Some contractors dubbed this the "aggravation tax.") One
of the chief reasons they cited for inflating costs was the slowness of getting paid for work done. The commission calculated that the aggravation
tax contributed to making it 300 percent more expensive to build schools
in New York City than in the rest of the nation on average. Taxpayers pay
the cost of six schools for every five built.[52]

Most striking, some law enforcement agencies have begun to permit
contractors to pass this "tax" back to the districts that "levy" it. When the
LAUSD inspector general tried to have one contractor prosecuted for
billing the district for about $295,000 for work he had not done, the
prosecutor refused to take the case. Although the prosecutor acknowl-
edged that the billing was false, he agreed with an arbitrator to regard it as
legitimate "advanced billing."[53] The prosecutor bought the argument that
because the LAUSD was slow to process payments and reluctant to reim-
burse contractors for change order expenses that it had not authorized
beforehand, regardless of whether the expenses were justified, contractors
could make up for their losses by inflating charges or billing for work they
never did.

The upshot? The legitimation of a totally unmonitored way of paying
vendors that at worst invites fraud and at best passes along the costs of red
tape back to the schools and ultimately taxpayers and children.

To some degree, these problems are part of a wider phenomenon in
government. Frank Anechiarico, for example, shows how New York City's
tough Procurement Policy Board, established by Mayor Ed Koch in 1990
after embarrassing fraud indictments, has driven many contractors away.[54]
But while creative agencies have begun to address these problems, most
urban school districts are stuck in the scientific management principles of
a bygone era.

THE COST OF MANAGERIAL PARALYSIS

Perhaps the most important cost of the top-down oversight machinery is its paralysis of those in the best position to improve learning. Economists and scholars of organization since Friedrich Hayek have observed that the most efficient organizations are those that place authority at the level where all information essential to decision making is immediately available.[1] "Decisions must be left to the people who are familiar with these circumstances, who know directly of the relevant changes and of the resources immediately available to meet them."[2] Thus decisions about long-term strategy, which require information about the organization as a whole, would best be made at the top. But decisions requiring highly specific information from the field would best be made closer to the bottom. What counts is that decision-making knowledge be necessary and available at whatever level the decision is made. So if, as James Q. Wilson notes, specific information available in the field is not necessary to decision making, as at the Internal Revenue Service, which requires uniformity of procedure, authority should not reside in the field.[3]

In school districts, long-term education strategies devised at the top should leave room for information about what works best for the particular students in every school. Districts in large, multicultural centers are among the nation's agencies with the most varied and unpredictable constituent needs. Numerous uniform, districtwide mandates will likely shortchange many children since their issues—from language to safety to drugs—vary from one grade to another, one school to another, one neighborhood to another. Mandating the same class size for every fifth grader, for example, glosses over the real differences between poor, non–English-speaking fifth graders, who are likely to benefit greatly from smaller class sizes, and affluent, English-speaking ones, who tend to do just fine in regular larger classes.

City school districts also need flexibility in the field because children's needs are changeable and unpredictable and must be met within the unique short school cycle. After a three-month summer break in which schools and pupils lose contact, schools have to be ready by the first day of class with the right kind of teachers and specialists on board and the right programs in place. Yet many principals may not know until the first day what kinds of and how many students will enroll. As neighborhood populations shift and new immigrants arrive, incoming students pose different challenges from one year to the next.

Principals also may not know until the first day what their staffs will look like. Teachers often quit, and the principal may not find out until the end of August. And it is not just at the start of the academic year that principals face uncertainty. Children come and go during the year. Some are homeless and drift from school to school as they move from shelter to shelter or from one foster home to another.

Forcing principals to take orders from the central office on personnel hiring, firing, and transfers and follow lengthy procedures on advertising vacancies in such high-pressure, unpredictable circumstances is not just an education issue—possibly putting the wrong teachers and programs in place—but also a safety issue. If the central office assigns a slew of novice teachers with no classroom experience to a rough school, that can pose dangers, because teachers there have to know how to manage a class. For all these reasons, while the school district's chief executive must be able to steer the district's overall direction, the person best situated to deal with the challenges of day-to-day urban education is the principal.

Yet both these key players—the chief executive and principal—have become casualties of school oversight machinery and command-and-control management in the three largest districts. The same root causes that foster waste and abuse also handcuff the principal and the chief executive.

HAMSTRINGING PRINCIPALS

Education experts agree that strong principals are crucial to successful schools. But to be strong leaders, principals need freedom to make decisions. One study of education in poor neighborhoods found that schools where students performed in the top 25 percent of students nationally all had strong principals who used whatever decision-making authority they could muster to mold their schools.[4] Experts such as John Chubb and Terry Moe argue that principals need freedom from central controls to improve their schools academically.[5] National surveys show that most public school principals believe that one of their biggest impediments is the lack of authority to make basic decisions.[6] Teachers and principals in charter schools say that their freedom from central controls enables them to better channel efforts toward academics.[7]

But antiwaste and anticorruption reforms and myriad collective bargaining rules, school policies, and state and federal laws that lodge decision-making authority in the central bureaucracy in New York City, Chicago, and Los Angeles impede principals from being strong leaders. As a New York City high school principal, whom I will call Mr. Alexander, notes: "The principal doesn't run the schools. The union chapter chair, the collective bargaining contract, Board of Ed policy and practice, and state, federal and city law do. . . . I can't hire and fire [and] get rid of the rotten apples. I can't manage the budget. . . . Much of my time is taken up with paperwork. We're at a stage in time where the last of our priorities are the kids we teach."[8]

SCHOOL BUDGETS

Money is probably the single most important tool through which to exercise leadership. As the old adage goes, money is power. Yet in the three largest school districts principals control very little of it. When legislators allocate money to public schools, they usually speak in terms of dollars per child, conveying the impression that districts divide the money by their total enrollment and push the resulting number of per-pupil dollars down to each child to be spent as teachers and principals deem best for him or her at the school.[9] This is a gross misimpression. What really happens, to begin with, is that a portion of the money that districts receive arrives earmarked by the federal, state, or city government for a multitude of specific purposes.[10] How this money is spent is thus determined not by the principal in consultation with the child's teachers but by officials and politicians who have never met and who know little about what particular children may need.

As for the money that arrives at schools relatively unfettered by state or city,[11] district headquarters quickly tie most of it up to suit their prerogatives before it reaches schools. After deducting its overhead, the central office parcels out money for various central services, from transportation and curriculum development to building maintenance.

The three largest districts then parcel out the remaining unfettered money through strict enrollment ratio formulae that use various tables to determine how much money each school gets, an amount based on the number and category of students enrolled in it, and how the money is to be spent. So, for example, each district will allocate a fixed number of teachers and a certain sum for supplies per pupil. The formulae and tables drive most operating expenses, from crossing guard and nursing posts to copy machines and computers. The LAUSD's Norm Tables, for instance, spell out how many teachers and other personnel a school must hire for every certain number of children. Norm Tables exist for every major category of school and student, such as special education, magnet, adult education, elementary, and secondary programs (see table 2).

TABLE 2.   Sample Los Angeles Unified School District norm tables, 2001–2002

Secondary Norms

Certificated (Based on District Norm Charts)
1	teacher per 41.25 students in middle or high schools
1	teacher per 40.5 students in senior high schools
1	principal per school
1	assistant principal per school with enrollment of 1,299 or under
2	assistant principals per school with enrollment of 1,300 or over
1	librarian per school
1	assistant principal, secondary student services per school with enrollment of 1,601 or over
1	assistant principal, secondary counseling services per school

Classified
1	school administrative assistant per school plus:
4	clerical positions for middle schools with enrollments of 1,400 or less plus 1 additional for each additional 400 students over 1,400
6	clerical positions for senior high schools with enrollments of 1,900 or less plus 1 additional for each additional 300 to 400 students over 1,900
1	financial manager per junior high school
1	senior financial manager per senior high school

Elementary Norms

Certificated (Based on District Norm Charts)
1	teacher per 20 students in kindergarten
1	teacher per 20 students in grades 1–3
1	teacher per 39 students in grades 4–6
1	principal per school
1	assistant principals for schools with 950 or more students
2	assistant principals for schools with 1,650 or more students
3	assistant principal for schools with 2,200 or more students

Classified

1	school administrative assistant per school plus:
1	clerk for schools with enrollments up to 999
1.5	clerks for schools with enrollments of 1,000 to 1,199
2	clerks for schools with enrollments of 1,200 to 1,350
3	clerks for schools with enrollments of 1,351 to 1,850
4	clerks for schools with enrollments of 1,851 to 2,350
5	clerks for schools with enrollments of 2,351 and above

Instructional Material Allocation Formulas

Regular K–6	$24.00 per enrolled student
7–8	$29.00 per enrolled student
9–12	$33.00 per enrolled student
New Special Education Schools	$2,487 per class

Custodial, Gardening, and Other Operational Supplies Allocation Norms

Adult	$88.00 per custodial hour (separate site) + .80 per enrolled student (shaded sites) + 1.22 (separate sites)
Special Education	$52.90 per custodial hour + 6.58 per enrolled student
Administrative Sites	$155 per custodial hour

The formulae and tables do not allow principals and local managers discretion to vary allocations on the basis of student learning needs (for example, students who are or are not prepared for school) or physical needs (for example, abused children, children who suffer from asthma, and so forth). Once money is allocated for a certain purpose, it is funneled into *silos*, each for a specific purpose (money for computers, money for other instructional goods, and so forth). The LAUSD, for instance, funnels money into eighty different silos. Money from one silo generally cannot be transferred to another (although New York City recently loosened some of these restrictions). The districts enforce silo restrictions by assigning object codes and budget codes to money and by requiring that money assigned to one code be spent only for its assigned purpose.[12] The central office develops the categories and subcategories into which money is funneled—general supplies, instructional supplies, computer supplies, and so forth—and sends the district offices a budget code grid directing them how to allocate money.

Moreover, to the extent that principals have discretion over tiny fractions of their budgets, the central office closely oversees these expenditures, usually requiring approval beforehand of any deviations from standard operating procedures. Although the New York City schools have recently relaxed somewhat the stringency of preapproval requirements for schools with good financial track records, they continue to scrutinize the spending of the majority of schools.

Little wonder, then, that, as William Ouchi and I report,[13] principals in the three largest districts, particularly New York City and Los Angeles, perceive that they control just a fraction of their budgets (see table 3).

TABLE 3. Percentage of school budgets that principals report to be under their control

District	Percentage of Budget under Principal Control
New York	6.1%
Los Angeles	6.7%
Chicago	19.3%

SOURCE: William Ouchi, Bruce Cooper, Lydia Segal, Tim DeRoche, Carolyn Brown, and Elizabeth Galvin, "The Organization of Primary and Secondary School Systems" (unpublished paper).

A window into how central funding formulae and other mandates have become surrogates for principals' decision making is provided by the experience of a principal of a large New York City high school, whose name has been changed to Mr. Alexander. Alexander's school has over three thousand students, a staff of over four hundred, and a budget of over $17 million (exclusive of operating and other costs such as security, maintenance, food, pupil transportation, and electricity). If his position were in the private sector, Alexander would be the chief executive officer of a medium-sized corporation. But in the New York City public school system, he has very little say over how his school is run.

First, even though New York politicians say they provide about $10,000 for each general education high school student, Alexander rarely sees any real money. Virtually all he sees are *units*. After subtracting about 60 percent of what the government allocates per student to pay for services such as maintenance and food, the school system converts the remaining money into units. Using a formula by which average teacher pay (about $60,000) equals one unit, it divides the number of children by fifteen, its unit price for high school classroom instruction, to calculate the total number of units a school will receive. The central office then allocates these units to the various high school superintendent district offices (now to be merged into ten regional superintendent offices), which, after shaving off their share, distribute what is left to high schools in their jurisdictions.

Units are very restrictive. Suppose a principal has 200 units total (the equivalent of about $12 million). First, he or she has to pay his or her own salary. A principal's pay is worth about that of 2.0 teachers, or 2 units, leaving 198 units. Next the principal must hire assistant principals. New York City high schools typically have about ten assistant principals, each of whom costs what 1.75 teachers do. So the principal subtracts 17 units to pay for ten assistant principals, leaving 181 units. Next, according to central mandates, he or she may need, say, four librarians, each of whom costs a little more than a teacher. So the principal would have to use a little over 5 units for four librarians, leaving 176 units. And so on, until he or she gets to zero.

But the bigger problem is that most units are tied up. For example, class size rules dictate that every high school principal must provide at least one teacher for every thirty-four students—even if the principal and the teacher want to vary class size to suit the nature of the course and student ability, with smaller classes for students who need intense attention and larger ones for others. High schools must also hire one librarian, at a little over one unit each, for every one thousand students, even if school aides, who cost much less, would do "just fine."[14] In fact, since librarians must be pedagogues, principals have to pull teachers out of the classroom to serve in the library. High school principals also have to pull teachers out of classrooms to fulfill a central mandate requiring them to have a certain number of attendance coordinators, even though secretaries, who cost less, could easily do that job.

SCHOOL PERSONNEL

The other major impediment that principals in New York City (as in Los Angeles) face is that they cannot freely hire and fire, despite widespread agreement that having staff who share a common vision is critical to successful organizations.[15] A study of charter school principals in Massachusetts, for instance, shows that these principals regard their discretion over personnel as one of the most crucial ingredients to hiring "go-getters who fit their school's mission."[16]

First, most school staff are not even hired by the principal. Food services workers and janitors are hired centrally; paraprofessionals are hired by district or central offices, depending on what program they are under. Either way, principals often have no say in who they are.

Second, even if principals can technically fill a post, that does not mean they can pick whom they want. They must give the job to minority transfers from other schools until their school meets the systemwide minority target. Once the target is met, the central office can force them to take staff who have been excessed, or removed from their previous positions because of a surplus of faculty. If an excessed teacher with more seniority than and with the same license as a junior teacher applies for the same job opening, the excessed teacher has precedence.[17] Yet such teachers, Alexander suggests, are precisely the kind most principals wish to avoid.

Third, principals must hire on the basis of seniority. The veteran principal of a kindergarten through eighth grade school with over one thousand children in Brooklyn, whom I will call Mr. Alberts, calls seniority hiring "a disgrace." He had been trying hard to improve his school's test scores but could not hire the people he believed could best help him achieve that goal. "Sometimes an energetic, new, vibrant person is willing to do more than the person with lots of years in the system."[18] In 2001, for instance, Alberts was told to cut one paraprofessional from his school. He had to let his best one go since he was the most junior. In the spring of 2002, Alberts wanted to hire a qualified junior reading teacher whom he felt would connect with students. But he knew that if a more senior teacher with the same qualifications came along, that is whom he would have to take.

Personnel rules, moreover, have become less flexible in New York City in the past five years. In 2000, after a fierce battle in which the New York State education commissioner sued the New York City schools chancellor, a consent decree mandated that schools on the state failing list, known as Schools Under Registration Review (SURR), hire only certified teachers.[19] Because there are not enough certified teachers to go around, many of the unofficial, under-the-table methods that non-SURR schools used to hire the certified teachers that they wanted were shut down. Certified teachers have since been hired almost exclusively on the basis of seniority. Principals in Los Angeles are similarly constrained in hiring teachers, although they are less so in Chicago.[20]

As for firing teachers who should not be in the classroom, procedures in almost all districts are laborious, lengthy, and tricky. In New York City, Los Angeles, and Chicago, elaborate due process procedures require principals to take time from their very busy days to observe and meet with problem teachers numerous times over the course of many months, each time giving the teacher proper notice, documenting their observations, and giving the teacher a chance to respond and grieve. Dismissal proceedings additionally require extensive efforts at remediation. Yet even after all this, there is no guarantee that the teacher will leave.

In the LAUSD, a principal who wants to fire a poorly performing teacher needs to evaluate the teacher for two years and ninety days from the time he or she first gives the teacher a below-standard evaluation.[21] Only at the end of this period can the case go before an administrative law panel (ALP). But since the law does not say how many years of negative evaluations a teacher must receive to be dismissed, the ALP, on which two teachers sit, may judge that two years and ninety days of negative evaluations is insufficient, especially if a veteran teacher is involved. The ALP may also blame the teacher's problems on the principal. Or the ALP may reject the case on the grounds that the principal did not devote the same level of scrutiny to every other teacher in school. As Dale Ballou has observed in similar cases in the New York City schools,[22] if a principal cites a teacher for lateness, say, twenty times but does not review everyone else's punctuality, the case may be thrown out for insufficient documentation. Most principals do not have the time to document a case to meet such standards.

Principals in New York City and Chicago[23] face similar hurdles. Alberts says that the process to fire underperforming teachers in New York City, codified in state education law 3020(a), "doesn't work" despite recent efforts to streamline it somewhat. Although 3020(a) hearings are supposed to be completed within four months, the average hearing lasts more than a year. Alberts sums up his experience trying to remove such teachers in over twenty years as a principal: "You can write the bad ones up 'til you're blue in the face! . . . Even if you give them an unsatisfactory rating, they come back next year. They always do."[24]

Nor can principals get rid of someone by eliminating the position and writing the line out of the budget. Alberts once tried that, but his district office prohibited it.

Other rules hamper hiring in other, subtler ways. For example, rules effectively prevent principals from replacing a teacher who has gone on maternity leave when there is a tacit understanding that she will not be returning. The teacher has no incentive to state her intentions officially up front because she wants to get paid maternity leave. In the meantime, however, the principal cannot declare a vacancy until the teacher has exhausted all her sick days (New York City allows ten sick days per year, although teachers usually accumulate more) as well as her maternity period days (thirty days). It can take two or three months to fill such a position. In the meantime, the principal needs to rely on substitutes.[25]

BASIC EDUCATION DECISIONS

Aside from budget and personnel, though, there are many other ways in which top-down controls hamper a principal's decision making. School and union rules intended to protect employees and children make it illegal for principals in public schools in New York City and Los Angeles to determine their school schedules and keep pupils in school after closing bell even if a class assignment calls for it. Principals cannot easily arrange field trips in these districts because the bus drivers, bus matrons, and other personnel whose cooperation would be needed report not to principals but to central school divisions that control the money for these activities and call the shots. Most high school principals, unless they are in charter-type or exam schools, cannot pick their students. Even if they are supposed to have some choice, complex central formulae greatly limit discretion.

Most principals also have limited control over the physical condition of their buildings. Say a fluorescent light bulb burns out in a classroom, a student kicks a large hole in a plaster wall, graffiti mars a school's outside walls, or the sound system breaks. Union work rules and central mandates make it illegal for principals to hire someone, ask parent volunteers, ask their school janitor or handyman, or even fix the problem themselves.

Instead, work rules mandate that only licensed central school electricians, plasterers, and painters do tasks labeled *major repairs,* which include all the foregoing, including changing a fluorescent light bulb. Principals must wait for months or years until the central office processes their work orders and assigns them central skilled workers. Principals cannot act alone or hire whom they please. The irony is that many of these repairs could easily be handled by the school handyman, who costs a fraction of what central skilled workers cost.

What about control over purchasing? In most large school districts, with the exception of New York City, principals cannot buy items they need on their own. They must purchase them through the central office, follow detailed procedures, and select from among preapproved items from preapproved vendors. Districts such as New York City allow principals to peruse the DOE supply catalogue and order on line, greatly speeding up purchasing. But in other districts such as the LAUSD, principals still pore over hefty catalogues and mail paper orders of what they want to a heavily backlogged central office.

But while some districts offer speed in purchasing, principals are often still restricted in the choice of items to buy. Even New York City, which has drastically improved procurement, does not let principals buy technological equipment of their choice, for instance. Principals need to buy centrally prepackaged offers, even if they can show that they would save money by purchasing their own choice of equipment.

One high school principal tried to buy a computer with a large monitor because he had students with limited vision. But headquarters would not let him, even though he had negotiated a steep discount with a reputable store.[26] Another principal wanted a certain model of printer to suit the computers already in his office. But the central office prohibited him from buying it even though he had negotiated a better price and warranty than what the DOE offered.[27] As Alberts added, "Whenever they [central headquarters] negotiate, you can get it cheaper elsewhere. . . . I could go to Best Buy or P.C. Richards and get a better price." The message implicit in the school system's refusal? If saving money requires individual entrepreneurship, it must take a backseat to the centralized drive to fight potential corruption.

Prepackaged central deals not only restrict principals' choice. They also remove any incentive they have to save. As Alexander noted, if principals "negotiate deals, we get discounts" and put the saved "money back in the school."[28]

HAMSTRINGING SUPERINTENDENTS AND CHANCELLORS

Schools' anticorruption apparatuses even hinder the top executive. Superintendents may be at the helm. But they do not necessarily have the authority they need to steer the ship.

FILLING POSITIONS, PUTTING TEAMS TOGETHER

Civil service, seniority, and bumping rights (the automatic precedence given to senior personnel over junior personnel)—measures intended to defeat patronage and favoritism—drastically limit the superintendent's ability to fill positions with people of his or her own choosing. The LAUSD "exempts"[29] only 0.04 percent of the classified workforce, about twenty people altogether, or 10 senior managers out of every 25,000.[30] So, for example, only the chief administrative officer and the general manager of the LAUSD Facilities Division are exempt. But the branch chiefs below the general manager are part of the civil service.

The New York City DOE exempts roughly the same percentage of central employees: about 0.047 percent, or a total of about fifty-seven central employees (mostly nonpedagogical division heads and certain special assistants and deputies).[31] This means that the superintendent or chancellor must fill all the management and coordinator positions below the very top levels from established civil service lists, making it harder to align the organization with his or her goals. These officers cannot be easily removed if they resist their boss's policy direction or underperform.

In New York City and Los Angeles, however, the paralysis is even worse than it appears on paper. Even though the New York City chancellor and the LAUSD superintendent are technically permitted to fill top spots in their district, in practice it is difficult for them to fill all division directorships and deputy directorships with new people of their choice. These school systems' size, complexity, and level of diversification and regulation inherently put any top executive who is recruited from outside at a disadvantage vis-à-vis the "permanent administration." The more regulated, complex, and large an organization, the more information and knowledge the chief executive needs to steer the system. This is where existing senior administrators are crucial. The top school executive in New York City and LAUSD requires about one year to get his or her feet wet, develop a set of goals, and figure out how to move the organization toward them. To navigate their districts, chancellors and superintendents need the deep reservoirs of institutional knowledge that senior administrators possess. In effect, the chief executive must rely on these people and cannot afford to alienate them.

Furthermore, since superintendents and chancellors tend to turn over very quickly, to succeed they need existing senior administrators to trust them and buy into their goals as quickly as possible.[32] Opaqueness in schools, particularly the LAUSD and New York City DOE, is further aggravated by the high turnover of superintendents and chancellors at the top. The top executive depends on the bureaucracy's entrenched senior officials, who guard their turf fiercely. The less time they have on the job, the less chance they have to develop the kinds of trusting relationships with senior administrators that can relax defensiveness and mitigate communication dysfunctions.[33]

The position of the New York City chancellor is particularly precarious. Joel Klein is the thirteenth chancellor to serve in the twenty-three years since 1980.[34] Two of these thirteen chancellors lasted only eighteen months: Richard Green and Anthony Alvarado. The longest any chancellor has served since 1978 is four years and a few months: Frank Macchiarola (1978 to 1983) and Rudy Crew (1995 to 1999). Chancellors can be easily toppled for any number of reasons, including falling out of favor with city hall (Rudy Crew), never getting into favor with city hall (Raymond Cortines), being investigated (Anthony Alvarado), and being ousted by a hostile board over diversions such as condoms and the rainbow curriculum (Joseph Fernandez). The picture looks remarkably similar in other large urban districts around the nation. Los Angeles, for instance, had four superintendents in the six years from 1995 to 2001.[35]

In this environment any chancellor understands that if he alienates senior school administrators, they will likely resist his goals and wait out his time in office until his replacement arrives. Now that the mayor picks the chancellor in New York City, the tenure of the average chancellor may extend to four or possibly eight years, the maximum any mayor can serve in that city. But given the lifetime tenures of many senior school administrators, waiting four years or even eight is still not that long. Thus, the precarious nature of the top job—together with the size and complexity of the bureaucracy—all temper any new leader's ability to steer the school system in any way that might shake it up too much.

But even if a chancellor or superintendent is willing to assume the risk of bumping down a senior administrator who is particularly intransigent, he or she still may not realistically be able to do so. Most people who have reached the upper echelons of large school systems have usually had a chance to make powerful friends in city and state politics and the teachers' union, whom they can call on for help when threatened. One former high-ranking New York City school official who served at the pleasure of the chancellor reported that several times during that chancellor's tenure, influential people would telephone to tell him to "lay off."[36] Given their political fragility, most chancellors will comply, especially at the beginning of their terms, when they need all the friends they can get.

LACK OF VITAL INFORMATION

A second, related factor that can hamper the chief executive's ability to steer is the possibility that the permanent bureaucracy may refuse to give him or her crucial information. One former chancellor said that when he took over the helm of the New York City school system, he asked his top administrators to report to him on how many people were on the central staff and where certain sums of money were being spent, among other things. But the senior administrators repeatedly failed to provide the information. "They wouldn't give me the numbers." His explanation? "[They are] there before you get there. There after you leave. . . . Division heads were very protective of their turf."[37] It was only after an enormous amount of digging, persistent demands for the information, and going around the recalcitrant division chiefs that this chancellor was finally able to find out "where they hid the money"—"I talked not just to the division heads but also to the people who were accountable."

Investigators examining the Belmont Learning Center construction fiasco found that various officials in the LAUSD Division of Facilities were similarly reluctant to share information with their nominal superiors. When members of the central school board asked senior officials for information about the multimillion-dollar construction proposal to build the learning center partly atop an old oil field, senior Facilities Division officials either did not supply the information requested or supplied partial and inaccurate information.[38] These administrators even deflected requests for information from an external panel established to oversee their work.[39] The school superintendent was kept in the dark, too. Unfortunately, much of the information withheld concerned the fact that the oil field emitted hazardous fumes: methane and toxic gasoline by-products. When the extent of the problem came to light, construction had to be halted halfway through. By then, about $160 million had been sunk into the project, making Belmont the most expensive high school in the state of California and an unusable one.[40]

CHAPTER TEN

CREATIVE NONCOMPLIANCE:
INFORMAL POWER NETWORKS

Top-down urban districts, like virtually all clogged bureaucracies, provide incentives for the development of informal ways of doing business. In a series of case studies of specific industries, scholars of white-collar crime have been pointing out since the mid-1960s that when professionals are denied the discretion they need to reach their goals legitimately, they may search for alternative routes.[1] Scholars showed how excessive economic pressure to meet profit targets and increase sales in industries with outmoded business and legal practices generated fraud. Most scholars focus on the crime that can result from such alternative routes, particularly bribery and extortion. They describe crooked officials taking advantage of red tape to extort payoffs[2] or vendors paying off officials to speed up approvals. This kind of corruption is sometimes referred to as *bottleneck corruption,* harking back to the bureaucratic delays that prompt it.[3]

But people who find ways around school bureaucratic bottlenecks need not necessarily commit crimes or be crooked. Their conduct may be legal or at least semilegal. And if they break the rules, they often seem to do so despite little official pressure to perform or attain goals—in contrast to many other criminogenic industries where pressures to attain financial success are pervasive. School officers who illegally break bureaucratic bottlenecks do not generally do so because they want more money or their boss is threatening to fire them if they do not meet goals. In fact, most enjoy solid job protection and could not get a merit bonus no matter how good a job they did. Instead, they generally break bottlenecks because they want to save time, reduce irritation, or believe that breaking the rules is the best—or only—way to get their jobs done well. Among school employees, then, it is usually more a question of personal satisfaction and a job well done than of straining to meet profit targets.

It is probably no coincidence that some of the most successful principals and school managers in New York City, Los Angeles, Chicago, and other large districts have waged what Colman Genn of New York's Center for Educational Innovation refers to as "creative non-compliance" or what Seymour Fliegel, the center's president, more bluntly terms "guerrilla warfare."[4] In most cases, their primary motivation seemed to be putting children first.

The bottom line is that congested school bureaucracies invite, sometimes necessitate, creative solutions of different kinds, at different levels of the hierarchy, and for the use of different people within and without the district. Employees have developed some semilegal methods within the central hierarchy to get around the bureaucratic process as a whole, methods that can both help the district and sometimes lead to waste and abuse. Vendors and employees together have devised other solutions at lower levels of the hierarchy to get around clunky rules, which too can help and harm a district.

THE NEED FOR STRATEGICALLY LOCATED FRIENDS

Unofficial ways of doing business arise in response to needs. The more headquarters becomes involved in detailed operational matters and compliance, the clumsier the organization's decision apparatus will be and the greater the need for informal power structures, concealed alongside formal procedures, to expedite business. Interviews with dozens of principals and managers in America's three largest districts suggest that one of the most pervasive needs is for a friend in the central office who can cut through red tape. These connections must be at headquarters because that is where the power is. As the former Chicago school inspector general observed, the Chicago Public Schools (CPS) "creates 'gatekeepers.' . . . You get through these gates by building relationships with the bureaucracy."[5] Or, as a high-level community school district administrator in New York City summed up, "You develop friendships with central to do what you need to do."[6]

Having strategically located friends helps with all sorts of things. In the Los Angeles Unified School District (LAUSD), auditors noticed that employees who had contact with the Payroll Division had a better chance of getting their expenses reimbursed than those who did not. In New York City, community school district administrators with friends in the Budget Office can get a little more bang out of their budget allocations. As one community school district administrator explained, most managers prefer tax levy funds, which come from the city, to federal categorical funds because tax levy money is more flexible. So if an administrator charges an expense—say, $500,000 for overtime—to his tax levy budget when he could just as well have charged it to his categorical budget, he can, if he has help from on high, shift the expenditure to categorical, thereby saving those tax levy dollars for future use. The administrator would get on the phone to his friend, who would change the journal entry to shift the charge to categorical.[7]

The more stopped-up official channels are, the more indispensable a well-positioned friend at the central office becomes for just about every major task. In the LAUSD, a former principal whose name I have changed to Marina Sanchez to protect her privacy, explained that "whether purchasing or fixing windows or anything else, . . . you need to know someone at central or their secretary. . . . If you don't use connections to get what you want, you've got to go into the line—and you'll be number 600 in line! . . . People don't answer the phones in these districts."[8]

Sanchez recalled that when she first became an LAUSD principal in the early 1980s, the parents at her school desperately wanted the graffiti on the walls to be painted over. The official way to do this would have been to submit to the central office a work order for a paint job. But Sanchez saw that, because she had no connections at the central office, the graffiti would likely be there for years if she went that route. So she decided to raise funds from the school's parents and its poor, mostly Latino neighborhood. After holding days of popcorn sales, she eventually mustered enough money to hire some local painters. But, Sanchez recalled, "right before I was set to go, . . . the lead guy arrived from the District Office." He was "at my office within minutes. He said, 'No, you can't do this!' " He insisted that she go through the proper course and use central painters, who belonged to the painters' union. But Sanchez stood her ground. Eventually, they reached a compromise: she could hire community painters, but the job had to be inspected by LAUSD inspectors.

As time wore on, Sanchez, like most successful principals, forged alliances in the central office. Once when she was in a hurry to buy something for her school, she actually dictated the required letter over the telephone to a top central official's secretary. "It got done quickly."

The danger latent in unofficial power networks is that they may be abused for personal gain at the organization's expense. Only one small step separates a friend who helps principals get their jobs done from someone who bends the rules for colleagues at the district's expense.

In a publicized case in the early 1990s, a group of senior New York

City school officials used their authority to help a colleague who had been convicted of child abuse. The school system requires any employee convicted while employed to go through an elaborate hearing to determine fitness to continue working. The top-flight group designated themselves as their friend's official review panel and conducted a sham hearing to bury the matter. One official filled in the forms; the others signed them. None probed the details of their colleague's conviction. One of the officials, the director of Appeals and Review, who enjoyed enormous informal discretion in the school system, then tucked the file away in the top drawer of his desk.[9] Investigators found it there four years later, stuffed in with some other people's personnel information, including the BOE "invalid list," a list of dismissed employees who were not to be rehired.

SURVIVAL IN U-FORM ORGANIZATIONS

Amassing power and bending rules for friends can happen in any setting; they are not peculiar to any organizational structure. As Moss Kanter has observed, most organizations are filled with people looking to "grab and use power."[10] But what is significant about large top-down districts is that they feed such people and give them incentives to accumulate and misuse power.

First, such systems make the accumulation of informal power virtually essential to their ability to function. Second, particularly in hard times, these bureaucracies make the accumulation of informal power for personal ends almost a question of survival. In all large organizations, divisions jockey to maintain and expand their staffs and vie for resources, particularly when they are under stress (such as the threat of budget cuts).[11] In a performance-driven organization, where component units have some autonomy, unit heads can point to their unit's performance and what they contributed to make their case for more—or at least no fewer—resources.

But in a large command-and-control U-Form organization,[12] where divisions have little autonomy and are not meaningfully held accountable for performance, division chiefs cannot realistically point to job performance to make their case. In lean times in particular, given the human instinct for self-preservation, officials' only sensible option is to play up the value of what makes them most needed in such organizations: usually their technical expertise over complex rules.

School districts facilitate this in several ways. First, given the specialization of modern urban schools, expertise inherently comes at a premium. As one veteran in the New York City school Human Resources Division put it regarding school civil service, "Unless you've *lived* this, you won't get it. You won't know how it works."[13] Or as the New York City community school district administrator quoted earlier said about managing the budget, "It is an art, not a science. You need experience to get the budget right and know what to charge to what. . . . You need to learn it over time."[14]

Second, the compartmentalization and difficulty of seeing into divisions in large districts make it easy for officials there to enhance their indispensability. With few people able to review the substance of their operations, they can hoard technical know-how and foster others' dependence on them. So instead of being true friends to the organization and helping field administrators do their jobs better and faster, central officials may have incentives to amass informal power for themselves, especially in hard times. In so doing they may end up hurting the agency through waste and abuse.

Indeed, some large school bureaucracies have survived and flourished by refusing to teach lower levels how to do things on their own. Scholars have often observed that, as school regulation increases, so does the size of headquarters.[15] As school budgets become more complex, there are "demands for more school district bureaucrats."[16] But what experts do not generally probe is how much of this growth is due to self-preservation rather than true need.

TURF PROTECTION

An insight into how the incentive to amass informal power for selfish ends can deliberately squander precious resources is provided by New York City's school procurement division before it was revamped in 1996 and 1997. Procurement personnel navigated a vast sea of complex rules on how to bid and purchase goods and services. Historically, whenever New York City's community school districts ran into difficulty with purchasing, central procurement officials would be dispatched "to rescue the locals in the field," as the veteran Mr. Rossi observed.[17] They would clean up their specific problem. But "they made sure not to teach them how to do things," Rossi said. That way they could justify their existence and show "how much worse things would be without them. Central will always stay in control as long as [it] can show that things are not working well."[18] Indeed, the record is full of examples of central experts dashing off to extricate employees from all kinds of troubles in the field, only to be sent back a few months later when the next crisis struck.

Meanwhile, however, these short-term "solutions" to local deficiencies masked the need for real reform and came at the cost of tens of thousands of dollars of potential savings wasted in central services year after year. It was only after a major scandal in the school system's main warehouse in 1995 that the school system began radical reforms requiring the central office to help local officials help themselves. Since then a significant number of local districts have enjoyed some measure of local expertise in procurement.

The turf-protection mentality pervaded various areas of the central office. Until recently, for example, New York City's internal school audit unit made sure not to teach custodial supervisors in the school Facilities Division how to catch errors in custodians' requests for reimbursement. That way, the audit unit stood to catch more errors and show that it had recouped a larger amount of money in improperly spent funds. As a high-level official in the audit unit said, the unit, which had suffered cuts under a succession of chancellors, was eager to show that it "would pay for itself."[19] The trouble was that, aside from wasting personnel who could have been used for other purposes, the auditors did not generally get to the custodial reimbursements until two years after the fact—when the money had already been reimbursed and was much harder to get back.

In another example, internal auditors similarly refused to teach payroll officers how to calculate lump-sum payments to retiring school employees. Auditors almost always found mistakes in these tricky calculations, which involve adding half the sick leave and annual leave and taking into consideration all the posts the employee held during his or her DOE employment and doing different calculations for time on pedagogical posts versus administrative posts. But, as the official from the audit unit noted, rather than teaching payroll employees how to do the calculations themselves, auditors would recalculate the payments post factum and then point to how much money they had saved. Under the direction of the new auditor general, internal auditors are now showing custodial supervisors and payroll employees how to do their own work better.

Similar patterns have surfaced in the LAUSD. The central Accounts Payable Division, for instance, was supposed to help local district offices and schools become independent in various fiscal matters. But four separate independent studies have reported that Accounts Payable procedures were so byzantine and cumbersome[20] that regional and school officials were forced to rely on central officials for continual help. Every major study of Accounts Payable since 1993 recommended that it simplify, clarify, and modernize procedures. But the division persisted in its "historical resistance to change and lack of openness to new ideas and new ways of doing things."[21] One possible reason, according to investigators: the division lacked a "strong commitment" to make local officials independent.

USING CONTROL OVER RED TAPE TO AMASS POWER

The drive to protect one's expertise and use it to make oneself indispensable can lead to out-and-out power grabs, as illustrated by the late Bruce Gelbard, a twenty-two-year veteran of the New York City school system, who climbed his way up from a classroom aide in 1974 to the $161,000-a-year post of secretary to the seven-member central board of education in 1990.

Gelbard's official duties were largely clerical: preparing the official central board calendar, maintaining its books and documents, executing board contracts, and reading roll call. But Gelbard's ability to wield crucial information, as reported in numerous newspaper articles and confirmed by various officials during interviews, enabled him to amass enormous unofficial power during his six years as central board secretary.[22] His power depended on the existence of red tape. His ability to call on administrators throughout the bureaucracy to do him favors and cut through lengthy procedures made him invaluable to his friends and a bane to his adversaries.

When new chancellors and board members arrived, they would reportedly turn to Gelbard for information on matters big and small. He knew where money and people were hidden in the sprawling school system and understood many of the system's obscure bylaws and rules. He would prepare thick briefing pamphlets for board members on upcoming votes. Soon they came to rely on him for major policy decision making, as some later told reporters.

Gelbard also knew about the small perks that could make board members' lives so much more pleasant. He knew how to get them school car service, cellular phones, and office furniture. He knew where to get new school stationery printed with their names on letterhead, how to get their offices painted, and how to make sure their expense forms got processed quickly.[23] He knew where to lodge school business guests from out of town and how to get the system to foot thousands of dollars in hotel and peripheral bills—food, telephone calls, and so forth—apparently without any fuss.[24] This know-how is crucial in a system draped in red tape, where the more permanent employees sometimes act as if the chancellor or superintendent and central board members, who come and go in quick succession, work for them, not the other way around.

Life can be perplexing at the top of such a system, as Chancellor Harold Levy learned on his first day on the job. In a speech for the Center for Educational Innovation in Manhattan, Levy recounted that when he was first settling into his new office, he asked the custodian in charge of maintaining his building, 110 Livingston Street, where the men's room was.[25] The custodian motioned toward the men's room far down the hall from his office. A few hours later, however, Levy noticed that the thick black lacquered door just outside his office, which had been locked until then, was ajar. Curious, he pulled it open. Inside was a beautiful, exquisitely decorated marble bathroom, obviously intended as the private bathroom of whoever occupied his office. But the custodian was using it to store his mops and cleaning products. When Levy asked the custodian about the bathroom, he told him he could not go in there; it was reserved for custodial staff.

Gelbard parlayed knowledge of rules and quirks like this to amass power. If you were his friend, he would cut through the red tape for you; if you were not, you would suffer. Over the years, he had allegedly cemented the loyalty of crucially positioned midlevel administrators throughout the bureaucracy by using his influence to protect and promote their employment. In return, they would allegedly cut through red tape when he asked.

So when Chancellor Joseph Fernandez wanted the board quickly to approve a philanthropic couple's $1-million donation to open a new school in Brooklyn, the donation languished amid the usual bureaucratic concerns and objections. Weeks later, when an official working on the donation passed Gelbard in the hall, Gelbard reportedly told him, "When are you going to learn to talk to me first? Then you wouldn't have to fight so hard."[26]

Gelbard used red tape as a weapon to protect his own perks too: a school car and a staff of five full-timers, five part-timers, and a group of interns. When someone in the Division of School Facilities tried to get him to return the car, crucial school repair paperwork went unapproved by his office for months.[27]

Gelbard also used knowledge of information to intimidate adversaries. He would reportedly collect damaging information on people and later threaten to reveal it, if necessary.[28] When some central board members tried to remove him from his job as secretary in 1996, for instance, Gelbard's lawyer threatened to disclose embarrassing information about them.[29]

Gelbard even created new red tape when it suited him. When Chancellor Rudy Crew was trying to streamline the central bureaucracy in the mid-1990s, Crew said that Gelbard demanded to know which people's jobs would be affected, raised multiple procedural objections, and repeatedly delayed putting the proposal on the central board's agenda. Fernandez reported that Gelbard had used similar tactics against him—repeatedly rescheduling central board meetings, scheduling them when Fernandez was out of town, or revising the board agenda so that the chancellor would not be prepared.[30]

Eventually, however, after a major shakeup of the central board in which the majority coalition lost power to a new faction backed by Mayor Rudolph Giuliani, the new faction was able to muster the votes to oust Gelbard from his position as secretary, pushing him back to his previous civil service position.

WHEN ANTICORRUPTION MACHINERY BREEDS CORRUPTION

Informal power networks work only if people have connections. What about employees who do not have friends in the central office or who do not want to have to stoop for a favor every time they hit a bump in the road? And what about vendors who do not have access to the right people at the center?

To circumvent red tape, employees at the lower levels in the school hierarchy may take the law into their own hands and act alone, or they may collude with vendors. Their *creative noncompliance* may be legal, semilegal, or illegal. But they are usually motivated by legitimate and charitable goals and, much of the time, help the district achieve its mission more effectively. Of course, there is the danger that creative noncompliance be abused for personal ends. If this happens, what was *bottleneck corruption* may be said to degenerate into *occupational corruption*.[1] While bottleneck corruption helps the organization accomplish its mission in the short term, occupational corruption comes at its expense. But for the most part, the examples in the record suggest that creative noncompliance helps achieve legitimate ends.

Anthony Alvarado, the entrepreneurial former chancellor of the New York City school system, had earlier served as superintendent in Community School District 4 in Manhattan's East Harlem, where he created what was one of the first public school choice districts in the country. The students, predominantly minority, could choose from a number of small alternative schools, oases in an otherwise failing district. He made sure that principals had discretion to shape their schools in response to student needs and hire appropriate teachers. Under his auspices, the district became a national showcase for some of the best public schools in America's inner cities. Student achievement soared.[2]

But to get there, Alvarado had to find creative ways around a slew of central bureaucratic rules. In fact, the very concept of alternative schools, from the central office's perspective, pushed the limits of central rules. Central computer systems did not recognize the existence of the fifty-two alternative schools that Alvarado had established, many on floors of school buildings or other unofficial locations. As far as the school payroll and other central divisions were concerned, there were only twenty schools in the district. Deborah Meier, the star director of one of the most successful alternative schools, Central Park East, observed, "We're living a fiction."[3]

So, not surprisingly, getting the choice program to work required a good deal of inventiveness. Alvarado had to get around union seniority hiring rights to enable talented junior teachers to bump worn-out senior ones. He had to get around overtime restrictions to pay people who were working late and weekends. He had to find ways around payroll and contractual job descriptions and create new positions to put senior teachers in charge of running some of his new alternative schools. He had to pay for programs not conceived of under the rigid budget system. Alvarado needed flexibility, not the line-by-line permission that he would have had to seek every time he wanted to apply for a budget modification. If children were going to come first, as one assistant put it, following protocol would have taken "too long."[4]

Under the rules for overtime, for example, no recipient could get more than 270 hours a year or five hours a day overtime without a waiver. Overtime work had to differ from the employee's regular assignments. Overtime lines had to correspond to the employees's actual title. But since Alvarado's goal was to motivate and remunerate staff and since teachers were often doing principals' jobs and vice versa, observing every regulatory detail regarding overtime caps,[5] descriptions of work, and official titles would have been difficult and at times practically impossible.[6] Unfortunately, some of Alvarado's inventiveness went too far, and a probe by investigators eventually caused him to step down from the chancellorship years later.

BOTTLENECK CORRUPTION

In other cases, employees collude with vendors and vice versa to devise creative solutions. In 1994 the U.S. Attorney's Office, Federal Bureau of Investigation, New York City Department of Investigation, School Authority

Inspector General, and New York State Organized Task Force announced the indictment of eighteen people caught in a web of bribery and racketeering in the New York City schools. The investigation painted a picture of a system in which it was natural for contractors to bribe school officials in order to expedite legitimate payments and to inflate bills and bribe officials to process them.[7] Defendants would meet in restaurants across the city, at school headquarters in Brooklyn, in lawyers' offices, and in parked limousines to discuss and make payoffs of up to $40,000 at one time.[8] The defendants were additionally accused of fixing leases and contract settlements and influencing contract awards.[9]

The case stunned many because of its magnitude (eighteen defendants), scope (millions of dollars' worth of contracts and leases), duration (at least thirteen years, from 1981, when the probe started, through 1994, when indictments were issued), and the high-level officials it implicated. Sheldon Rosenblum, the school's deputy counsel and the second-highest attorney at the BOE, who had taken hundreds of thousands of dollars in bribes from contractors, became a key informer for the government.

The probe started in 1985, when investigators were looking into why construction costs at Fiorello H. La Guardia High School near Lincoln Center were $85 million, $50 million higher than the original estimate.[10] Their big break came when they discovered that one company responsible for the construction, Mars-Normel, had inflated bills for $4.5 million. When they confronted the owner with the evidence, he implicated Rosenblum, acknowledging that he had paid Rosenblum between $150,000 and $200,000 and agreed to tape their conversations. When the FBI confronted Rosenblum with the tapes, he too agreed to cooperate. His cooperation, together with that of the assistant deputy director for technical services in the Division of School Facilities, who had also taken bribes, led to hundreds of hours of secretly video- and audio-taped conversations with dozens of engineers, architects, and contractors and finally broke open the seamy underworld of leasing, construction, and renovation. Since the indictments in 1994, eleven defendants pleaded guilty, two died pending trial, one was convicted after trial, one was acquitted, and three cases were dismissed.

What most people glossed over in this case, however, was that a number of the defendants had their backs against the wall because, as a result of procedural delays, they were not getting paid for work they had done. They hired "expediters" and consultants to help them speed up their payments. These expediters arranged for bribes and were subsequently convicted of bribery, along with their clients.

Several of the defendants—consultants, lawyers, and engineers—had been successful because of their ability to maneuver through the school construction bureaucracy. It is thus not surprising to hear from the New

York City School Construction Authority inspector general that all eighteen defendants in the case "perceived bribery as a normal part of doing business with the board" and that none "showed the slightest hesitation or compunction about offering bribes."[11] One, a senior partner at one of New York City's oldest construction law firms who had worked in school construction law for over forty years, was charged in four separate complaints with arranging bribe payments by his clients to board officials.[12]

One architect, Nicholas Sensey, together with other subcontractors, had done extensive work—nearly $70,000 worth—for a landlord who was repairing and renovating a building that he was leasing to the BOE. When the landlord failed to complete the repair work, the BOE took it over, thus becoming responsible for paying the architect and other subcontractors for work they had already done for the landlord. With no time frame regarding when he was going to get paid, Sensey, as some of the other subcontractors did, hired an expediter, who accordingly met with school officials in November 1992 to discuss bribes to move his check along.

To complicate matters, however, the BOE had lost track of a huge pile of unpaid invoices after a reshuffling of responsibilities between it and the School Construction Authority. So it froze all payments and sent letters to contractors asking them whether they were owed any money and, if so, to resubmit bills and documentation for their work, thus practically inviting fraud. The BOE also established committees to review and research the large influx of documents it was receiving in response to its letters before releasing any money—not the most reassuring sign for vendors hoping to get paid before long.

Some vendors were genuinely concerned that they were in for a real fight to get the BOE to release their money. Unfortunately, what started off in some cases as an effort to recoup legitimate payments from the BOE degenerated into outright fraud. Asked to resubmit invoices, a number of contractors inflated their old bills and fabricated corresponding backup documentation, while their expediters arranged for bribes to push the phony bills through the bureaucracy. While Sensey's expediter initially arranged a bribe simply to get Sensey paid for his actual work, five months later he met with school officials to discuss how to inflate Sensey's invoices to far in excess of what they actually were.

Neither red tape nor BOE ineptness justifies the commission of crimes. But it is important to consider how the system can invite bribery and bill inflation. While some contractors are crooks out to bilk the school district from the outset, others can get drawn into corruption as a result of genuine frustrations. Moreover, the prospect of having to go through the additional review procedures that are often necessitated when large numbers of unpaid invoices accumulate[13] spurs an adversarial attitude that can easily decline into efforts to take as much money from the system as possible.

COMPLEX PROCUREMENT RULES

The degree to which complex regulations can spur creative corrupt scams is further illuminated by the New York City school district's record with procurement fraud. Before procurement rules were streamlined in 1996 and 1997 under the direction of Rossi, they gave rise to repeated cases of bottleneck and occupational corruption. Since Rossi revamped them, however, relatively few problems have emerged.

Investigators described the rules prior to the reforms as torturous and paper driven—"something out of the Dark Ages."[14] Most supplies had to be purchased centrally, usually through the Bureau of Supplies (BOS).

Items were either *list, nonlist,* or *regulated nonlist.* List referred to items for which the BOE had an exclusive contract with a particular vendor on its master list. Employees could order list items from the BOS or sometimes from the vendor. Nonlist items were those for which the BOE had no existing contract. Employees could buy these directly from the vendor but had to follow strict competitive bidding procedures. Regulated nonlist items were the most difficult to buy. Employees had to order them through the BOS, which had to solicit competitive bids before ordering.

Employees had to obtain approval from different sources and supervisors, depending on which program the money came from. For regular items, employees needed their supervisor's approval; for reimbursable programs, they needed the approval of the director of funded programs; for unusual purchases, they had to get written authorization from the director of the business office at central.

To buy computer diskettes, an employee first had to peruse the BOS's voluminous catalogue to determine whether there was a master list for diskettes. If not, the employee had to determine whether diskettes were considered a "regulated nonlist" item. If so, she had to order them from the BOS and wait, sometimes for years, to receive them.

If diskettes were not regulated nonlist, the employee could solicit bids herself, but then she would have to apply to the BOS for the paperwork to order the diskettes. Once the paperwork was complete, her school would forward it, along with the three bids, to the district office for review. From there, the forms would go to the Financial Management Center, where they would remain "buried on a desk . . . , under dozens of similar documents" before they were processed and the funds were encumbered.[15] Only then could the BOE mail the order to the vendor, who required a minimum of between three and seven weeks for delivery. If there was a mistake in the paperwork, it would go back to the school.

Tales of teachers ordering supplies that never arrived or receiving something different from what they had ordered were legion for decades. Veterans described procurement fraud as "prevalent" in New York City. A

1994 Special Commissioner of Investigation probe conducted with the help of a high-level school purchasing officer whom investigators called "Fortunoff" and a vendor called "Sales" opened a window into how the cumbersome procedures spurred fraud. Twenty-four employees and one vendor were accused of participating in fraud and abuse in procurement.[16]

CREDIT POOLS

To get around the rules, people created illegal slush funds known as credit pools to buy what they needed quickly without having to go through the official procedures. A school official and vendor would collude to order supplies from the central office; these the vendor would either not deliver or deliver in lesser quantity than what was ordered. The conspirators would select any fungible office supply readily available from the central office and submit a set of three bogus bids and a bogus purchase order.[17] More often than not, the vendor would take care of fabricating the bids and filling out the purchase order. The central office would process the fictitious order and pay the vendor, who would deposit whatever was left over after expenses in an account known as a credit pool.

Credit pools made life "simple and painless."[18] Employees could use the money in the credit pool to order whatever they needed—list or nonlist—directly from the vendor, who controlled the account, without bother. Also, since credit pool money could be spent any time, employees could use it to avoid the BOE's *use it or lose it* rule that required employees to spend specified funds by the end of the year or return them. (The BOE has since rescinded that rule for various programs, but the state and federal government and many other school districts, such as Los Angeles, still have it, prompting spending frenzies at year's end.) As one school employee explained to Sales, who was secretly recording the conversation for investigators, " 'We have to spend the money [$25,000] by the close of business tomorrow . . . , and we need your help in spending it.' "[19]

Vendors too benefited from credit pools. They could do business with school administrators without hassle and would get paid instantly for delivering supplies.

The central office never had to know about the arrangement. Central officials could never tell from looking at the paper trail that supplies had not arrived as ordered because someone—often the same employee who ordered the goods—would sign a packing slip, falsely indicating that the goods had been received. Moreover, because of the BOS's remoteness, teachers and local office workers usually had no way to find out why they did not receive supplies and rarely knew whom to complain to.

A number of people initially set up credit pools to do their jobs better and faster. Consider the assistant principal of a new high school who needed to wire a classroom for computer use and install a bell system in the school by the first day of class. The BOE had refused to send electricians to work on an emergency basis, meaning that the assistant principal would probably have to wait many months, by which time it would be too late. So he arranged for a vendor to advance him some cash from their credit pool and used it to pay BOE electricians under the table to wire the classroom.[20]

Others used credit pools to buy specialized supplies that were hard to get through official channels. When Fortunoff's boss, a top central administrator, needed some free-standing dry-erase markerboards in a rush, Fortunoff's vendor, Sales, used the credit pool. The markerboards arrived soon thereafter. When a secretary in the Office of Legal Services needed special file cabinets, she used her credit pool.[21] As with all credit pool arrangements, the deals could easily be concealed from the central office by putting down "office supplies" on the purchase order and packing slip.

A number of officials used the discretion afforded by illegal credit pools to negotiate hard for discounts from vendors, something impossible under official procedures. One teacher who had won an $8,000 grant to create video libraries in five schools persuaded her credit pool vendor to give her a discount so that she could buy as many videocassette recordings as possible for her money.[22] In another example, a supervising school psychologist for severely disabled children solicited bids from other companies for office partitions before approaching his credit pool vendor to match the price of the lowest bidder.[23]

A secretly recorded conversation between the assistant principal trying to get his classroom wired in time for the start of school and his vendor, Sales, illuminates how some educators became creative in fighting for students' welfare when they had the chance to make spending decisions. The electrician had told the assistant principal that he would wire the classroom for $1,300 cash. But the vendor, Sales, told the assistant principal that he would have to charge their credit pool $2,800 to give him $1,300. The assistant principal's response was noteworthy: "How can we work it so it doesn't, you know, cost 115 percent more? . . . Can you, umm, instead of paying me in cash, if cash is gonna cost this much, if you paid, paid me in Visa, if you wrote another check in Visa, instead of the cash, could it, would it be less?"[24] This kind of bargaining is practically unheard of under official procurement regulations.

OCCUPATIONAL CORRUPTION

The danger of bottleneck corruption, however, is that because it establishes a totally unmonitored, unofficial method of doing business with an organization, it makes theft a real possibility. So, as in the case of some of the defendants indicted in connection with the school construction case, some people used credit pools to steal from the school system. While the majority of officials in the case did not try to enrich themselves, about one fourth, or six out of twenty-five, did.[25] Of these six, two seemed motivated to bilk the system from the outset. From the beginning, the acting director of the Early Childhood Program in the Bronx's District 12 used most of her credit pool for personal items and a vacation to Puerto Rico, including airfare, hotel, and car, with her sister-in-law and the latter's three children. Another officer used her credit pool to support her desired lifestyle, including paying the mortgage on her Poconos vacation home.[26]

The other four offending officials, however, at least started out using credit pools for legitimate purposes and only gradually descended into theft as they realized how easy it would be to get away with. One special education administrator initially used her credit pool to order needed computer software, but eventually she began ordering questionable items such as kitchen appliances, a refrigerator, microwave, and coffee maker.[27] Similarly another administrator started out purchasing legitimate office furniture, such as bookcases and file cabinets, but eventually began to buy personal office furniture for herself and other offices she administered.

Recalling his own experience, the confidential informant Fortunoff explained how he, like a few of the administrators in the case, went from buying legitimate items to waste to theft. He first bought only legitimate, hard-to-get office supplies. Then he started buying questionable appliances for his boss's office: a television, videocassette recorder, microwave, refrigerator, and coffee pots.[28] Eventually, he bought a clock, radio, and compact disc player for himself, as suggested by the clandestine nature of the vendor's time and place of delivery—on a Saturday morning in a McDonald's parking lot near the Manhattan Bridge.[29]

Los Angeles exhibits similar patterns. In fact, in the Los Angeles United School District (LAUSD) procurement regulations are as, if not more, cumbersome than those in prereform New York City.[30] In its 2002 annual report, for example, the LAUSD inspector general describes how a teacher and vendor colluded. The teacher put in an order for a certain amount of computer equipment from the vendor. When the initial purchase was reduced by $1,380.62, rather than adjust the invoice, the teacher requested a "credit memorandum" with the vendor. She used the credit to buy more equipment.[31]

THE WRONG MEDICATION: HOW NOT TO FIX THE PROBLEM

CHAPTER TWELVE

LESSONS FROM LOCAL POLITICAL SCHOOL CONTROL

The pathology suggests the remedy. Since the roots of fraud, waste, and mismanagement in America's biggest school districts lie largely in their command-and-control structures, the solution is generally to decentralize discretion and shift from a virtually exclusive concern with compliance accountability to a balance between compliance and performance accountability. Because there are many ways to decentralize, reformers should heed the warning of some previous experiments in decentralization.

Throughout the history of urban public education, there have always been diehards who struggled against the stampede toward centralization. Every once in a while, usually after a major scandal at headquarters or mounting racial pressure for grassroots control, these holdouts would manage to wrest a modicum of power from central offices and hand it to parents and communities, at least for a while. From the 1960s through the early 1990s, such efforts generally focused on creating locally elected boards of community and parent representatives with a say in how schools were run. In one of the nation's best-known experiments in local control, New York City gave thirty-two (initially thirty-one) locally elected community school boards authority over elementary and middle schools; each board oversaw one school district. This experiment holds a valuable lesson in how not to decentralize.[1]

NEW YORK'S SCHOOL DECENTRALIZATION LAW

New York State inaugurated radical local political control of schools in 1969, when it passed what is known as the school decentralization law.[2] The law followed over a decade of turbulence in which minority school enrollment grew dramatically, citywide reading scores plunged, and dropout rates soared.[3] During most of the 1950s, reformers pinned their hopes for improvement primarily on racial integration. The Board of Education (BOE) came up with a number of proposals to integrate schools but, in the face of bitter resistance by white parents and teachers, repeatedly gave excuses, leaving behind a string of broken promises. Citizens, particularly minorities, increasingly perceived the BOE as an entrenched remote bureaucracy concerned with perpetuating its own power.[4] The corrupting influence of local politics was no longer perceived as the problem with urban public schooling. Instead, the problem was the elite corps of central educational professionals whom progressives had touted as the panacea for the ills of urban public education. This corps was now perceived to be the problem precisely because it excluded local public participation from education policy and operation.

Fierce racial antagonism pitted black parents against the mostly white teachers' union and school bureaucracy, both seen as obstructionist. By 1966 community control became the rallying cry of New York school reformers. The Ford Foundation added impetus to the idea of community-controlled schools by establishing three demonstration districts in the city. Although community control meant abandoning integration efforts, by the late 1960s New York City activists had come to see integration as an implicit rejection of minority culture. Schools that were predominantly minority were branded as inferior simply on the basis of their racial makeup.[5] Community control, on the other hand, affirmed minority values by enabling schools to reflect them.

After devastating teacher strikes, lawmakers eventually agreed to give inner-city minorities greater influence over their children's elementary school education.[6] The plan was for thirty-one (later thirty-two) nine-member community school boards, elected every three years from their districts, to oversee the city's elementary and middle school pupils. The BOE retained control over high schools, special education, and a host of other programs. Local boards replaced the central office in hiring most district staff, from the district superintendent to nonpedagogical employees (known as "nonpeds") to principals. Although teachers remained outside board patronage, boards controlled their promotions.

The short-term goal of local school control was to appease minorities and avert a race war. But the widely shared long-term hope was to force schools to be politically accountable to their communities and thus improve education for minorities.[7] The assumption was that, since school boards picked key pedagogues such as superintendents and principals, they would make sure children got a good education. If children did not, residents would vote their local boards out of office.[8]

Unfortunately, the reality turned out to be quite different. Over two decades of exposes by grand juries, investigators, civic watchdog groups, and journalists reveal that many community school boards, with their vast reservoirs of jobs and money, quickly became centers for power and patronage, harking back to Tammany Hall.[9] These boards carved their districts into fiefdoms where jobs were doled out to loyal campaign workers, lovers, and family members or sold for cash. The way for a teacher or assistant principal to get ahead was not to create excellent lesson plans or find better ways to teach math but to work on campaigns and run errands for board members. As one board member from Brooklyn's District 27 put it in a secretly recorded conversation for investigators, "I'm a political leader, that's why I'm here. . . . I make sure my people get f—ing jobs."[10] Children meanwhile were pushed out of the picture: "I've never heard the word 'children' or 'education' enter into our discussions in the last few years . . . with anybody," another board member laughingly told an informant cooperating with this commission.[11]

By the 1980s, scandals surfaced every few months. In January 1988 two community school board members—a state assemblywoman and her husband—were accused of stealing a $10,000 piano from a school. (However, the case did not go anywhere.[12]) In March, Miguel Diaz, the chairman of District 12's school board, and Jose Cruz, a board member, were indicted in connection with separate incidents of soliciting bribes.[13] The chancellor suspended the entire board. About four months later, two board members from District 9 pleaded guilty to petty larceny for using school property for personal political campaigns.[14] And in the fall of 1988, Anthony Losacco, a teacher's aide from District 4 in Manhattan who allegedly had firsthand knowledge about secret slush funds and missing money there, was found dead with a gunshot wound to the head the day before he was to testify before a grand jury investigating the fund.[15] Media exposes suggested that the superintendent and a city councilman who represented the area had stolen the money. Losacco was distraught about testifying.

Problems were so widespread that, by the end of the year, four of New York City's five district attorneys were investigating school district corruption.[16] A Bronx grand jury examining all school districts in that borough concluded that fraud and political patronage were a "way of life."[17] Children, needless to say, were pushed out of the picture.

To appreciate how community school control was vulnerable to fraud, it is helpful to look at one of the most dramatic investigations into school board wrongdoing, a 1993 investigation by the Special Commissioner of Investigation (SCI) of District 12, an impoverished area in the South Bronx near the bottom of city test scores.

In 1991 an early-retirement incentive opened up forty-six principalships and assistant principalships in District 12, presenting a tremendous opportunity for renewed educational vitality. Instead, a six-member majority alliance on the school board, known as "the caucus," began an all-out struggle for the vacancies and awarded them to campaign workers, friends, and lovers. The positions were divvied up in a series of secret meetings at which every opening was brought up for negotiation as the different factions on the caucus sought to improve their positions in the district. The superintendent, jockeying to secure the votes to renew his contract, mediated between the different sides. Parents and the board minority, which the caucus did not need to consult to pass its initiatives, were left in the dark.

HOW LANGUAGE ILLUMINATES THE PATHOLOGY

The pathology was illuminated by the language used to refer to board members and their spoils. Board members who obtained jobs for people were known as their *godfathers* and *godmothers*. The people for whom they obtained jobs were called their *pieces*. Pieces earned their jobs through nepotism, sexual favors, and bribes but most commonly by doing political work for board members. Always referred to in the possessive, pieces were regarded as their godparent's property. Board members relied on them to perform all kinds of favors after giving them jobs.

Pieces were not only single individuals. Some pieces gave their godparents control over multiple jobs. For instance, by placing his or her piece as coordinator of a program, the board member controlled all the jobs that that program generated. As the acting District 12 superintendent explained, "Coordinators . . . control a budget. So when I put you in that position and you're my piece, you'll find a way of providing for me. . . . That's how the job bank is created."[18] Thus schools and a host of education programs were referred to as pieces. As one former District 12 board member put it, "Everything is a piece."[19]

Critical to board members' bargaining for spoils was the understanding that pieces had different values depending on their potential to turn out votes. Thus principals were considered "plum" pieces because they had "access to parents . . . the people that vote," as one official explained.[20] Elementary schools were worth more than middle schools because parents were more likely to accompany younger children to school, providing more opportunities to garner votes. Education programs were ranked according to a similarly perverse criterion: the size of their budget. What makes a program "a big piece . . . is where the big money's coming in. The more jobs pay, the better, because you can get people big salaries."[21] Far from the ideal of concerned citizens, the terminology *godfathers, god-*

mothers, and *pieces* told of a perspective in which board members saw themselves as mobsters vying to expand power by gaining as many jobs as possible.

Illustrating how politics distorts hiring, a ferocious struggle broke out over the district's biggest elementary school because, with 1,160 pupils, it drew the largest number of parents. The caucus member who won the school appointed her campaign manager as principal. At another point, one faction traded several principalships for a program to counsel students at risk of dropping out because, one informant explained, it had "money in it . . . and people wouldn't get laid off. You could get more jobs through that."[22]

Official corruption findings were likely only the tip of the iceberg. When one woman from Brooklyn's District 19, in the midst of paying an informant board member an installment on a $8,000 to $10,000 bribe for a principalship, was asked how she knew to offer money, she replied: "Nobody said it. But you know . . . I've been around a long time, and I know a lot of board people . . . across the city."[23] Indeed, the jargon—*godfather, piece,* and *caucus* (or *coalition*)—was used to refer to the players in the patronage game in several districts.

NO REAL ACCOUNTABILITY

Why did local school control go so far awry? The answer illustrates the critical importance, as explained by microeconomists such as Oliver Williamson, of decentralizing down to the level where managers have all necessary knowledge to make decisions for which they and their units can be held accountable for performance. Community control pushed power down to the wrong level—a community political group—and erected a flawed form of accountability—local political accountability. Without safeguards, the system's structural vulnerabilities made corruption alluring and easy to engage in and get away with.

Consider first the lack of accountability. The 1969 decentralization provided for minimal performance accountability and minimal compliance accountability; thus, political accountability did not work as expected. Central oversight was minimal by law. But nothing ever happened to superintendents, principals, or boards if students did not learn.

Political control did not work as expected because voters did not vote board members out of office. First, as with most local elections,[24] few people bothered to vote in the city's obscure school board elections, which were held at different times from general elections. Turnout averaged 7.5 percent.

Second, some of those who might have voted were turned off and confused by the complex, arcane school board electoral system in which candidates were elected through proportional representation. Proportional representation was devised to ensure minority representation, but ironically it was so complicated that it probably scared a lot of minorities and other voters away. Voters had to vote for multiple candidates, ranking them in order of preference. Many people did not understand that they could vote for multiple candidates or how their votes would be counted. The wide array of candidates made it hard for most people to learn anything about them. Further, city parents had to fill out special forms to register to vote, which did not constitute registration for general elections.

Third, the way many board members got and stayed elected was not necessarily by doing a good job but by handing out jobs and buying votes. The more corrupt board members were, the more impervious they were to political removal. Since a couple of hundred votes was all that was needed to win a board seat, some board members could win just with the votes of people to whom they doled out jobs and perquisites. Moreover, as in most local elections, voters were more willing to trade their votes for the tangible rewards of patronage in local elections than in highly publicized national elections, where issues are of wider importance.[25]

Board members and superintendents were also insulated from education performance accountability to the central office. The chancellor could not remove them if children failed. He could not enforce education standards by law. Although the 1969 decentralization law permitted the chancellor to oust board members for specific violations and crimes, most chancellors who attempted to do so on academic performance grounds alone were slapped with time-consuming lawsuits, which they often lost.[26]

Sometimes even the federal government stood in the way. In 1996 Chancellor Rudolph Crew ordered the District 12 school board not to appoint a superintendent who had performed dismally when he was a teacher and assistant principal. When the board defied his order, the chancellor replaced three board members with three of his own trustees. The board countered with a lawsuit charging that the chancellor had violated the Voting Rights Act (1965). The U.S. Department of Justice agreed with the board. It found that the trustees altered the board's racial balance, making it no longer representative of the community. The Department of Justice therefore not only required the chancellor to select different trustees but also required him to obtain preclearance from it anytime he wanted to replace elected board members with his trustees in the future.[27]

Local boards were also barely held to account for how they spent money. Internal audits merely sampled a small number of district expenditures. District record keeping was generally so poor that it was difficult or impossible to get to the bottom of fraud and abuse. Although central administrators were sometimes dispatched to clean things up, they usually fostered local districts' dependence on the central office.

STRUCTURAL VULNERABILITIES: USING THE SCHOOL HIERARCHY

Without meaningful accountability for how they spent money or performed on the job, winning a school board seat proved very alluring to many people with financial, political, or even social ambitions.

Although they paid members only $125 a month, school boards provided numerous other tangible benefits. Board members got to go on conferences to exotic locales such as Honolulu at taxpayer expense.[28] They hired relatives with a mere two-thirds board vote. In District 12 board members agreed to rubber-stamp each other's relatives for jobs and not to interfere with their perks. "You know the rule we have," one former District 12 board member angrily complained to another when an official questioned his wife's unapproved leave of absence from her district job. "We don't mess with family."[29]

Boards could also be used for illicit profiteering, from bribery to kickbacks. One board member collected over $18,000 from a textbook publisher and meals, cash, and a white cashmere coat from other vendors; another got cameras, television equipment, and other items.[30]

But school boards, like many other community-controlled programs of the 1960s, were most valued as sources of power and status. In poor areas, they even enhanced sex appeal. As one District 12 board member told investigators, he ran for "the power and the women." Board members have used their influence to secure jobs for lovers.[31]

A board seat was also a way out of the inner city not encumbered by civil service regulations. Schools provided a treasure-house of everything politicians needed: campaign staff, office space, supplies, and equipment. Board members did not pay a dime for any of it. They rewarded campaign staff with school jobs and perks and used school supplies and equipment, despite regulations prohibiting this. Because it cost them so little, numerous members campaigned repeatedly for higher office, and many succeeded.[32] And those who did continued to use schools as a job bank for their supporters after they moved up.[33]

Board members expanded their political horizons in other ways, too. By lending their school patronage networks to higher politicians, they curried favor with them. They also "drafted" employees to campaign for relatives, augmenting their family's influence.[34]

Board members could also make money from patronage. One board member from Brooklyn's District 21, for example, orchestrated a massive teacher letter-writing campaign to support the construction of a $300-million condominium in which he had a financial stake.[35] Members also pressured staff to perform errands, such as planting their flowers and packing their boxes.[36]

Like the big city political machines of the last century whose successes were largely attributed to efficient organization, the school hierarchy could easily be turned into an efficient campaign base. Board members could assign campaign tasks to staff depending on where staff was stationed in the district. When a group of District 12 board members decided to hold a fundraiser for their school board campaign in 1991, they enlisted employees to perform every task.[37] A worker in the district printing office printed tickets on school stationery. Principals sold quotas of fundraiser tickets. A secretary in the district office did the bookkeeping. Others collected money at the door and took attendance.

A textbook example of how easily the school hierarchy could be put to work was Sheldon Plotnick's 1993 city council campaign.[38] To try to catapult himself from his seat on Brooklyn's District 21 board to the city council, Plotnick conveyed his aspirations to his beholden principals. To wrench control of the local Democratic club from his rival, he had principals orchestrate a massive club membership drive. At one school the principal sent subordinates to recruit the rest of his staff to join the club. Within a month, most had signed up. On the day of the vote, the principal's loyalists herded staff to the club en masse after school, giving Plotnick a big victory. Faculty who did not attend were deprived of valued preparation time.

A month later, when the club was to vote to endorse candidates for city council, the principal's subordinates circulated a sheet with the question "Are You Going?" followed by staff members' names. The previous month's "punishments" understood, virtually the entire staff attended the club meeting. Several school employees testified they did not know why they were there. With staff from different district schools sitting together, some teachers simply copied one another's ballots; others consulted palm cards. The result was a resounding endorsement for Plotnick. Although he lost the city council election, without the school machinery he would not have got as far as he did.

THE EASE OF BUILDING A PATRONAGE ARMY

School board members built patronage networks by rewarding people who campaigned and punishing those who did not. Illuminating the quid pro quo implicit in virtually every job in corrupt districts, one former District 12 board member running for reelection promised an aspiring assistant principal a lavish array of jobs if he could turn out one hundred votes. For this many votes, the board member said, "You could just about write your own meal ticket. . . . Deputy, principal, superintendent, whatever you want to call them—Director of Programs."[39] These deals bound employees to their godparents. As the board member added, "My attitude only changes if I lose, of course."[40]

In various insidious ways that often escaped the grasp of the law, board members punished those who did not campaign. They could fire probationary employees. They could deny tenured ones promotions. After supporting one District 12 board member for years in the hope of getting a promotion, an assistant principal "got tired of being demeaned" and eventually stopped doing the board member's errands and campaign work. He foolishly believed that when the principalship at his school became vacant he would get the job because the parents supported him. Instead, the board member appointed a woman who had hygiene problems and no parental backing but who had been a staunch campaign supporter. When the assistant principal asked why he had not received the job, he was curtly told, "We missed you," alluding to the campaign.[41]

Board members could also punish professionals by simply making their lives miserable. As a former District 12 board member said in a secretly recorded conversation: "Just like you can get up, you can come back down. . . . I mean a principal be out there, minding his business, trying to do a good job. But if a superintendent or his deputy who's in charge of principals is not supportive of you, you know, hey, you don't get textbooks, you don't get little grants, . . . or you don't get your conferences, your seminars. You know all the little things that can be done to principals. Your life can be made very, very miserable."[42]

Once corruption set in, board members no longer needed to twist arms to garner support. Employees already knew what to do. Everywhere they looked they saw that people who campaigned got ahead; people who did not fell behind. Thus when a board member in the Bronx's District 9, long beleaguered by corruption, sent quotas of fundraiser tickets to district schools addressed "Attention Principal," principals knew from experience to sell them.[43]

But secretly recorded conversations unmasked the deeply coercive nature of patronage and its demoralizing effect on those close to the classroom. As one assistant principal told an informant about working on her godmother's city council election, "I hated doing all that sh—."[44]

CONTROLLING THE TOOLS FOR PATRONAGE

School decentralization facilitated patronage by making it easy for board members to create jobs and perks and dole them out. Without any accountability for results, board members and superintendents could virtually invent jobs as needed. When a board member from District 27 in Queens wanted a $42,000 post for his campaign manager and another wanted a job for his wife, they instructed the superintendent, who was wearing a wire, to create a $75,000 "satellite" office from the district budget.[45]

Decentralization also made it easy for board members to control hiring without considering merit. To give communities room to select professionals who better reflected their values, centrally mandated requirements for several professional positions were eliminated. Principals could be appointed on the basis of a qualifying rather than a competitive exam, so that boards did not need to select those at the top of the civil service list. Superintendents could be appointed on a contract basis without tenure rights.

The only potential obstacle to board control over the hiring of nonpedagogues was the superintendent, whose job was to ensure the district's educational quality. However, because they were hired on a contract renewable at the board's discretion, superintendents were vulnerable to board coercion. Although most boards hired superintendents who reflected the majority's wishes, they could easily be pressured if that changed. The Joint Commission's 1989 investigation in District 27 in Queens shows how such pressure was brought to bear thanks to the cooperation of then-superintendent Colman Genn, a thirty-year school veteran outraged by the corruption he witnessed.[46]

Once boards usurped their superintendents' professional integrity, they could easily jettison merit as a requisite for hiring nonpedagogues. As one board member bluntly put it when Genn questioned the qualifications of one of his candidates, "Unqualified? Qualified? Bullshit. That's my recommendation."[47] Another board member put it even more graphically: "If we recommend somebody," he said regarding staff for children with special needs, they should be hired so long as "they're not illiterate or deformed or something [is] the matter with them."[48]

EXPLOITING PARENTS' POVERTY

To dictate the hiring of principals and assistant principals, unlike the hiring of nonpedagogues, school boards additionally had to control parents. Because of these officers' importance, the process for hiring them was carefully designed to elicit input from parents, the superintendent, and the board. First, a parent screening committee selected five candidates from the applicant pool and forwarded their names to the superintendent. The superintendent then chose two of these five and sent their names to the board, which voted on the final appointment.

This intricate process would have appeared to make corruption difficult: to get their principals and assistant principals appointed, board members, after coopting the superintendent, would have additionally needed to ensure that the parents included their piece in the top five choices they sent to the superintendent. However, with so much riding on their ability to dole out these top jobs, board members devised numerous ways of manipulating parents.

One was buying parents with jobs, money, and gifts. In impoverished neighborhoods, as one assistant principal observed, "to offer money or a job is hard to resist."[49] In District 12, where 89 percent of children qualify for free lunches, buying parents was widespread. When a board member was asked how she would secure a principalship for a campaign supporter in a school where the parents did not know him, she impatiently responded, "Go over there and buy 'em. . . ." Questioner: "Give 'em jobs?" Board member: "That's the way. . . . "[50]

The depth of the problem is illustrated by the fierce bidding war for parents' support that erupted between two candidates for principal in another District 12 school. As each candidate outdid the other with successively better offers, which included offering parents jobs and paying their telephone bills, the parents kept shifting allegiance from one candidate to the other depending on whose proposal was more remunerative. In an illuminating last-minute shift, the parents abandoned one candidate after it turned out that a key PTA parent did not qualify for the job he had promised her.

GETTING AWAY WITH PATRONAGE

Board members knew they could get away with patronage because patronage is hard to prove and the laws proscribing it are equivocal and easily frustrated.[51] Most laws that criminalize official coercion of subordinates

reach only the grossest types of misconduct, not the subtle influence ped-
dling prevalent in city schools and most other patronage-ridden programs. For instance, to convict board members for pressuring subordinates to campaign under the New York City Charter, board members had
to request them for political support.[52] However, the more corrupt a district, the less board members needed to request subordinates, who knew
what to do without being asked. For the same reason bringing board
members up on charges of extortion involving the use of fear or force was
difficult and thus rare.

Indeed, because it is so easy for public officials to pressure people
without overt coercion, some extortion statutes, like the federal Hobbs
Act (1945),[53] have been interpreted to dispense with the need to show the
use of fear or force when the defendant is a public official acting "under
color of official right." However, if the payment is a campaign contribution, the state must still prove that the official explicitly promised something as a quid pro quo for the contribution.[54] Deals in city schools, as in
any political machine, are seldom so clear-cut.[55]

Bribery statutes are also limited in their use against patronage. Although many state bribery statutes might, if taken literally, encompass patronage, they are generally ambiguous in scope and provide little guid-
ance as to whether such conduct should come within their purview.[56]

The civil law approach to tackling patronage is also limited. The U.S.
Supreme Court has held that hiring and firing on the basis of partisan af-
filiation, where it is irrelevant to the job, violates employees' First Amendment rights of free speech and association.[57] However, to win a suit, plain-
tiffs must show that the employer failed to hire or fired them primarily as
a result of partisan politics. Employers needed merely show that they had
other legitimate reasons for their actions. Like most employers, board
members could easily come up with plausible reasons.[58] These difficulties
perhaps explain why no suits based on the First Amendment were brought
against New York City board members.

Even if officials were convicted, moreover, cases were usually pleaded
down. Imprisonment was rare. In District 27, where board members
pleaded guilty to felony counts of coercion and mail fraud, no one went
to jail.[59]

As corruption became entrenched, it became necessary to engage in.
School staff had to campaign to avoid punishment. If well-intentioned
board members, usually in the minority, did not wheel and deal, they were
excluded from decision making by the caucus. "We've all sold out to a certain extent . . . out of necessity," explained one such District 27 board
member. "I was gonna get absolutely nothing, you know?"[60]

Even politicians got sucked into the cycle of corruption. One state assemblyman, for instance, said he had to use schools for campaigning simply to keep up with his competition, who were using school staff to run against him.[61]

Further fueling the problem, officials in corrupt districts saw corruption as their right. As a District 12 board member remarked, "I mean, you know, we're making 125 [dollars] a month, and they're [principals and assistant principals] making all this big money. They can do something when we're putting their names up."[62]

THE BACKLASH TO BOTCHED POLITICAL DECENTRALIZATION

Eventually, perceived inadequacies with local control provoked backlashes. In New York City, years of outraged editorials and school reform proposals led to a 1997 state law, known as the governance law, which stripped school boards of most of their powers and concentrated authority in the center.[63] The law was a compromise for Mayor Rudolph Giuliani, who had been pressing for full mayoral sway over the schools in a bill vigorously opposed by the state assembly. When Giuliani saw that the narrower governance bill had a real chance to pass, however, he dropped his bid for control and threw his support behind it.

Signed by the legislature in December 1996 and the governor in January 1997, the governance law stripped school boards of most of their powers and concentrated authority in the chancellor and his administrators.[64] Under it, the chancellor had the authority to remove academically floundering principals, superintendents, and board members and take over underperforming schools and districts. District superintendents, who were now accountable to the chancellor, gained control over all the district personnel and programs that local boards used to command.

The only significant power that boards retained was a role in selecting superintendents. Board members could submit a list of up to four candidates to the chancellor, who made the final selection. If the chancellor was dissatisfied with the choices, he or she could send the list back for more names until a satisfactory one was presented.

Although the governance law unquestionably reduced corruption at the school board level, as evidenced by the reduced number of school board cases investigated and substantiated,[65] stories of board member misbehavior, nepotism, and patronage kept seeping through.[66] There was also the sense that the central administration, besieged by its own problems, did not have the solution to student performance on standardized tests, which remained depressingly low. And the chancellor was not fully in charge anyway, as local school boards strove to assert whatever autonomy was left to them. One board, for example, chose to remain without a superintendent for three years as it locked horns with the chancellor over candidates for superintendent.[67] In another case, a board member whom the chancellor had ousted for financial malfeasance defiantly won his seat back in the next board election.[68]

For all these reasons, it was not long before the battle cry for yet further centralization sounded again. Support swelled for a governance change that would put the mayor firmly in charge, much as had happened in Chicago in 1995, when a state law centralized power in the mayor, a new school chief executive officer, and a new school board.

Mayoral control in New York City became law in June 2002, putting Mayor Michael Bloomberg at the helm of the school system. The idea was to introduce long-needed political accountability into what had been one of the most unaccountable bureaucracies in the state. In his public statements Bloomberg has repeatedly said he would stake his success on his ability to improve education, implicitly inviting New Yorkers to vote him out of office if he fails.

The chain of command in the New York City schools appears to have tightened significantly under the 2002 law. The mayor handpicks the chancellor, and the chancellor handpicks the district superintendents. The mayor also controls the central school board, which was expanded from seven members to thirteen. The mayor picks eight of the thirteen members, one of whom is the chancellor. The remaining five members are parents chosen by the city's borough presidents. As for community school boards, after four years on life support under the governance law, the 2002 law finally rang their death knell. The law called for their elimination by June 2003 after hearings to determine what should replace them, as a way of offering parents some say in education.

CHAPTER THIRTEEN

LESSONS FROM BUREAUCRATIC AUTONOMY

Another illuminating lesson in how not to liberate managers from bureaucracy is provided by the New York City school custodian system, the half-billion-dollar-a-year, 8,500-employee-strong system under the Board (now Department) of Education's Division of School Facilities that is the biggest, most expensive school cleaning enterprise in the nation.[1]

In contrast to the community school boards, the custodial system devolves a great deal of power to field managers who have the knowledge necessary to make relevant decisions: the one thousand school custodians, or building superintendents, who are responsible for cleaning and maintaining the school system's 1,200 schools. So the problem here is not power without knowledge; rather, it is power without accountability.

When people have power but no accountability, the results are not pretty. Scandals going back to 1924 paint a picture of school custodians, who control millions of dollars in building maintenance budgets and employ dozens of helpers such as cleaners and handymen, systematically transforming their schools into enterprises for bribery, extortion, theft, and nepotism. With little accountability, custodians gave family and lovers no-show jobs as helpers and handed them thousands of dollars in fraudulent overtime. They used school maintenance budgets to renovate their homes and boats. They extorted kickbacks from emergency contractors. A number did not even maintain a presence at their schools, pursuing lucrative second jobs instead. Meanwhile, some supervisors turned a blind eye to custodians' abuses and sometimes shared in kickbacks from contractors.

At the same time, reports described children sitting in filthy classrooms surrounded by peeling paint, falling plaster, and broken windows. Water dripped on their desks from holes in the ceilings; rodents sometimes ran over their feet. As a commission headed by Harold Levy before he became chancellor put it, some schools were "more suitable to prisoners than academics."[2]

But the school custodial system highlights much more than what can go wrong when managers have power but not accountability. This chapter illuminates these roadblocks through a description of the custodial system and how it invited abuse until 1993, when state legislators passed a comprehensive law designed to reduce fraud and make custodians accountable to principals. The next chapter examines how and why the custodial system has been able to derail one remedy after another, including the latest attempt in the 1993 law.

THE NEW YORK CITY CUSTODIAL SYSTEM: A RECIPE FOR ABUSE

Since the New York City school system began hiring custodians—before the Civil War—it has maximized their discretion to enable them to respond quickly and with minimal red tape through a management system known as the "indirect system."[3] Under this system, custodians controlled their own annual school maintenance budget, which today ranges from $80,000 to over $1.2 million, depending on the school's size. Custodians were expected to use the money to buy supplies and hire helpers, such as firefighters to operate school heating systems, handymen to perform repairs, watchmen to provide security, and cleaners. Custodians had discretion to pay helpers as much overtime as their budgets afforded. They also negotiated wage and fringe benefits with their helpers' unions.

Although the school system's budget allocation formula assumed that the bigger a custodian's school, the more helpers and supplies he would need, custodians did not have to hire a particular number of helpers or buy a particular amount of supplies. So long as they complied with the system's cleaning standards, how they spent their money was up to them.[4] But cleaning standards, a bare-bones list of custodians' minimal duties, granted them total latitude in deciding how hard to work beyond the mandated minimum. In effect, the only way the system could know where custodians' money went was by auditing their expenditures after the fact.

Custodians were also expected to pay themselves a salary from whatever was left over in their budgets after cleaning and maintenance expenses.[5] Administrators hoped that allowing custodians to determine their earnings would encourage them to be frugal and efficient. They reasoned that custodians would not waste money because the more they wasted, the more they would have to spend to clean their schools and thus the less they would have for their salaries.[6] In 1964, when a scandal revealed that custodians earned more than most U.S. governors and mayors,[7] the BOE imposed caps on custodians' salaries. The caps were proportional to the size of the custodian's budget, and custodians were required to return any balance remaining above their caps at the end of the year to the BOE.

FLAWED ACCOUNTABILITY MECHANISMS

Giving custodians broad discretion may have made sense when the BOE first hired them in 1856 because they lived in the schools and had incentives to care for their buildings as they would their own homes. But once custodians moved out, in 1900, their incentives became similar to those of independent contractors, who also control funds, hire their own workers, and buy supplies. But while contractors, like many regular government employees, are held in check by constraints such as performance accountability and bureaucratic oversight, checks on custodians were nonexistent or too flawed to be meaningful.

With independent contractors, school system supervisors see that they comply with standards that ensure safe and satisfactory service. But in the custodial system, oversight mechanisms did not ensure compliance and BOE standards did not guarantee clean or well-maintained buildings even if custodians followed them to the letter.

One reason was that standards, known as work rules, describe custodians' minimal tasks and serve as guides to inspire them to do more work.[8] Although work rules have been minimal since the BOE first started issuing them in 1903, they became increasingly so after the 1960s, as the BOE pared them down further and further in successive collective bargaining sessions with the custodian union, Local 891 of the International Union of Operating Engineers. Work rules issued in the 1970s and 1980s, for instance, required custodians to scrub toilets and mop cafeteria floors no more than once a week[9] and sweep classrooms only every other day.[10]

Adding to the inadequacy of the work rules, custodians used them not as an inspiration to work harder but as an excuse to do no more than the mandated minimum. So if a child threw up in the bathroom on a day when toilets were not due to be scrubbed or spilled food in the lunchroom when it was not due to be mopped, custodians did not see this as their problem. Indeed, Local 891 would threaten custodians who volunteered to do more than was in the work rules; if the BOE wanted more, it would have to pay for it.[11]

At the same time, the BOE's mechanisms for ensuring that custodians complied with the work rules were marred in several respects. First, conflicts of interest between custodians and their immediate supervisors, known as plant managers, compromised oversight. Plant managers were supposed to inspect custodians regularly and evaluate them annually. But until 1993, plant managers belonged to the same local as custodians and had "friendships and loyalties" to them; as a result, they rarely inspected custodians and gave them excellent ratings even when they were chronically absent, openly engaged in fraud, and had filthy schools.[12]

Second, the Division of School Facilities, which was supposed to oversee custodians and plant managers, was too big and removed from schools to supervise them effectively. So despite some able managers, unless a problem was an emergency, had the potential to attract negative press, or was brought to their attention by individuals with political or other clout, DSF managers were unlikely to learn about it. In one school, for instance, for six months parents repeatedly complained to the DSF that their children were feeling faint because the school had no ventilation and that they could not use bathrooms because toilet bowls were missing. But until parents contacted their city council representative, who called the DSF director to arrange a public meeting with reporters, the DSF did not respond.[13]

The BOE also had no reliable machinery to police custodians for fraud and abuse (the Special Commissioner of Investigation was not up and running until 1991 and even then had limited resources). Although the BOE had in-house investigators, exposes showed they were so dependent on BOE management for their jobs and raises that, to avoid embarrassing their bosses, they usually swept findings under the carpet.[14]

The BOE also had in-house auditors, but they did not aggressively ferret out fraud either. Although they audited each custodian yearly, their audits were compliance audits, not fraud audits.[15] While fraud audits require auditors to visit schools to verify whether signatures on receipts are genuine and items were delivered, compliance audits merely require auditors to check paperwork to see that the proper forms were filed and signed in a timely manner. Since fraud audits were rare, custodians knew they could usually avoid detection for fraud by supplying auditors with phony canceled checks and receipts.[16] Moreover, unless auditors found evidence of theft that could be proved beyond a reasonable doubt in court, the school system did not punish custodians whose money was missing.[17] It simply required them to pay the money back without interest—in effect, rewarding sloppy and possibly crooked custodians with interest-free loans.[18]

PERFORMANCE ACCOUNTABILITY

Unlike independent contractors, who are held in check by the risk of being fired for poor performance, custodians faced no such risk. Until 1993, custodians enjoyed full civil service protection, making it practically impossible to fire them for incompetence or abuse. In one instance, the BOE fired a custodian who regularly locked teachers out of school. But after four years of administrative proceedings, a court held that the BOE had to hire him back because it had not documented its case for a long-enough period (eighteen months) under state civil service laws.[19]

In addition, custodians were not held adequately accountable for performance to "customers"—those who used schools, such as students and principals. As for pupils, there was no formal mechanism to solicit their views on custodians.[20] As for principals, although the BOE had methods to solicit their views, it was widely understood to be a waste of time for them to state them.[21]

First, although before 1993 principals could evaluate custodians once a year, their input in these evaluations was limited. Principals could rate custodians only either satisfactory or unsatisfactory on one question—the custodian's cooperation with the principal—out of many questions on the evaluation.[22] All other questions were completed by the custodian's plant manager, whose objectivity was questionable. So a custodian could easily get high marks even if his principal thought he was unscrupulous.

Second, evaluations had no impact on what mattered most to custodians: their ability to transfer to schools with bigger budgets where they could earn higher salaries. Seniority, not merit, counted for this.

But principals' evaluations were meaningless for yet a third reason: most principals were terrified of what some dubbed custodians' "reigns of terror."[23] If a principal became at all troublesome, the custodian could "fix" her in various ways. He would, for example, turn off the heat or hot water,[24] lock auditoriums and bathrooms when after-school concerts were scheduled,[25] leave school when a flood broke out, or tear down instructional materials that teachers had spent hours designing.[26] Some custodians even intimidated their principals physically. In one school, the custodian had his boiler operator curse at the principal and block her path whenever she walked through the halls.[27] The upshot was that most principals gave their custodians the highest ratings regardless of their performance.

POLITICAL ACCOUNTABILITY

Finally, until the mayor won control over the BOE (which he renamed the Department of Education) in 2002, custodians were not politically accountable to voters in significant ways. The executive director of the DSF reported to the BOE chancellor and deputy, who answered to a seven-member appointed central Board of Education in charge of the entire city school system. But the board members were appointed by so many local politicians with different constituencies that voters could not realistically hold any single board member or politician responsible for school problems.[28] Each of New York City's five elected borough presidents appointed one member to the board, while the mayor appointed the remaining two members. If voters were unhappy with the condition of the schools in their borough, they could not expect to have much impact by refusing to reelect the mayor or their borough president, because neither politician decisively controlled the board.

THE RESULTING FREE-FOR-ALL

The custodial system displays the multiple ways in which power, unaccompanied by accountability, can result in the use of freedom from red tape not to improve efficiency or reduce waste but to profiteer. Instead of paying themselves a salary from what was left over after cleaning expenses, custodians pocketed the maximum permitted under their salary caps and found myriad ways to enrich themselves from what remained in their budgets.

Until 1992, for instance, custodians could pocket money directly from their budgets because it was legal to commingle funds from their school accounts with their personal accounts. Custodians also diverted resources by using their staff to work on personal projects. One custodian had his helpers renovate his home, boat, deck, and woodshed. They would clock in at school on their way to his house and clock out on their way back.[29]

In addition, with discretion to hire whomever they wanted as helpers, custodians boosted family and friends' incomes by putting relatives and lovers on payroll. A 1977 audit found that three out of four custodians had at least one relative on payroll.[30]

Custodians further showered family and friends with no-show jobs and overtime, a lucrative perquisite that pays time-and-a-half in addition to a fixed minimum, just for showing up on weekends and holidays. One custodian gave his son, who never showed up, overtime for working seven days a week, nine to ten hours a day, with no lunch break or vacation for a whole year.[31] Another custodian allowed a family member to bill an average of ninety-seven hours a week—over twice the regular forty-hour week.[32]

Custodians also took kickbacks from their staff in exchange for giving them overtime. One custodian borrowed thousands of dollars from his fireman, paying him with fraudulent overtime until the loan and the income tax due on it was repaid.[33]

Meanwhile, many custodians, whose duties were minimal to begin with, barely did any work. A 1990 study found they devoted less time to cleaning than custodians in any other U.S. school system.[34] In fact, custodians did not necessarily maintain a presence at their schools. A 1992 investigation disclosed some of the activities they pursued while they were supposed to be at work. One custodian flew corporate jets around the country and operated his own pay phone company.[35] When investigators asked how he could do his job at his Brooklyn school when he was miles away in the sky, he pointed to his nationwide beeper and explained that the school could beep him no matter where he was. Another custodian operated a real-estate law practice, using his staff to run court errands.[36] Others relaxed on their yachts, visited mistresses, took drugs and alcohol at school, or engaged in target practice in their school basements.[37]

Some custodians resented coming to school even to pick up their paychecks. As one custodian remarked to another in a conversation secretly recorded for investigators, "All I do is sign checks," to which the other wistfully replied, "I remember the old days when we didn't even come in. We picked up our checks at the bar."[38]

CHAPTER FOURTEEN

LESSONS FROM RESISTANCE TO REFORM

Although a key part of combating corruption in large, entrenched districts is decentralizing properly, if serious wrongdoing exists, the rotten apples and the rotten infrastructure that nurtures them must be dislodged. Otherwise reforms will be sabotaged from the inside and the ensuing scandals will lead to greater centralization. But to do so, reformers will need to surmount a recalcitrant subculture and a host of union rules. This chapter illustrates through the example of the New York custodians how insidiously these roadblocks can undermine change and how crucial it is for reformers to deal with them head-on.[1]

Since 1994 the custodial system has been headed by a charismatic new high-level manager, James Lonergan, director of Building Services, who is the first person in recent memory to come to that position from outside the ranks and who has dedicated enormous effort to change the system. Yet the custodial system has resisted outside reform as well as inside reform.

REFORM STRATEGIES FROM THE OUTSIDE

Consider some of the many reforms that the Board of Education pressured the Division of School Facilities to try to reduce custodial abuse, from rules to reduce absenteeism and poor record keeping to bans on nepotism and the commingling of funds between custodians' personal and school accounts. Administrators also pushed structural reorganizations on it. From

1900 through 1953, the BOE experimented with centralization. It stripped custodians of discretion at some schools and moved power to central headquarters. It hired custodial helpers, bought supplies, and gave custodians and helpers civil service status.[2] But the experiment proved to be too expensive: the BOE had to hire large numbers of personnel to oversee and process the paperwork for custodians and their helpers.[3] By 1953 it had reverted to the indirect system, under which custodians bore responsibility for their staff and cleaning operations.[4] Despite all these reforms, however, scandals persisted.[5]

In 1993, after a highly publicized investigation, state legislators passed one of the most comprehensive anticorruption laws in the history of the custodial system. To strengthen performance accountability, legislators gave principals major input in evaluating custodians.[6] Custodians could be fired for poor performance if their principals gave them two consecutive unsatisfactory ratings. Legislators streamlined the procedures for firing them. In addition, lawmakers sought to improve oversight by stripping plant managers, the custodians' supervisors, of civil service status so that they would no longer belong to Local 891.

The 1993 law was fleshed out in the BOE's 1994 custodian contract. That year Mayor Rudolph Giuliani, a former U.S. attorney who owed little to organized labor, broke with the city tradition of acquiescing to whatever agreement the BOE struck with Local 891 and became directly involved in negotiations. The 1994 contract accordingly put a premium on making custodians accountable to principals and strengthened existing prohibitions against many custodial abuses. To curb theft, the 1994 contract required custodians to record their expenditures, itemizing quantity, vendor, and check number, and to keep original receipts. The contract also prohibited custodians from commingling personal and school accounts. To stop absenteeism, custodians had to record the times they arrived and left school and had to notify their principal before leaving. To curb fraudulent overtime, custodians had to file timely records of their staff's overtime schedules with the DSF at the end of each pay period.

But the 1993 law and 1994 contract did not appear to stem the flow of scandal. Two years after the contract went into effect, investigators caught custodians giving one another fraudulent overtime to work on personal projects. Custodians also used staff to work on their homes and looked the other way as helpers falsified time cards, tampered with time clocks, and worked on private projects during school.[7] A year earlier, city auditors uncovered the fact that in 1994 alone helpers racked up $31 million in questionable overtime, doubling and tripling their salaries.[8] Needless to say, custodians' record keeping was still nonexistent or inaccurate. And 34 percent of custodians continued to mingle personal with school funds.[9]

Meanwhile, maintenance costs soared, schools were still dirty, toilets were chronically clogged, sinks did not work, and bathrooms lacked soap and paper.[10]

Why did corruption persist after all these reforms? Conventional wisdom would probably blame loopholes in the 1993 law and 1994 contract. But the history of custodial reform suggests that even if controls were tighter, abuses would continue. After all, the DSF already had earlier versions of most of the anticorruption rules in the 1994 contract on its books. Custodians have had to record their hours and notify principals before leaving their buildings since at least 1903.[11] They have had to keep records of their expenditures and their staff's schedules since the 1920s. Nepotism had been prohibited since 1978, commingling personal and school funds since 1992.

THE ROLE OF MANAGEMENT IN FRUSTRATING REFORM

In the custodial system, as in any chronically corrupt agency, there are many often overlooked impediments that can derail even well-crafted reforms. One of these obstacles may be management itself. At the DSF, managers in the past did not enforce existing rules or use available tools to reduce corruption, sometimes even after multiple warnings from auditors. Classical organizational theory presumes that upper management has a stake in meeting official objectives, identifies with those objectives,[12] and will at least try to implement reforms that reduce corruption, particularly when it harms the agency's core mission. Indeed, a good deal of the literature on implementation assumes just this as it dispenses advice on how top officials can ensure that their initiatives are implemented[13]—such as by simplifying rules,[14] reducing the actors involved in enforcement,[15] or securing sufficient resources.[16]

But if top officials do not identify with agency objectives for whatever reasons, they may not enforce anticorruption rules, regardless of how clear and simple rules may be or how many resources they have. In the past, DSF managers often failed to enforce rules that were clear, simple, easy to enforce, and would have added money to the system's coffers; for example, they rarely enforced rules requiring custodians to return money they owed to the BOE.[17]

One reason top managers may not enforce anticorruption rules is that they are influenced by groups with agendas that conflict with those of the agency.[18] These groups, sometimes called the *dominant coalition*,[19] gain power over official decision making and set an organization's real agenda to reflect their own, not the public, interest. If corruption controls threaten its power, the dominant coalition will seek to block the enforcement of those controls.

The ease with which a dominant coalition can mobilize depends on many factors,[20] but public agencies may be particularly vulnerable to exploitation by such groups because managers may not have strong-enough incentives to safeguard the public interest.[21] Local 891's rise to power at the DSF illustrates the ease with which special interests can take advantage of such weaknesses.

The custodian union began exerting influence on the DSF well before it was recognized as a union for official collective bargaining purposes in the early 1960s. In 1930, the association that subsequently became Local 891 bargained informally with the BOE and DSF on custodians' behalf. But while the BOE and DSF had few incentives to protect students' and taxpayers' interests, they had many reasons to placate the union.

Consider how weak the DSF's incentives were to safeguard the public interest. Managers were not evaluated on agency performance and suffered no consequences if they fared poorly. Because the New York City school system was a virtual monopoly, parents would not remove their children, the system would not shut down, and officials would not be out of jobs if schools deteriorated.

In addition, unlike union negotiators, whose jobs and salaries depend on their striking deals favorable to their members, public officials are insulated from the consequences of making concessions against their customers' interests. No one ever demoted a BOE negotiator for striking a poor labor deal. In fact, BOE officials could afford to make abusive concessions because, as public choice theorists point out, monopolistic agencies such as public schools can always ask the legislature for more money without having seriously to compete with other providers.[22]

Further, until the early 1970s, the BOE could make union concessions behind closed doors because few paid attention. Before Watergate, the media probed the public sector less aggressively than it does today. The BOE was even more insulated from scrutiny than most agencies because, as neither a city nor a state agency, it enjoyed a quasi-independent political status.[23] So the mayor did not usually bring the force of his clout to the negotiating table, as he did for regular mayoral agencies.

Contrast this to management's incentives to appease Local 891. First, satisfying it ensured labor peace and averted school shutdowns. Even when New York State lawmakers passed the Public Employees' Fair Employment Act (1967),[24] known as the Taylor Law, thus restricting custodians' ability to strike, custodians could still intimidate the DSF with school shutdowns because they could persuade their staff, many of whom were their relatives and were not covered by the act, to strike.

Second, the DSF had reason to placate the union because a number of managers were former union members. Local 891 gradually infiltrated the DSF as current and former members worked their way up the ranks there. Historically, for example, the executive director and deputy director of the DSF's Bureau of Plant Operations, the office responsible for overseeing custodians, have been former Local 891 members. While revolving-door legislation blocks public employees from taking jobs in the private sector within certain time periods after leaving their agencies, nothing prevents former union members from assuming jobs in the agencies they worked for or vice versa.[25] Although custodians would lose their membership in Local 891 when they were promoted into upper management, to the extent that they remained loyal to their union they assured it of a voice in policy making.

Local 891 even secured a foothold in BOE collective bargaining because some top DSF officials who used to belong to Local 891 would help the BOE's Office of Labor Relations negotiate contracts against the very union they once belonged to. One high DSF official, who had been a member of the custodian union's executive board, helped the BOE negotiate its 1988 custodial contract. Not surprisingly the contract, although trumpeted as a "historic settlement" with the union, was filled with false promises.[26]

The union's capture of the DSF did not result from a conspiracy to systematically exploit management's weaknesses. Rather, as opportunities presented themselves and the union won concessions, victory fed itself. The more the union won, the more formidable it became at the negotiating table. The more formidable it became, the more the DSF treated it as a partner in policy making, eventually losing the ability even to recognize what was in students' best interests.[27] In one example of just how much managers saw themselves as the union's ally, when auditors recommended that they try contracting out custodial services to save money, they said they could not make such a decision without consulting the union.[28]

One of the union's biggest early victories came in the 1950s. During the BOE's experiment with centralization, it made custodians civil servants. In 1953, after centralization proved to be too expensive, the BOE gave custodians back their autonomy. However, instead of revoking the custodians' civil service status, the BOE let them keep it. This gave custodians the best of both worlds: the freedom of independent contractors as well as the job security of civil servants. After this triumph, Local 891 easily won many others, ranging from unlimited sick days to free jeeps to free income tax return preparation.

Management's alienation from its mission eventually reached the point where it would side with the union against even the most sensible law enforcement suggestions against abuse. Even during one of the BOE's toughest financial periods—New York City's fiscal crisis in the mid-1970s—the DSF refused to cut perquisites that auditors said were particularly wasteful, such as free preparation of custodians' income tax returns.[29] Although its budget had been cut and it had reduced custodians' duties, the DSF insisted on keeping this unusual frill.

MANAGERIAL SABOTAGE

Once captured, management can frustrate corruption controls and disguise what it is doing in many ways. One way the DSF did this in years past was by pretending to embrace reforms but then failing to implement them after the pressure subsided. In 1988, after exposes of waste, for instance, the BOE publicly announced that it would no longer give custodians free jeeps. In fact, however, it merely imposed a one-year moratorium on the practice, during which it was to study the problem. After the media attention died down, the BOE never completed the study and allotted $2.5 million to buy two hundred jeeps for custodians during the following two years.[30]

Managers used similar tactics to stall auditors. They explicitly assured auditors that they would implement various reforms but then did not. After audits revealed that custodians' records of their helpers' schedules were nonexistent, auditors asked the DSF to discipline custodians who did not comply with record-keeping rules. The DSF explicitly agreed.[31] But almost twenty years later, custodians' records were still nonexistent or so poor as to be "audit-proof," as the DSF had never properly checked them, let alone disciplined custodians.[32]

Even if controls were implemented, managers sabotaged them in various ways. One year after the 1993 law made it more likely that plant managers would evaluate custodians objectively—by preventing them from belonging to Local 891—the DSF emasculated plant managers by ensuring that their evaluations would have no impact on whether custodians were promoted, disciplined, fired, or denied transfers to larger schools.[33]

A graphic illustration of how managers could subvert their own reforms was the DSF's pilot program to privatize custodial services. Auditors had long urged the DSF to contract out custodial services to save money. They hoped that the DSF would learn how private contractors saved money and force their own custodians to copy them. Local 891, however, opposed contracting out and demanded that the DSF not conduct studies comparing contractors to BOE custodians.[34] Managers resisted privatization as long as they could. When pressure finally forced them to try it in 1963, they implemented it so as to minimize any threat to BOE custodians.

First, officials made it nearly impossible to compare private custodians to BOE custodians.[35] Until the mid-1980s, the DSF privatized at too few schools to provide a statistically significant basis for comparison. The DSF also gave private custodians many more duties than BOE custodians, making comparison difficult. The BOE did not cooperate with auditors trying to compare BOE custodians to contractors.[36] These reasons probably explain why, after forty years, the DSF still cannot say for sure whether contractors are more efficient than BOE custodians.

Second, the DSF prevented contractors from being as successful as they might have been, thus lessening their potential to make BOE custodians look bad. For example, managers required contractors to hire skilled mechanics at the same rates as the DSF's civil service mechanics, although the non–civil service mechanics that contractors wanted to hire would have been cheaper. The DSF also gave private contractors no choice in selecting their buildings, so they often received schools in neighborhoods where vandalism put them at a comparative disadvantage to BOE custodians, who had choice.[37]

Further undermining the program's success, the DSF would sometimes hire the same contractors whose contracts it had previously refused to renew because of incompetence.[38] Perhaps as a result of all these impediments, the DSF has been unable to attract many qualified bidders, creating yet another obstacle to successful privatization. Today, as in the first twelve years after the start of the program, only two corporations offer the BOE custodial services.

THE ROLE OF CULTURE IN UNDERMINING REFORM

Another hidden barrier to reforming corrupt agencies is their culture, or shared values about appropriate behavior.[39] A deviant culture can foster resistance to reform in many ways. It can encourage employees to regard wrongdoing as their prerogative, or it can make them fearful of trying change and new powers. The more entrenched the culture and the more alienated employees are from society's values, the more fiercely they will fight corruption controls.

Many factors can contribute to the tenacity and virulence of a deviant culture. Management, for instance, can set a corrupt example. In one telling instance of how rank-and-file workers absorbed the DSF managers' skewed priorities, employees in the custodial payroll unit saw themselves primarily as serving Local 891—to the point that they would return telephone calls of union officials but not those of BOE higher-ups who were not directly involved in the custodial system.[40]

Management can also fuel a culture of deviance and estrangement from society's norms by not punishing misconduct. After years of getting away with abuses, many custodians could barely even conceive that their conduct might be considered objectionable from society's perspective. Three examples provide a window onto that alienation. One custodian brazenly announced to his principal shortly after he was transferred to her school that, since he had two other jobs, she should contact his secretary, not him, if she needed anything.[41] Another custodian let his boiler operator store his gun collection near the lunchroom and live in the basement, where he slept, entertained women, and kept a dog.[42] Yet another custodian used his school basement to raise chickens for cockfighting, telling inspectors that the hundreds of labeled eggs he was incubating there were to feed students.

Culture has foiled many custodial reforms. It was an important reason that legislators' measures to improve custodial accountability for performance did not work. The 1993 law gave principals more power than ever before to evaluate and affect custodians' careers.[43] But after years of watching the DSF do nothing as principals suffered the consequences of standing up to derelict custodians, principals refused to use their new power to evaluate custodians honestly because they still feared reprisals and had little faith that the DSF would support them. Custodians, after all, remain in their schools while dismissal proceedings are pending, creating an even worse nightmare for the principal should the custodian not be fired. If the custodian is fired, moreover, the principal cannot choose his successor; the DSF does.

Not surprisingly, surveys conducted after 1993 show that principals continue to give custodians top ratings, most likely without regard to performance.[44] While fifteen principals gave their custodians two consecutive unsatisfactory evaluations shortly after the law went into effect, these principals all capitulated when forced to confront their custodians during arbitration and raised their ratings. Administrative hearings accordingly found the custodians competent, and most returned to their schools, while a few transferred to new ones. Needless to say, out of a workforce of one thousand, not one custodian has been fired for incompetence or abuse since the 1993 law was passed.

The culture of fear, moreover, is self-perpetuating, making it an even more potent obstacle to reform. The further principals retreat from giving custodians unsatisfactory ratings, the less likely it is that custodians will be fired, further feeding principals' fear that they are invincible. In fact, the easiest way for principals to get rid of custodians is to give them high marks because this helps them transfer to bigger schools. The worst thing principals could do is give custodians average or below-average marks, since these would be low enough to antagonize them and dim their transfer prospects but not low enough to fire them.

In addition to managers' conduct, history and the size of the profits at stake can also foster a deviant culture. In the custodial system, history has reinforced custodians' notion that certain misconduct was their prerogative, while the large sums of money at stake strengthened their determination to persist in wrongdoing. These factors buttressed the culture of corruption to such a degree that even when managers wanted to enforce controls, the culture blocked them.

Consider how culture foiled the DSF's efforts to fight nepotism. Nepotism has been an integral part of custodians' lives since the 1850s, when their families, who lived in schools with them, helped with school chores. Sons apprenticed with their fathers, learning skills such as how to operate school coal furnaces. Indeed, some custodians today have forefathers who trace their custodial lineage back to the Civil War. Nepotism, furthermore, was very lucrative. Experts estimate that in 1991 alone nepotism cost the BOE about $4 million and boosted an individual custodian's family income by thousands of dollars yearly.[45]

When the DSF passed a rule in 1978 prohibiting custodians from hiring their wives, custodians got around it by hiring one another's wives.[46] In these deals, referred to as "wife swapping," one custodian would hire a second's wife and the second would hire the first's wife. Then, in 1994, the BOE prohibited wife swapping between two custodians. But custodians found ways to circumvent this rule, too. Many swapped wives among three custodians: the first custodian would hire the second one's wife, the second would hire the third's wife, and the third would hire the first's wife.[47]

One of the most revered strategies in the literature on public administration and white-collar crime for turning around corrupt agencies is to "reorganize" them by replacing the dominant coalition and leaders with new, honest personnel.[48] Research certainly suggests that leaders are critical to an agency's success[49] and that removing the old guard is important to changing its culture.[50]

But the custodial system suggests that even if reformers can neutralize an agency's dominant coalition, neutralization may not be enough. After a number of senior administrators left the DSF in the 1990s (one for a top job at one of the custodial helpers' unions, another to become custodian of one of the city's largest high schools), some new, dedicated managers such as James Lonergan arrived to improve the system. But they faced numerous obstacles, including special interests, deeply embedded in the system's policies and modus operandi.

At a certain point, the problem with an agency whose management has once been captured by special interests becomes bigger than the dominant coalition or any single interest group. The sheer accumulation of concessions that reflect special interests creates an organizational infrastructure so enmeshed in its own selfish advantage that it takes more than even new dedicated personnel to change it.

UNION CONCESSIONS AND ARBITRATION DECISIONS

Consider how various union concessions undermined legislators' 1993 efforts to require custodians to be evaluated on the overall condition of their buildings. The reality was that custodians could not take responsibility for their buildings because the DSF, in a concession to the fifteen unions that represent the skilled trade mechanics, such as electricians, plumbers, and carpenters, precluded custodians from handling any major repairs. These repairs were to be the exclusive domain of civil service, skilled trade mechanics who worked at the DSF.

Many so-called major repairs, however, were basic to school operations and could easily have been handled by custodians—at a fraction of the cost of skilled mechanics. Whereas a custodian could replace a regular light bulb, only a skilled electrician, who cost $32 an hour, could replace a fluorescent bulb, although a custodial handyman, who cost $15 an hour, could easily have done it. Whereas a custodian could patch up a hole in a wall if its diameter was less than three inches, a carpenter, at $45 an hour, was required for a larger hole. And should a skilled mechanic have needed an assistant to hold up his ladder or shine a flashlight, he was entitled to a skilled maintenance worker, who cost twice as much as a handyman but did essentially the same work.

These restrictive labor policies often made it impossible for custodians to keep their buildings in good condition for several reasons. First, the policies prohibited custodians from making many fundamental repairs even if they wanted to.[51] The skilled trade unions, with jobs and union dues at stake, fiercely guarded their members' work fiefdoms.

Second, although custodians could request skilled trade mechanics to make repairs at their schools, it could take years for them to arrive. Custodians had to fill out a work order that had to be reviewed and signed by various supervisors before it was sent to the DSF, where it would queue up behind a backlog of over thirty thousand orders.

Custodians' dependence on skilled trade mechanics directly hampered their ability to maintain schools, as illustrated by their wall painting duties. Custodians were allowed to paint up to a height of only eight feet on exterior walls and only ten feet or the picture molding, whichever was lower, on interior walls;[52] anything higher required a skilled painter. But since 40 percent of schools had interior and exterior walls over ten feet and since it usually took long for painters to arrive, walls looked half-done for months. One custodian, for instance, could not paint over the upper parts of graffiti on a wall because it went above his permissible limit.[53]

Could a new slate of managers simply repeal these union concessions? James Lonergan, the dedicated head of the Building Services since 1994 and the only person to hold that post in recent memory who has not belonged to Local 891, is relentlessly trying to get custodians to do more work. The problem with winning concessions through collective bargaining, he explains, is that previous DSF administrations have "given away so much . . . there [is] nothing left to give" in exchange.[54]

So Lonergan tries to use whatever managerial power he can muster to win battles on matters not explicitly covered by contract. Management is entitled, for example, to dictate policy. But even here arbitrators limit Lonergan's ability unilaterally to revoke any practice, no matter how wasteful, if it has become a "policy and practice." In such cases, management must go through collective bargaining, even if the practice was never included in any labor agreement. When Lonergan tried to discontinue custodians' free coffee machines, coffee, and tea—perquisites never mentioned in any contract—arbitrators held that he could not because these frills had become "policy and practice" over the years.[55]

Managers often try to make or change policy that the contract leaves unclear, through policy meetings with the union, where each side makes a recommendation about what the policy should be to the chancellor, who then decides. But the union often walks out of such meetings because, if there has been no policy meeting, the matter goes to arbitration, which tends to favor the union. Fighting for change this way is very time consuming: Lonergan spends two to three days in court or arbitration every week.

ELUDING PROSECUTION AND EXTERNAL OVERSIGHT

The usual presumption for agencies as corrupt as the custodial system is that prosecutors and investigators will step in, clean them up, and remove the rotten apples.[56] But the custodian case shows that some corrupt agencies can largely elude criminal sanction and independent oversight, even in cities with a vigilant media such as New York City.

Consider how the custodial system has largely escaped criminal sanction. Despite the city's establishment in 1990 of the SCI, a powerful, independent school inspector general, prosecutors have focused on major custodial crimes, such as extortion and bribery, but not on minor corruption, which is more prevalent, more expensive, and more central to what makes the agency systemically corrupt.

There are several reasons for this. First, some misconduct, no matter how abusive or costly, is not necessarily criminal.[57] In the custodial system some of the most prevalent and costly abuses, such as nepotism, are administrative violations but not crimes.

Second, other misconduct that ought to be criminal has been sanitized through collective bargaining, arbitration decisions, discretion, and tradition. In most agencies, employees who take equipment home—even old, broken equipment—can be prosecuted for theft. But until 1994 the custodial contract permitted custodians to keep millions of dollars in capital equipment such as jeeps and snowplows after five years' use.

Third, conduct that is clearly criminal may escape prosecution because it does not appeal to prosecutors. The most prevalent custodial crimes are hard to prove, resource-intensive to investigate, and easy to conceal. To determine if a custodian is hiring relatives, for instance, investigators need to scour payroll records that are often illegible or nonexistent. Custodians can easily hide phony overtime by handing it out during holidays when few witnesses are around. With the keys to clean time clocks, they can also easily cheat schools on time worked.

PART V

THE PRESCRIPTION: HOW TO FIX THE PROBLEM

CHAPTER FIFTEEN

ESTABLISHING INDEPENDENT INSPECTORS GENERAL

How do school systems deal with all the impediments to real reform—unhelpful union rules and arbitration decisions, a deviant subculture, corruption, and powerful, uncooperative unions? If serious wrongdoing exists, as in the custodial system, the first order of business should be a crackdown; districts probably cannot thoughtfully reform themselves while scandals keep making headlines. This chapter lays out the first steps to help break the cycle of corruption. Any crackdown on systemic corruption should involve efforts to remove the dominant coalition and change the subculture.

Inspectors general go way back in our nation's history—to General George Washington's Continental Army in the late 1700s.[1] But the office came into vogue in earnest in civil agencies only after Watergate, with the passage of the Inspector General Act (1978).[2] The idea behind the civil inspector general movement was to create an office dedicated to auditing and ferreting out fraud and waste in each major federal agency and to make the office at least somewhat independent of management. Under the 1978 law, the president, not the agency, picked the inspector general heads, with the advice and consent of the Senate.[3]

Although a number of states as well as municipal agencies in some cities have established inspectors general, they are a rarity in school districts, even though some districts have budgets bigger than those of many states. New York City, Chicago, and Los Angeles and a few other districts such as Miami-Dade,

Florida, have independent inspectors general, but most districts in the country do not. To be sure, some have internal audit units and some might have a few investigators on staff. But such units are generally small and do not conduct fraud audits. And investigations are usually geared toward sex abuse or corporal punishment, not fraud, waste, or abuse.

Yet if a district is dysfunctional and corrupt, having an independent inspector general is crucial. Internal auditors and investigators, who usually depend on management for everything from raises and promotions to their budget and office space, are unlikely to pursue cases boldly. In fact, the record of internal investigative units in America's three largest school districts, before these districts were forced to accept inspectors general, shows that school management essentially used those units much as the notorious Mayor Jimmy Walker of Tammany Hall once used New York City's Department of Investigation—as a burial ground for mischief.

The New York City school system had established an internal investigative unit in 1981. But while district scandals abounded, virtually none of the cases was made by its internal investigators; almost all were unearthed by state and federal prosecutors, state and city auditors, legislative committees, or investigative reporters.

So in 1988, Mayor Ed Koch appointed the Joint Commission on Integrity in the Public Schools, a temporary commission known as the Gill Commission after its chairman, the attorney James Gill, to look into the matter. The commission issued two reports. The first, "Investigating the Investigators," focused on the internal investigative unit, concluding that it swept cases under the carpet to avoid embarrassing its bosses.[4]

The report described an internal unit[5] staffed by ill-equipped, illtrained investigators who seemed to be interested primarily in being able to say that they had looked into an allegation, not in making cases. The unit seemed to interpret the complaints it received in the most narrow, rigid manner, usually looking only at whether there was some minor regulatory violation and not considering the impact of the alleged conduct on a program or the district as a whole. The Joint Commission's report was not, however, a reflection of internal investigators' intelligence or talent. Rather, their behavior was a reflection of the "pass the buck" culture in the rest of the school system at the time. But the upshot was that most of the school workforce did not take the unit seriously.

At the Los Angeles Unified School District (LAUSD), the internal audit and investigative units that preceded the current inspector general were similarly hamstrung by a lack of training and technology, and a "don't rock the boat" mentality, according to a 1993 Arthur Anderson study. The LAUSD would repeatedly hire high-level executives from the private sector to audit the district, only to have them quit in frustration or be fired amid clashes with management over its unresponsiveness to their reform recommendations.[6] Local papers ran a series of stories noting the run-ins of one such executive, Wajeeh Ersheid, with the LAUSD over issues ranging from meddling administrators to an absence of monitoring technology to unqualified auditors.[7] At one point, Ersheid allegedly fired off a terse memo to the director of spending after the director refused to act against an employee who was swindling the district: "Audit is not a political football game."[8]

Ersheid was fired after a total of seven months on the job amid a flurry of bitter allegations by both sides. But a 1998 report by KPMG Peat Marwick confirmed a number of his complaints. The audit unit, it said, squandered large amounts of time pursuing trifles, as it had no budgeting or tracking procedures to manage its work, no standards for reports, and only one staff member trained as an electronic data processing auditor, when it should have had five or six. But the report's conclusion was that, regardless of who was in charge of the unit, internal auditors and investigators could not do their jobs objectively or intelligently because they reported to the chief financial officer,[9] creating a conflict since auditors were essentially there to keep tabs on their boss's spending decisions.

As public pressure mounted, both districts were eventually forced to accept independent school inspectors general. New York City heeded the Joint Commission's recommendation to create the Special Commissioner of Investigation (SCI) in 1990 to monitor the most serious misconduct within the school system. The system's existing internal investigative unit was renamed the Office of Special Investigations, and its focus was limited to minor misbehavior, such as minor cases of corporal abuse of students.[10] A mayoral executive order gave the SCI the power to issue subpoenas, make arrests, grant immunity, and take testimony under oath.[11] The New York City Board of Education approved a resolution allowing it to dismiss those who refused to cooperate with it.

In Los Angeles, the school board heeded the advice of KPMG Peat Markwick and in November 1998 approved reforms to professionalize, expand, and revamp the structure of the internal audit unit.[12] The board also created a unit charter that outlined the unit's authority and empowered it to audit and investigate any functions within the LAUSD as well as private entities doing business with the LAUSD.

Less than two years later, however, following a major school construction scandal, another outside auditor recommended that the unit be further strengthened, its mission be expanded to include performance audits, and it be given law enforcement powers similar to those enjoyed by inspectors general in other agencies. In 2000 the California legislature accordingly passed a law renaming the unit the Office of the Inspector

General and giving it the power to issue subpoenas, administer oaths, and take testimony.[13]

But the two inspectors general had different reporting models. The commissioner of the New York City SCI was to be selected by and accountable to the commissioner of the city Department of Investigation (DOI), which in effect meant the mayor, since the DOI commissioner was a mayoral appointee. To remove the head of the SCI, the DOI commissioner had to present him with written reasons and give him a chance to respond. The head of the LAUSD inspector general, on the other hand, was chosen by and accountable to the central elected school board; his contract has to be renewed every three years.

Some measure of investigative independence is necessary if a school district is dysfunctional. Only since New York, Chicago, and Los Angeles established independent inspectors general could someone focus on exposing problems in the central office with some measure of reliability and regularity and a chance of getting convictions. As a *New York Daily News* editorial noted about Edward Stancik in 1997, "Before Stancik, no school worker was ever convicted of a sex crime in schools. Since Stancik, there have been 41 arrests, with 31 convictions and four cases pending. There were no sex crimes before Stancik got his job?"[14] Even if slightly overblown, the editorial was essentially correct.

The importance of independence can apply to any district, not just the three largest. In Detroit, criticisms of school headquarters led to the hiring of an auditor who was supposed to suggest ways to reform the central office. But so long as the auditor answered to the superintendent, he was made to focus on the local school community organizations, not the central office.[15] Only after the auditor's contract was amended to make him accountable to the school board was he able to look at the center.

INITIAL HURDLES

Establishing an independent inspector general is just the beginning. New inspectors general in beleaguered districts have formidable hurdles to confront, such as an entrenched culture of resistance to external review.

Although tensions between inspectors general and the agencies they oversee are legion in state and federal government,[16] the tension seems to be particularly pronounced between school districts and their inspectors general. School districts have fought their new inspectors general on practically every front, from budget and staff to jurisdiction and law enforcement powers, often refusing to cooperate. They have tried to undermine the inspectors general in various ways, from ignoring their recommendations to taking physical action to oust them from their offices.

One possible explanation for the high level of tension goes back to the progressive creed that schools should be run by experts and be above politics.[17] It is easy to imagine how this belief might translate into the notion that people without education credentials cannot understand school operations and therefore should not scrutinize them.

This belief was the explicit reason that the New York City school system balked when the city comptroller wanted to audit its vocational program's success rate in placing students in jobs after graduation as long ago as 1978. The president of the central Board of Education objected on the ground that auditors had no expertise in evaluating curricula or performance.[18] He ordered school administrators not to cooperate with the audit,[19] insisting that the BOE be the one to evaluate its vocational program. After days of trading angry letters leaked to the press, the parties went to court. The comptroller won, but the bitterness lingered for years.

To get a sense of the ferocity of resistance that school inspectors general may face, it is instructive to recall the experiences of two pioneering school inspectors general: the late Edward Stancik in New York City and Don Mullinax in Los Angeles.

After his first week on the job in 1991, Stancik later told a class of graduate students at John Jay College, he had no idea what lay in store for him in his second week.[20] He and his staff had spent the first week settling into the high-rise offices that the Board of Education had cleared out for them at 65 Court Street, Brooklyn, one of the central office's buildings. Stancik recalled that as he was walking down the corridor toward his new office on the Monday morning of his second week, he passed heaps of boxes piled up against the walls. Never did he imagine that those boxes were stuffed with his and his staff's belongings and that someone else would be sitting in his chair at his desk when he got there. Yet over the weekend someone had apparently ordered all of his and his staff's possessions removed and had other officers occupy the space.

That was just the beginning. Shortly thereafter, Stancik went to introduce himself to the chancellor. But the chancellor had him "kicked out of his office," as he put it. Some days later, the chancellor summoned Stancik back but not to apologize. Instead, some reporters from the *New York Post* had called Stancik the previous day to get biographical information from him and ask about a sex abuse investigation they had heard about. The next morning the city woke up to the headline "School Sex Shocker" and a racy story that quoted Stancik. So when Stancik walked back into the chancellor's office that day, a furious chancellor and a group of his deputies sat him down and told him that he could not go to the media; he had to go through them. "When I told them 'I don't work for you,' they were shocked," Stancik recalled.[21] The chancellor was "used to having a peon," referring to the previous internal investigator.

Some of the three subsequent chancellors with whom Stancik served seemed also to be set against him and his office. One tried to have Stancik fired while he was on vacation in London. An ABC affiliate called him in his hotel room to give him the news. As Stancik summed up, it is "hard to change things and be 'Mr. Popular.' You are threatening their world."[22]

Don Mullinax, the LAUSD's new inspector general, has also endured efforts to undermine his office. One superintendent allegedly lobbied state legislators to disband his office, arguing that there was no need for it, while another tried to persuade board members not to renew his three-year contract. Repeated attempts have been made to cut his office's budget. One superintendent threatened to file a defamation suit against him.[23] Another told him he could not conduct financial audits of education programs[24] (the superintendent lost). Contractors sued to stop him from issuing reports that commented on their performance (they too lost). Officials have been "uncooperative" and "slow to answer or produce documents" for the inspector general.[25] And all this, even though Mullinax has made substantial efforts to forge a cooperative relationship with management, as evidenced by his professional, balanced reports, his always giving managers a chance to respond to his audit findings before publishing them, and his giving the superintendent a "heads-up" on investigations as soon as feasible.

MEDIA USE AND PUBLICITY

A problem with a recalcitrant school district is that it can force an inspector general to rely on adversarial measures such as using the media. New inspectors general in beleaguered districts must confront enormous obstacles, such as cynicism that nothing will change and that the inspector general is just another charade. As Stancik, who used the media extensively during his tenure at the SCI, told students at John Jay College, publicizing cases can help overcome such obstacles. It "helps win the trust of potential witnesses, who take big risks in coming forward." They know that the "office is professional and will take their complaint seriously."[26] Or, as he told *Education Week*, publicity appeared to have "a significant deterrent factor."[27]

Publicizing cases can force people to pay attention to the inspector general and thereby eventually change the culture.[28] In March 1995, Joan Salvatore, a school administrator in one of New York City's community school districts, stepped into a car owned by a vendor who sold supplies to schools. She was there to receive a $1,500 cash installment on a kickback—including more than $11,000 in cash, two Rolex watches, a gas barbecue grill, and a paid vacation to Puerto Rico—in return for giving the vendor a lucrative school supplies contract. Unknown to her, however, the vendor had agreed to wear a wire and let SCI investigators install a hidden camera in the backseat of his car.

The SCI had used this same technique the year before to videotape a consultant paying an $8,000 bribe to a school board member from the same community school district. The board member had agreed to have his car wired and a camera installed in the backseat. The resulting video-tape had been widely publicized on television.

As Salvatore took the money from the vendor, she laughed nervously and, glancing around, asked in an apparent reference to that earlier case, "Is this gonna be on video?"[29] The vendor skillfully sidestepped her question (to the relief of investigators listening in), and Salvatore proceeded to count out her cash from him. She eventually pleaded guilty to embezzlement and was sentenced to four months in jail.

Another school official also being secretly taped by a vendor around the same time displayed a similar reaction. After she and the vendor had agreed on how he would deliver her cash kickbacks, she suddenly became nervous as she sat next to him in his car and recalled the District 12 case. "You don't watch the news?" she asked. "They were in a car just like you and I are and they had a tape of him offering her a job . . . and saying you gotta do this and that and the other for me."[30] But like Salvatore, she forged ahead with the deal and eventually pleaded guilty to embezzlement. She was ordered to repay the school system $21,260.

Although publicity about the SCI investigations did not stop the commission of these crimes, the cases suggested that school employees were at least aware of the threat of detection from the SCI—a worry that probably never occurred to them when the internal investigative unit was on the job. Building such awareness is a crucial first step to changing the culture. If we accept that people are self-interested, then organizational cultures can be changed through incentives that appeal to people's self-interest.[31] Detection and punishment, if perceived to be real, can be such incentives.

OVERSIGHT AND CHANGING FOCUS

Although use of the media and a zero-tolerance assault on corruption may be appropriate tactics for an inspector general at the beginning of the fight against corruption in a district, the marginal benefit of such tactics and priorities declines as the district improves over time. In the beginning, if the corrupt district is hostile, the inspector general may have little choice but to go to the mat with management by aggressively publicizing cases and investigating every crime possible to break down the aura of invincibility of those used to profiting from corruption.

As the district improves, however, a shift in the inspector general's priorities, tactics, and relations with management is in order. Priorities must expand to include getting rid of not just the rotten apples but also the rotten terrain—the dominant coalition of abusive work rules and built-in structural incentives for fraud. To accomplish this the inspector general's role must grow to encompass program evaluation, outcomes assessment, and risk management.[32]

As a district improves, the inspector general also needs to consider that repeated headlines and a zero-tolerance policy may discourage the kind of risk taking and entrepreneurship needed for decentralization to work and may in fact promote the narrow, compliance-obsessed mentality that is the source of many districts' problems to begin with. As managers become genuinely interested in breaking down bankrupt central structures, inspectors general should forge more cooperative relations with them to reduce waste and monitor performance and expenditures in schools. Because inspectors general can only make suggestions, not give orders, management is far more likely to heed their policy recommendations in an atmosphere of trust.

Realigning the focus and tactics of school inspectors general will not be easy. In a sense the task reflects the broader challenge in public administration today: how to remold inspectors general from a law enforcement, compliance-oriented model of oversight appropriate to top-down Weberian bureaucracies to a model that accommodates the decentralized, horizontal, entrepreneurial, customer-driven agencies of the postbureaucratic paradigm. As Paul Light notes, there are many impediments to changing the role of inspectors general in this way, from finding the political will to do so to making necessary changes in inspector general staff, expertise, and culture.[33]

That inspectors general must adapt to changes in the agencies they monitor cannot be clearer than in the context of large urban schools, where top-down structures are often the root of the problem. School inspectors general should accordingly be subject to periodic review. Every year they should reevaluate their own goals and tactics and undergo cost-benefit justification review by a body that has an interest in the welfare of the school system but does not directly run the system on a day-to-day basis.

The LAUSD inspector general offers a good model for school districts. The office is audited for effectiveness once a year by a private auditing firm. Its head serves on a three-year contract renewable by the elected school board that assesses his performance. The office also reports annually to the California legislature on its use of subpoenas and must issue public annual reports setting forth the audits and investigations it worked on and their outcomes.

The inspector general, Don Mullinax, appears to have risen to these performance challenges. His office goes after not just crooks but also embedded waste and abuse, returning about $19 for every dollar it has spent since the fall of 1999.[34] The office conducts analyses of the district's organization, pinpointing weaknesses and recommending sweeping reforms such as privatization of some areas. Most noteworthy, the office also tries to help the district accomplish its educational mission, recently convincing top managers to issue a strategic plan for the first time in district history.

REMOVING THE DOMINANT COALITION

Once the inspector general has ousted the crooks, top management should remove as much of the dominant coalition and as many abusive work rules as possible. Otherwise, as with the surgeon who cuts out a tumor but not the surrounding infected tissue, the disease will grow right back. While no one should underestimate the challenges of dealing with public-sector labor groups, the experience of some school districts suggests possible solutions even in large cities where labor is most powerful. If regular collective bargaining negotiations do not yield reductions in abusive work rules, management should privatize or threaten to privatize to win concessions. Armed with audits pinpointing areas of waste, management should also lobby the legislature for legislation that exempts as many classes of employees as possible from civil service, tenure, and other provisions that make performance accountability a virtual impossibility. Management should take advantage of layoffs and reorganizations to declassify employees when possible. The point is not to fire people but to transform the old workforce into one that can be motivated through performance incentives and that will be open to entrepreneurial decision making rather than just input-oriented compliance.

One of the best illustrations of a school district that has removed much of its dominant coalition and cut many wasteful work rules despite being in one of America's strongest labor towns is the Chicago Public Schools (CPS).[1] One of the most illuminating accounts of how the fat was trimmed concerns its Division of Facilities.

THE CPS CUSTODIAL SYSTEM

The Division of Facilities had for years been one of the most notorious fiefdoms in the central offices of the Chicago Public Schools. It was in charge of maintaining school buildings and overseeing school custodial engineers, known as engineers. But with broad discretion over school maintenance budgets and a history going back to the nineteenth century, Chicago's engineers had a record of abuses reminiscent of their New York City counterparts, the custodians. Abuses included theft, kickbacks, bribery, questionable overtime, waste, and recalcitrance.[2] Schools were filthy and decrepit.[3] One engineer let pigeons live in his school.[4] Another stopped painters from painting his school because they had not started with his office first.[5]

As in New York City, principals complained about not having power over delinquent engineers, who reported to the CPS's unresponsive Division of School Facilities, now the Division of Operations.[6] That division appeared to exist to serve primarily central administrators, engineers, and unions—everyone but children. It was controlled by the engineers' union, Local 143. James Harney, the division's director for eight years until 1994, had been an engineer in nearly fifty schools and was regarded as the union's de facto head. The division routinely awarded millions of dollars of work to companies run by former engineers.[7] Companies would submit bills without detailing work done and administrators would pay them without asking questions, often in exchange for bribes, to an estimated loss of over $7 million yearly. As Harney would later explain to a federal judge, "The deal—the thinking was, as we did the work we'd share the profits."[8]

Waste was built into the payroll. As of 1995, the CPS retained 1,100 firemen and operating engineers left over from the days of coal furnaces at a cost of $14 million a year—even though schools had stopped using coal heat and very few had boilers.[9]

Waste was also entrenched in costly work rules built up because, as one highly placed official explained, "the central office [had] caved on this for years and years."[10] Overtime was built into engineers' pay schedules, so they would receive it any time their school was open after or before regular hours, regardless of whether they could have avoided it through better scheduling.[11] In 1990 this rule forced the CPS to cut back on the number of times local school councils could meet after school because it could not afford to pay the overtime for engineers at more than two meetings per year at each school.[12] To make ends meet, the CPS further had to give engineers time off for each four-hour permit issued for the meetings. Engineers also scheduled their cleaners so as to make overtime a necessity. They scheduled them during the day, when they could not clean classrooms because pupils were in them, so the CPS was forced to pay them overtime to clean after hours.[13] Meanwhile, questionable overtime was rampant,[14] and engineers' salaries were among the highest in the nation's public schools, second only to New York City custodians' salaries.[15]

The initial step in fighting corruption and waste in Chicago came in 1993, when the legislature authorized the formation of an independent inspector general, known as the Office of Inspector General.[16] The inspector general was given subpoena power and access to all information, documents, buildings, and personnel. Investigators could require employees to be interviewed, so long as the evidence did not show a crime. Headed by Kenneth Holt, a former FBI agent, it quickly began to issue reports detailing wrongdoing and millions of dollars in waste.[17]

However, because the dominant coalition still reigned in the district, most of Holt's findings and recommendations went nowhere. Entrenched interests coopted and de-fanged them. So although divisions were forced to accept shallow reorganizations, such as the replacement of the director of the facilities division in 1994,[18] and traditional controls, such as the requirement to label equipment with bar codes to prevent theft,[19] waste and abuse remained rooted in the organizational culture.

The dominant players in the system made sure that when abuses were uncovered, no one would be punished. After two schools allegedly "lost" over $400,000 in equipment, for instance, managers promoted all three employees responsible for overseeing the equipment.[20] The message to the new watchdog and the employees he was investigating? "The IG can't touch us." As Holt wrote about the CPS at the time, "lack of accountability stems from a cavalier mindset that certain employees in the system can do whatever they please without fear of BOE imposed sanctions, that incompetence will be tolerated, and that a person will not be held responsible for his or her actions. This mindset . . . leads to and justifies abuses in the system."[21]

Needless to say, managers were not exactly eager to cooperate with the inspector general. Mirroring Mullinax's difficulties in the LAUSD, when Holt requested records for his investigations, he said it sometimes took three tries and the threat of a subpoena before anyone produced the information.[22]

A NEW MANAGEMENT TEAM AND A NEW STATE LAW

Resistance toward the inspector general began to melt away, however, when the Illinois legislature passed the School Reform Act (1995), which allowed the mayor to pick a new school chief executive officer, central school board, and various other school executives and gave the new leaders the power to privatize entire classes of unionized employees.[23] The new management team headed by Paul Vallas, chief executive officer, and Gery Chico, board president, worked with the inspector general and took a no-nonsense approach, relentlessly ferreting out wrongdoing and waste and removing crooks.

The new management team concentrated at once on ousting crooks and incompetent personnel through tough, flamboyantly visible sanctions. Vallas hired Maribeth Vander Weele, a former reporter with the *Chicago Sun Times* who had written a book on corruption in the CPS,[24] to be his chief of investigations. After Holt stepped down as inspector general, Vallas put Vander Weele in the post, where, after some changes, she reported to the school board president, Chico.

Vallas and his deputies publicized the inspector general's cases and moved quickly on its recommendations for disciplinary action. Vallas doubled the size of the inspector general, established a fraud hotline, and privatized the school internal audit unit to ensure that it would perform rigorous desk and field audits.[25] Further, the school board reached out to the Cook County state attorney's office, agreeing to pay it to dedicate a team of attorneys to prosecute school fraud.[26]

In January 1996, in one of the biggest crackdowns in the Chicago schools in twenty years, Vallas announced plans to fire thirty-two employees and discipline twelve others for wrongdoing.[27] In May 1996, he moved to blacklist forty school repair vendors who had overcharged the system.[28] He also moved to remove principals for cheating, for not reporting sex abuse, and for nepotism and gross waste.[29] Adding to the message of no tolerance for corruption, in 1996 James Harney, former facilities director, was sentenced to forty-one months in federal prison for extortion and kickbacks.[30] The judge additionally required him to pay $300,000 in restitution to the CPS.

The new leaders also sent a message that waste would not be tolerated. They did away with warehouses, including the one holding about $250,000 in equipment that had been apparently forgotten, and distributed supplies to schools.[31] They reduced waste in the school benefits programs, which had been paying three thousand ineligible dependents, a number of whom had been dead for years, saving an expected $155.3 million over four years.[32] They cut overtime and staff in stadium and playground programs for a projected savings of about $19 million.[33]

Meanwhile, Ben Reyes, CPS operations chief under Vallas and a former commissioner of the Chicago Department of General Services, added to the tough message on a day-to-day basis by sending his "troops" into schools to crack down on slackers. When a principal complained that her custodian was absent, for instance, Reyes and his troops rushed to the school. They walked around looking for the custodian until they heard snoring coming from a bathroom. Kicking the door open, they yelled, "The wait is over!"[34]

PRIVATIZATION AND LEGISLATION BANNING WORK RULES

Vallas and his team used privatization and new and old state laws to sweep away as much of the old guard and its work rules as possible. The 1995 law gave the CPS the right to privatize various types of jobs. A previous school reform law passed in 1988 had stripped principals and assistant principals of tenure. Many central administrators who previously had tenure in their central posts as principals or assistant principals now lost it. But unlike his predecessors, who barely used their powers under the 1988 law, Vallas used it and the 1995 law to the fullest.

Vallas fired or transferred about 25 percent of the central staff, dismissed many career administrators, hired about one hundred new people in the central office who were loyal to his initiatives, and eliminated all of the system's five hundred union stationary engineers.[35] He also privatized all of the system's four hundred skilled trade workers, including firemen, and 75 percent of engineers' janitorial staff.[36]

By giving the district the right to privatize various jobs, the 1995 law significantly strengthened its bargaining position with unions. Fortuitously, Vallas was also able to exploit the rivalry between two warring engineers' unions in Chicago: Local 143, which served the CPS and represented its school engineers, and rival Local 399, which served city hall and various private contractors.[37] Vallas told Local 143 that if it did not make concessions, he would privatize school engineers and hire members of Local 399. The threat worked. Local 143 agreed to ease various work rules, including engineers' right to automatic overtime when a school was open after or before regular hours. It also agreed to allow principals to initiate action to fire engineers who did a poor job.[38]

PERFORMANCE AND COMPLIANCE ACCOUNTABILITY

What about accountability? Vallas issued policies embodying provisions in the 1995 law that made engineers accountable to principals, with checks by the central office. The law gave principals a freer hand to contract out for janitorial staff[39] and allowed them to discipline engineers for poor performance—a big change from the days when engineers had civil service status.[40]

Meanwhile, principals, who had been stripped of tenure in 1988 and served on four-year performance contracts, had incentives to keep on top of engineers and make sure that their schools were in good condition because they were accountable to their local school councils and the central administration.

The CPS additionally established information feedback loops between schools and the central management to help monitor repair work. It divided schools into six regions and hired outside "property advisers" to work closely with principals in each region to oversee repairs by general contractors and engineers. So oversight is conducted at both the school level and the regional level.[41]

Performance accountability that carries real consequences for failure helps address one of the key underlying reasons that agencies have been vulnerable to takeover by special interests: weak incentives to safeguard customer interests. Holding managers accountable to customers gives them stronger incentives to resist agendas that conflict with those goals and ensure that resources go where they were intended.[42]

These reforms likely contributed to the fact that, while audits found $7 million in theft and overcharges in 1995, they unearthed less than $500,000 in 1996.[43] The backlog of repair orders got smaller after 1995.[44] The CPS built more new schools in the five years after the 1995 law than it had in the five years before it.[45] In 1997 the district sold bonds for the first time in seventeen years using its own authority rather than another agency's.[46]

RESTRUCTURING SCHOOL DISTRICTS TO PUSH POWER DOWNWARD

Removing the crooks and dominant coalition is only the first phase of reform. Once the infection and surrounding tissue have been excised, the patient may seem fine. But unless his constitution and immune system are strengthened, it is just a matter of time before he gets sick again. To prevent the recurring bouts of corruption that affect some police departments,[1] for example, the goal of the second phase of reform is to help the school system help itself and fix its own problems. This may be done by restructuring the system to push power down to appropriate levels and infusing the system with a different balance of performance and compliance accountability. In contrast to the clean-up operations discussed so far, which depend on the intervention of strong executives such as Paul Vallas, the second phase of reform is all about pushing power downward and adding safeguards so that the school district can function with less regard for who is in charge at the top.

M-FORM SCHOOL DISTRICTS

A hypothesis about how to structure large organizations to improve oversight and management is offered by the microeconomist Oliver Williamson, who builds on Friedrich Hayek's thesis that decision-making authority should be lodged with those people who have the most information necessary to carry out decisions[2] and examines the success of certain giant corporations in America. Williamson predicts that if large organizations segmented themselves not into divisions based on function (for example, personnel, procurement, budgeting, and so forth), as U-Form organizations do, but into semiautonomous units whose performance could be easily measured, efficiency and oversight would improve.

This basic structure, which Williamson refers to as the *M-Form*, or multidivisional organization, was originally developed by Du Pont and General Motors in the 1920s and later adopted by Sears and Standard Oil of New Jersey.[3] Under it, the top officers delegate decision-making authority to the managers in charge of each quasi-independent unit, who are held strictly accountable for their unit's performance and audited for fiscal compliance. An elite cadre of specialists with no stake in any unit or division helps the executive coordinate, filter information flows reaching the top, monitor and evaluate each unit's performance, allocate resources, and ensure that each unit is audited for fiscal compliance.

Williamson's M-Form hypothesis predicts that M-Form organizations, once they reach a certain size, will always outperform U-Form organizations, which are carved along hierarchical, functional lines. Although M-Form organizations are not immune to fraud,[4] they promise to attenuate many kinds of corruption[5] through improved oversight and an effective reward and punishment system. First, since the top level oversees but does not run everything, it suffers less information overload and radial loss than U-Form organizations. The M-Form organization also releases the top level from having to rely so heavily on inputs since it offers alternative ways of controlling employees' behavior: by putting a premium on performance. Further, because each unit in an M-Form organization is like a minicompany that must show results, it is far easier to conduct performance audits of M-Forms than of U-Forms, where it is hard to see into divisions and gauge their performance.[6] Compliance oversight will likely work better, too. While top U-Form executives resist review of their area because they are disinclined to audit themselves, the M-Form's cadre of elite specialists is less likely to have a personal stake in any particular unit and so will be less likely to resist review.[7]

Second, the M-Form organization checks employee conduct by bringing marketlike pressures to bear on all its semiautonomous units. Those who meet or surpass their performance targets are rewarded with raises, promotions, or more resources for their units, while those who fail forgo these benefits and may find their jobs at risk. Unlike U-Form organizations, where the allocation of resources on the basis of bargaining power tends to foster the pursuit of subversive goals, the M-Form's allocation of resources on the basis of performance reduces the risk of goal displacement and develops a performance-oriented culture.

So what would an M-Form district look like?

THE INDIVIDUAL SCHOOL

Since the correct level at which to lodge authority is wherever the most relevant information lies to make the decisions, the most obvious unit for day-to-day decisions would be the individual school. Schools should have as much discretion as possible over their budgets, both how to spend money and what to spend it on. Categorical funds and grants should flow directly to schools. Schools should be able to hire, fire, and promote their staff, buy their supplies, including computers and photocopiers, make their repairs, and manage their daily affairs without interference. Schools should have flexibility in determining individual class size, class duration, and, so long as they do not violate the U.S. Constitution, the type of students they admit. There should be more room for single-sex schools, for instance. As long as they cover core subjects, schools should be free to develop their own extracurricular activities, themes, and academic specialties.

THE CENTRAL OFFICE

The central office should exist essentially only to monitor, support, plan for the long term, and operate those functions that it realistically must (such as dealing with legal matters, construction, and perhaps meals). Everything else should be decentralized to the level where the necessary decision-making knowledge lies. The central office's role should thus primarily include activities such as evaluating schools for performance, distributing that information to parents and schools, conducting audits for fiscal compliance, offering training to school staff, and providing intensive help to failing schools.

To the extent that any functional divisions remain centralized, the question should be whether the division's performance can be easily ascertained and the division chief held accountable for it. If so, the division chief should be given discretion over its budget, staff, and daily operations. Take a school construction division. Since it would be possible to evaluate it in relation to the number, quality, and cost of the schools it built over a given time, such a division should become semiautonomous and its chief held accountable for results.

Central divisions whose performance could not be easily determined and whose costs come from inputs resulting from internal allocation decisions rather than market competition would not qualify for semiautonomy.[8] A central cadre of experts independent of any divisions should coordinate between such divisions to minimize the risk of warring fiefdoms. To the extent that these divisions have discretionary budgets, they could be made to vary depending on their performance.[9]

But the point is that the central office must be there to serve principals and local school managers, not the other way around. Reformers can help ensure this by letting principals and local school managers evaluate central services yearly through surveys. They could also charge schools a predetermined fee every time they use these services, thus reducing the waste incurred from schools' overuse of certain central services because they are "free." Or they could follow the model of the Edmonton Public Schools described in the next chapter and transform certain central divisions into consulting operations. If principals had control over their budgets, they could decide whether to buy services from the central office or from private contractors, thus holding those central offices in check through marketlike competition. Central services that attract demand would grow in size and importance; those that do not would shrink.

A NEW BALANCE OF PERFORMANCE AND COMPLIANCE ACCOUNTADILITY

Performance accountability is one of the most powerful tools to motivate and restrain behavior in an organization.[10] It is essential when employees have autonomy and freedom from strict compliance; executives need to be able to evaluate people's work and hold them responsible for it. This is not to say that performance accountability will eliminate corruption. In fact, employees may have incentives to overrepresent their accomplishments. But if implemented with the proper safeguards, performance accountability will likely reduce incentives to engage in illcgal schemes that divert resources from official goals—the kind of corruption that is usually most harmful to districts.[11]

To make it possible to reward and discipline people for their work, reformers should strip managers and as many employees as possible of restrictive job protections such as civil service. But if all else fails, the district can establish a central unit dedicated to pushing through the due process hurdles that need to be surmounted to remove incompetent personnel. In Chicago, the Department of Teacher Accountability, established in 1996, has helped principals get through the thicket of hearings and procedures to remove teachers who should not be in the classroom. So, for instance, if the teachers' contract says that on the fifteenth day of what is called the E-3 removal process, the principal must visit the teacher's classroom, the department will telephone the principal the day before to remind him or her. The Houston Independent School District has a similar proactive unit dedicated to enhancing performance accountability in schools.

Executives should also use merit pay and internal resource alloca-tion to motivate and restrain employees.[12] The parts of the district that are doing well should be allowed to increase in size and importance; those that are not should get smaller. Students and parents should funnel in-ternal resource allocations to schools through a system of districtwide choice. Schools and principals should funnel resource allocations to cen-tral divisions.[13]

Schools should also be accountable for performance to parents in other ways aside from choice. Parents should have a forum in which they can bring complaints and force the school and the central office to listen. In fact, schools and the central office should proactively solicit parents' in-put through regular surveys used in teachers' and principals' evaluations. Parents should have full access to review their school budget, school bank accounts, and fundraising documents. Because this book is concerned with reducing school corruption and improving management, it does not discuss decentralization of governance, which is unnecessary from a busi-ness perspective, although desirable from a political and democratic one. However, school-based governance structures that give parents a voice in certain facets of school operations are compatible with what is proposed here.[14]

The development of a performance-oriented ethos in an M-Form dis-trict should arise naturally, from the bottom up, as schools and central units begin to enjoy independence in pursuing official goals. To help the process along, however, top officials should implement performance bud-geting and cost-benefit justification. By requiring officials to consider whether every expense is fulfilling a goal, these practices would further force a shift in focus from inputs and rote thinking to expected and actual results and innovative strategizing.[15] If officials had to systematically allo-cate resources on the basis of goals and measured results, details such as salaries and travel would take a backseat to the overall mission.

Further, to help replace the "gotcha" attitude of the old input-driven system by a culture of helpfulness and service, much as the private sector instills in its employees, the central office should have a unit devoted to helping vendors and principals navigate any complex rules and resolve any complaints or disputes. To discourage the kind of phony help that some central school divisions historically provided to the field, this unit should be evaluated on how well it teaches others to help themselves. The combination of simpler rules and genuine help from the central office is likely to reduce the need for bottleneck corruption. It is also likely to re-duce the number of vendors who overcharge or bilk the district out of frustration.

To give managers the leeway they need, rules that specify detailed procedures and earmark money should be streamlined where feasible. Some procedures are mandated by the state or federal government, but others are imposed by the district. The district should commission a cost-benefit analysis of these controls and cut those that are not worth it. Analysts need to consider not just the monitoring costs—the personnel who draft, interpret, implement, and enforce regulations—but also the apathy, rote thinking, fraud, waste, and abuse that may result when the organization becomes unmanageable.

At the same time, the central office must beef up oversight of a different kind. It should audit every school at least once a year for fiscal compliance and monitor schools' spending continuously. If schools move completely to on-line purchasing, their budgets will be transparent and technology can allow central monitors to see egregious expenditures virtually as they occur. If a school does not bring such expenditures into line within a reasonable time, the central office should offer help to preempt a potential problem.

STANDING DOWN PRESSURES TO RECENTRALIZE

In any large district that has tens of thousands of employees, someone is bound to get into trouble. And in a large city with an active press corps, some reporter will probably find out. So a decentralized district will invariably confront pressure—soon after the first employee is caught making off with money or the first administrator is caught abusing power—to recentralize and reregulate.

New York City's experiment with BlackBerries illustrates the kind of pressure at stake. BlackBerries are tiny portable computers that allow users to perform multiple tasks, including receiving and composing e-mails. In the spring of 2002, Chancellor Harold Levy bought them for a number of key central administrators and district superintendents. The bill came to more than $94,000 (over $43,000 for the BlackBerries and about $51,000 a year in monthly service fees). When the press found out, it jumped on the story, criticizing the Board of Education for spending so much on what looked like a frill.[16] Levy's response? An announcement that he would strip most of his staff of BlackBerries and attempt to get a refund from the manufacturer.

But with the average school manager making over $75 an hour, BlackBerries promised to save the school system time and money, especially over their lifetimes. BlackBerries would have allowed administrators to extend their productive hours. Administrators could have started to organize their day on their morning commutes to work, setting up meetings and reading e-mails. Because the machines use the Ethernet, they would also have allowed contact with administrators in the field when phones were unavailable.

Unfortunately, media-driven, high-pressured decision making like Levy's is common in public education and has helped shape the way districts are organized. Although the media performs an invaluable service by exposing school abuses, not every single question it raises about expenditures is thoughtful. By responding to exposes reflexively, without taking efficiency and the overall welfare of students into account, school officials encourage a bunker mentality that reduces risk taking and increases regulation.[17]

It is hard to immunize a decentralized district against these knee-jerk reactions. Chancellors and superintendents have a fragile grasp on their posts and need to be sensitive to public opinion. Nevertheless, as Johanna Neuman points out in the context of politics, the media is less likely to set the agenda if politicians offer strong leadership.[18] If decentralized districts institutionalize performance budgeting and cost-benefit justification, as suggested here, they will at least have the tools and hopefully the culture to insist that any proposed new rules and regulations be worth it. Cost-benefit analyses can help districts explain themselves to the public.

CHAPTER EIGHTEEN

THE MODEL OF EDMONTON, CANADA

M-Form school districts might sound a lot like some other popular school decentralization reforms today, but many types of decentralization are not real decentralization at all and should not be confused with the M-Form. New York City's 1969 community school decentralization, for instance, never devolved power to schools. As for school-based management (SBM), also known as shared decision making,[1] although it aims to devolve authority to schools, it comes in many different forms that vary widely in the locus and scope of decision-making authority,[2] most of which would differ substantially from M-Form schools. While SBM increases school discretion—often over marginal expenditures and issues peripheral to real school improvement[3]— most examples do not increase school autonomy. Moreover, a number of forms of SBM aim to empower not the principal above all but a group that may also include faculty, parents, students, and community representatives and is hard to hold accountable for outcomes. This may be why SBM seldom imposes real consequences for failure on school decision makers, unlike M-Form districts, which would hold principals strictly accountable.

M-Form schools would most closely resemble charter schools.[4] Consistent with M-Form schools, charter schools are propelled by the wish to empower principals, free them from top-down constraints and union rules, and hold them responsible for results. The key difference, however, is the scale and comprehensiveness of the reform. The M-Form district is not about turning one or two schools into charter schools; it is about turning the entire district into a charterlike entity. Every school in the district would become a charter school, and as many central office units as feasible would become semiautonomous, charterlike units. The overall effect of reform would be far more complete and profound and would give M-Form schools advantages that charter schools do not enjoy. M-Form schools would be closely monitored and trained by user-friendly central units in their districts, reducing the risk of school closings resulting from lack of financial training. M-Form schools could choose from a panoply of central services if they wished. And because M-Form schools would be part of a district filled with other schools like them, they would not endure the reduced or nonexistent funding for building facilities that many charter schools do today. Moreover, from students' perspective, there would be a broad and meaningful range of schools from which to choose, as principals use their freedom to shape their schools in different ways.

The Edmonton Public School (EPS) system, in Canada's Alberta Province, provides a graphic illustration of an M-Form district in action—a radically decentralized organization in which all schools and many central units are semiautonomous, accountable for their own performance, and held together by a small elite cadre of leaders dedicated to the system's overall mission.[5] With 209 schools, nearly 81,000 children, and a yearly operating budget of $465 million, the EPS is the paragon of site-based management in North America today.

Before the 1970s, the EPS was a top-down school district similar in structure to the school bureaucracies built up by the administrative progressives in American cities. The EPS had central supervisors for every subject, from art to French studies, who controlled most of what happened in the classroom in their subject. Principals and teachers had to consult them on every major decision. An upper-level officer in Edmonton's Planning Division recalled that, when she first started as a French teacher in the district in 1969, it took her two to three years to realize that the supervisor of French was not her boss. "He told me what to teach. He hired all of the French teachers. I saw more of him than my principal." Furthermore, he controlled the audio-visual equipment that she and other teachers borrowed for their classrooms.[6]

But starting in the mid-1970s a new M-Form-like organizational structure was gradually established that changed the culture from a compliance-driven, top-down model to a performance-based one driven by quasi-free-market pressures and customer needs.[7] The transformation was accomplished largely under the pioneering twenty-two-year leadership of Superintendent Michael Strembitsky.

LETTING PRINCIPALS CONTROL THEIR BUDGETS

Probably the single most cataclysmic reform, because of its repercussions throughout every corner of the school system, was making schools quasi-independent by giving principals control of about 90 percent of their school budgets. The bulk of the money that the EPS receives from the Province of Alberta flows right down to its schools, where principals decide how to spend it.

School autonomy was built right into the budgeting formula. The money is meted out not based on a strict enrollment ratio formula and Norm Tables but on a weighted student formula that allocates block grants to principals and lets them decide how to spend it.[8] Under the weighted student formula, which is also used in Seattle and Houston, the size of a school's budget depends on the type of students it enrolls, with hard-to-educate students, such as the severely disabled, receiving more money than easy-to-educate ones. But the key feature is that schools receive funds for numerous functions to serve those students—from money to hire teachers and librarians to money to pay for food, transportation, and building maintenance. And principals decide how to apportion it.

Moreover, most of the money is not tied up by central mandates, union rules, and detailed procedural requirements. Although the Alberta Teachers' Union, which represents EPS teachers, principals, and many other administrators, is formidable, Edmonton has managed to keep formal collective bargaining rules to a minimum through constant vigilance and skillful management.

Purchasing, for instance, allows for great discretion. Unlike the small, limited credit-card pilot programs in districts such as Chicago and New York City, the EPS had issued 1,200 credit cards as of the fall of 2001. All principals and many managers have one. Principals may charge up to $3,000 a month or $1,000 per purchase whenever they want without generating a central purchase order. The electronic order goes directly to the vendor, who delivers directly to the school, usually within a couple of days—without interference from the central office. When principals need to travel on business, their credit-card limit rises to $5,000. For orders over $1,000, the electronic order goes from the principal to the central office, which then sends it on to the vendor.

Consider what happens when an EPS school receives a government grant, say, to build a playground. Unlike in America's three largest districts, which would essentially grab the money and take over the construction, the central office in Edmonton hardly gets involved. The school applies for its own grants and receives the funds from its source, in this case the government. The central office sends the school a few documents to verify that the money was used for its intended purpose but does not get involved in construction. Nor does it impose contractors on the school. All it does is screen them; the choice of whom to hire for the project is the school's. Then, at the end of the process, the school sends the required records on the playground directly to the government—not to the central office.

HELPING PRINCIPALS HELP THEMSELVES

As much as principals need decision-making authority, they should not be forced to make decisions that transform them into business managers rather than instructional leaders. Running the academic side of a school is all-consuming. Principals may not have time to get deeply involved in building a playground or fixing a toilet. Even if they did have time, moreover, just because they are good at educating students does not mean they have a head for business.

In U-Form organizations like America's three largest school districts, central divisions are supposed to take care of noninstructional matters. On paper it works beautifully. A toilet leaking in a school? The Facilities Bureau will come to the rescue. Planning a field trip out of the district? The Transportation Bureau will dispatch a bus whenever and wherever required. A question about how to conduct competitive bidding to buy a school welcome sign? A central budget officer will walk the principal through the procedure.

Unfortunately, such scenarios are mostly mythology in large districts. The truth, as this book suggests, is closer to seemingly endless waiting on the telephone for a central officer to pick up and long, nerve-wracking waits while purchase and work orders wend their way through the bureaucracy. Moreover, if and when the central office finally does dispatch someone to help the locals in the field, the effect, if not the unspoken intention, can be to foster dependency on the central office, not to make schools self-sufficient. As we have seen, top-down organizations that rely wholly on rigid compliance accountability devices provide incentives for people to express their instincts for self-preservation in this wasteful, unhelpful manner.

So what should districts do to make sure principals are not overwhelmed while giving them more authority? A solution must force headquarters to respond to principals—to do what principals need when they need it—or give principals the power to run their own ship as well as a business manager, ideally situated right in the school, who works directly for the principal and who can coordinate the school's noninstructional affairs according to his or her vision.

The EPS does both. First, it allowed principals to force the central office to respond to them by giving them the power to buy goods and services either from outside industry or from headquarters. The fact that central bureaus suddenly had to compete for business with vendors and improve their services precipitated their transformation into semi-independent, accountable M-Form units. If a principal needs a computer fixed, for instance, he can get it serviced by either a central worker or a private vendor. If another principal wants her school painted, she can go to a private paint shop or give the school Purchasing Department her specifications and ask it to tender the job out. The Purchasing Department will invite its own skilled laborers to bid, but they have to compete with outside industry. Although by contract many central workers are guaranteed the opportunity to bid when the central office tenders out a job, they are not guaranteed to win. They must compete with industry to satisfy the principal. As the head of EPS Purchasing and Finance observed, "We are known as 'Central Services.' It's kind of like walking into a shopping mall and we're the vendors in the mall."[9]

The system thus puts marketlike performance pressures on headquarters. Central units such as information technology, electronics, curriculum, and maintenance do not receive a budget from the superintendent. They have to sell their services to the schools, which, if they choose, pay them from their own budgets.

The genius of the M-Form structure, manifest in the EPS, is that it harnesses the same human instinct for self-preservation so much in evidence in America's largest districts and channels it into furthering the system's mission, thus reducing the chances of goal displacement. Central officers have incentives to proactively figure out how to please principals. The message could not be clearer: If central experts satisfy principals, their units will grow. If they do not, their units will shrink and eventually fold. That is probably why the EPS is one of the few school districts in North America where the central office sends out annual questionnaires to principals asking them what they need. It is a matter of survival.

Two examples illustrate how this can play out for central units. First, recall those subject supervisors of art, French, and other subjects. No central school politburo pushed them out. Principals did—through the power of their purse. They paid to send some of their own teachers and assistant principals to professional development so that they could become in-house experts in various subjects.

In contrast with central supervisors, who fell by the wayside, the central professional development unit grew in importance. Today, the Consulting unit is one of the EPS's largest central units, offering training and professional development to meet whatever needs principals may have.

Now consider the EPS central Information Technology (IT) unit. In early 1998, school technology needs escalated dramatically. The budget office sent an infusion of IT funds directly to the schools, which then decided where to spend them. The IT unit, then a tiny, nearly moribund unit, realized that if it did not act quickly to attract that money, it would die out because of outside competitors. So IT became aggressively proactive, visiting schools and sending out questionnaires to find out what they needed. The unit set up a help desk. Within two years or so, so many principals were clamoring for central IT services that it grew from twenty technicians in 1998 to sixty-five in 2001. Today, the unit has contracts with 165 EPS schools for projects ranging from installing computer labs to installing virus protection software.[10]

This brings us to the second part of the solution to how to give principals authority without requiring them to become business managers: getting them in-house resident experts to manage the school in accordance with their vision. The EPS provides principals and their assistants with extensive, continuous training in budgeting, information technology, and management. Every school has an administrative assistant trained in bookkeeping and school-based financial management. At the same time, principals can use their own budgets to have staff trained in other areas, such as curriculum or computer software systems. The resulting contrast with traditional districts could not be starker. Survival in a top-down bureaucracy can mean withholding technical know-how from the field, but in an M-Form district such as Edmonton it means giving principals what they need.

A MIX OF PERFORMANCE AND COMPLIANCE ACCOUNTABILITY

To check misconduct and motivate employees, M-Form organizations use a goal-oriented balance of compliance and performance accountability devices. Let us examine how these devices apply to principals in the EPS.

PERFORMANCE

In return for the power they enjoy, principals are accountable for the performance of their schools as a whole—from the building's physical condition to the content of the curriculum to student achievement.[11]

First, principals are accountable to parents. Parents in Edmonton have the power of what Albert Hirschman called "voice."[12] The EPS provides a formal forum, known as the Parent Council, where parents can vent their complaints about schools and appeal to the central office for help. The central office also solicits parents' views about principals once a year and uses this input in their evaluations. In addition, the district facilitates parental evaluation of schools by making information about them accessible to parents. School budgets are available for scrutiny at the local library and on the EPS's web site, for instance. Principals are required to show parents textbooks if they ask.

Parents in Edmonton can also hold principals accountable indirectly through the power of "exit."[13] If they are not satisfied with their child's principal, they may change schools. Parents were first able to vote with their feet in 1972, when the school system let them choose their child's school within the district, but choice really took off after 1979, when principals were permitted to make major decisions about spending. Spending authority paved the way for schools to take on their own unique characters, enriching options for parents.[14] So unlike New York City and other districts that claim to have choice but actually have few seats open in decent schools and make the process very difficult, parents in Edmonton have many meaningful options.

Parents' ability to choose schools has the same sort of effect on principals as principals' ability to choose where to spend their money has on central officials. It makes them proactively responsive to their customers' needs. If enrollment drops below set levels in certain schools or in programs within schools, the School Board of Trustees may start proceedings to close them.[15] In 2001, for instance, two schools and two junior high school programs were closed because of low enrollment.

Second, principals are accountable for performance to the superintendent and Board of Trustees. The superintendent directly evaluates a third of the district's principals every year, visiting their schools for three days each. The central office also conducts yearly surveys of parents, students, and staff—Student-Parent-Staff Satisfaction Surveys and Community Surveys—which are used in principals' performance reviews with the superintendent or Board of Trustees. If principals have problems or fall short of their student achievement goals, they must explain why to the Board of Trustees.

COMPLIANCE

Superior transparency is a salient characteristic of M-Form organizations, where, because each component is carved out as a self-contained accountable unit, people at the top can more easily see through to the performance and compliance of each component. In consonance with such transparency, the EPS also uses extensive, continuous monitoring for compliance. Its focus is not so much on ensuring compliance with minute, detailed procedures (there are not that many) as on watching that transactions overall make sense and taking swift action if a problem is detected.

First, the EPS uses audits in a more effective, performance-oriented way than America's three largest districts do. Instead of having one unit audit a sample of schools at a fixed time once a year, the EPS encourages many different parts of the district to audit any and all schools at different times during the year, as needed. A small Internal Auditor Office that reports to the superintendent's executive assistant conducts yearly audits of the money that schools collect from children and parents to make sure it is deposited into school accounts. But various central units also conduct audits of schools in their own areas of expertise, whenever they see a need for it. So the Purchasing Office audits principals' purchases, for instance; the Budget Office audits principals' spending.

In addition, different parts of the central office review principals' budgets at different stages of the year. Before principals can touch their money, they draw up tentative budgets that are reviewed by the Board of Trustees. During the year, the central office closely watches school spending levels. If a principal goes into deficit, he has to submit a plan describing how he will pay his debts. After the school year ends, principals are asked to account for any unusual spending patterns (for example, more spending on staff than usual). If principals have a budget deficit, they may have to submit a full explanation. If the explanation is not good enough, trustees keep asking. Then they make recommendations. If a deficit is due to overstaffing, for instance, the superintendent or trustees will recommend solutions such as combining classes.

Most important, unlike command-and-control bureaucracies that scrutinize employees for compliance at preset points during a transaction—only if and when a rule tells them to—the EPS's central offices monitor school transactions continuously through state-of-the-art technology. The central Budget Office continuously monitors principals' expenditures to see if they are exceeding their budgets and where their money is going. Similarly the Office of Maintenance continuously monitors school utilities costs, which because of the climate consume a significant but steady portion of the overall budget, to spot any fluctuations.

Furthermore, unlike their counterparts in top-down districts, the EPS's central officials are encouraged to use their common sense and initiative to determine whether something might be amiss that warrants further investigation. So if the Budget Office notices that a school's spending "gets out of line, . . . [the principal] will be notified."[16] Such a case "might trigger an audit." Or if the Maintenance Office detects unusually high utilities costs at a school, it will dispatch a consultant to the site. If the consultant finds that the high costs are due, say, to inadequate insulation or windows that do not shut tightly, he will suggest appropriate remedies. The key is that the EPS's intense oversight is designed, as in total quality management,[17] to improve services and help principals, not to ensure compliance for the sake of compliance.

The monitoring is made possible by sophisticated technology that permits central offices to see expenditures soon after principals make them. The credit card technology allows each site to view its staff's charges but not the charges of other sites' staff. The central office, however, can view charges by everyone in the district. The software allows it to consolidate information by vendor, school, or employee to see every purchase, the store at which it was made, the amount, the hour, and even the store clerk's number.

PRESCREENING AND OTHER "PREVENTIVE MAINTENANCE"

The EPS also does as much as it can beforehand to make waste, abuse, and failure less likely. For example, it provides periodic training and continuous assistance to school personnel involved in creating budgets. It trains all 1,200 employees who have credit cards in their proper use.

Because it relies heavily on people to be honest, the EPS also invests significantly in prescreening of prospective principals, teachers, and vendors who wish to sell products on the EPS's on-line school supply catalogue for employees. For a vendor to be approved, the Purchasing and Finance Department audits it, making sure that it has a business license and liability coverage and that its staff members have workers' compensation coverage. The department also thoroughly checks vendors' references and does further financial checking as necessary.

But central officials are encouraged to use their judgment and take risks, not just blindly adhere to the prequalifying standards. So if officials encounter a company that is new, small, and inexperienced but also enthusiastic, officials might say, "We'll give you a job. But it'll be a small one and we'll see how you proceed until you increase your staff and knowledge."[18]

DISCIPLINE FOR WRONGDOERS

If an employee engages in fraud, the EPS has a zero-tolerance policy. Employees who use a credit card to steal are stripped of the card and never receive one again for as long as they work in the district. Vendors who engage in fraud have their names removed from the vendor bidding list, and are not allowed to work for the district again.

Ironically the EPS can afford to take a hard line with vendors precisely because it is so business friendly. It pays vendors' bills within thirty days. It goes out of its way to minimize red tape. Unlike New York City and the LAUSD, which scare away competition and thus often have to hire the same companies over and over again no matter what their past, the EPS can afford to take a hard line on vendor fraud because there are always plenty of other contractors who want to work for the district.

As the EPS's director of Purchasing and Finance noted, "Here companies are lined up at our door to bid. Vendors that don't have time to do a job [when we need it] are asking us to please keep their names on the [vendor bidding] list. 'Please just don't take us off,' they say. We have a lot of competition."[19]

CHAPTER NINETEEN

LOOSENED TOP-DOWN CONTROLS
AND TRUST

Urban schools have long been guided by fear that if they do not regulate operations from the top, a free-for-all will ensue at the bottom. Would implementing this book's recommendations prove them right? Although no one can answer this definitively, this book has provided many plausible reasons as to why the decentralization suggested here would probably not result in major scandals. This chapter examines some actual experiments in school decentralization that are consistent with this book's proposals to show what we might expect from principals, administrators, and central division chiefs.

HOW PRINCIPALS MIGHT ACT

What behavior—or misbehavior—should we expect of principals who receive control over large pots of money in return for accountability?

There are few examples of the kind of radical school-based decentralization proposed here. So far, Edmonton, Seattle, and Houston, all of which William Ouchi and I discuss at length,[1] are the best examples of districts that give principals a significant degree of budgetary autonomy and broad freedom from central mandates. But Houston's program is too new to evaluate. The district started giving principals broad autonomy only in 2000–2001, under the avant-garde leadership of its superintendent, Rod Paige, now U.S. secretary of education.

As for Seattle, although it started giving principals some

fiscal autonomy in 1997–98, its schools are not regularly audited internally. So although there is no evidence of any spike in misbehavior by principals there, the available data do not allow a considered judgment.

The Edmonton Public Schools (EPS) in Edmonton, Canada, on the other hand, has been letting its 230 or so principals control about 90 percent of their school budgets[2] for nearly two decades; in fact, some principals control as much as $10 million (Canadian) a year. Any major problems would quickly come to light since the EPS audits each of its schools at least once every year.

Stunningly, the public data show that corruption by principals in Edmonton is negligible. From 1984 through 2001, internal audits uncovered only four cases of low-level theft in the district's schools. Most involved a principal or a staff member failing to deposit a cash donation in a school account. Interviews with local newspaper editors and senior school officials and searches of electronic databases (Lexis-Nexis) reveal no other fraud cases during this period anywhere in the district.[3]

Of course, the EPS's pristine record does not guarantee the same results in America's three largest school districts because it is unclear how much of that record is due to its particular culture.[4] A relatively young pioneer town, Edmonton does not have the rich tradition of political machines, organized crime, and municipal corruption that cities such as New York and Chicago share. Research of newspapers and interviews with senior school personnel show that the Edmonton school system appears to have no history of corruption (although gross waste was reportedly a problem before the district was decentralized). Further, the EPS is a fraction of the size of these larger districts. So, while its record is encouraging, it probably needs to be viewed through the lens of its culture and size.

There are other signs as to how principals in America's three largest districts might react to autonomy. School inspector general reports in these districts show a relatively low incidence of theft, embezzlement, bribery, and nepotism or patronage among principals and assistant principals.[5] Although some principals do make off with money, such cases are few. In all of fiscal 2001, for instance, LAUSD investigators uncovered only one instance of a principal stealing (pocketing cash donations).[6] Of the three cases they uncovered of principals putting ghost employees on the school payroll, central administrators who pressured principals to give their cronies no-show jobs were allegedly responsible in every instance. In one instance a principal was pressured to hire three teachers who were relatives of high-level administrators.[7] In another, a high-ranking administrator instructed a principal to give full-time colleagues no-show school jobs.[8] In a third, an administrator obtained permission for teaching assignments at off-site locations for his colleagues who got paid but never showed up.[9]

These patterns hold true in the two other large school systems. In New York City, for instance, of the forty-six cases of fraud that the Special Commissioner of Investigation looked into between 2000 and 2001, only six involved principals and assistant principals.[10]

Second, inspector general reports suggest the three largest districts' biggest problems are not in schools but in regional, district, and central bureaucracies. It is in those offices, not individual schools, where the costliest and highest incidence of corruption and waste occur. In the Los Angeles Unified School District (LAUSD), the alleged waste and abuse uncovered in the central office was 99.8 percent more expensive and nearly twice as voluminous as that uncovered at schools, according to inspector general data from fiscal 2001.[11] Although there are 789 schools in the LAUSD, each with several accounts, the inspector general unearthed only eleven cases of theft and abuse of school funds[12] compared to twenty-one cases of theft and abuse in central operations.[13] This is striking because the LAUSD employs about five times as many people in schools as it does in central operations: 11,890 central employees versus 68,110 school-based employees.[14]

These data could, of course, be a distortion if it turned out that the inspector general arbitrarily conducted more audits and investigations of central programs than of schools—wherever investigators dig most is where they are likely to find the most dirt. But this does not appear to be the case regarding audits. As for investigations, the inspector general did launch more investigations of the central office than of schools. However, inspector general investigations are primarily reactive, launched only if the office receives allegations.[15] So either people at the central office are more likely to make allegations than people in schools or the central office actually has more problems, which seems more plausible.

Although it is hard to know if this pattern would hold up if schools received more power, the current data should provide at least some reassurance, because there are still ways principals could engage in theft if they wanted to, even without autonomy.

HOW CENTRAL DIVISION CHIEFS MIGHT ACT

HOUSTON'S DIVISION OF SCHOOL FACILITIES

What should we expect of central division chiefs handed autonomy in return for performance accountability? The example of Houston's Division of Facilities and Construction, researched for the School Design Project, may offer a clue. The division's reforms are recent, so there may not yet be enough time for a full evaluation. But the results so far may be valuable nevertheless: the reforms—turning the division into a semiautonomous M-Form entity—correspond precisely to what this book advocates, and the division's prereform culture was similar to that in some areas of the largest school districts.

The Houston Independent School District (HISD) is the sixth largest in the United States. It used to be an old-fashioned, U-Form, command-and-control bureaucracy with fiefdoms and built-in waste.[16] But when Rod Paige took over as superintendent in 1994, he methodically and relentlessly moved the district from a seniority-based, inputs-oriented system to a performance-based one. During his nearly seven-year tenure, Paige cleaned up much abuse, freed schools from many central mandates, and changed the culture in the central office and the schools by rallying the organization around a common mission, as described in Donald McAdams's *Fighting to Save Our Urban Schools* and William Ouchi and Lydia Segal's *Making Schools Work.*

In 1999, as part of these reforms, Paige gave the Facilities Division autonomy in return for performance accountability. To grasp the stunning results, it is helpful to have a picture of the division before, during, and after it became autonomous.

From the 1980s through the early 1990s, audits, investigations, and media exposes portray a division with three thousand employees and a $100-million budget that was the most troubled in the HISD. Newspapers churned out stories of alleged wrongs ranging from theft to phony overtime to racketeering.[17] At one point, in the early 1990s, officials were probing as many as ten burglaries in the Facilities Division and other areas. Poor supervision together with archaic, paper-driven procedures appeared to facilitate fraud.[18] A six-week investigation by a private law firm in 1992 suggested that some administrators were using subordinates to run their personal errands, making off with school supplies, and putting unqualified friends on the school payroll.[19] In April 1992, six employees were fired for alleged theft.[20]

Needless to say, facilities management did not effectively supervise construction and renovation.[21] Contractors would sometimes go over budget, miss deadlines, and do shoddy work. At one school, facilities managers failed to notice that cafeteria floor planks were not level and that outside concrete slabs contained deep hollows, which held pools of water after rainfall.[22] That renovation was supposed to take 270 days by contract; 658 days later it still was not finished.

Facilities managers also had little interest in getting input from principals. In the school renovation, no one bothered to explain the scope of work to the principal. All the principal saw was a schematic design "similar in detail to the home floor plans found in the Sunday newspaper."[23] When auditors informed facilities managers that the principal was unhappy with the job at her school, they suggested that auditors not talk to school staff.[24] Yet the absence of any feedback loop from the school to the central division was costly. It meant, for example, that the principal had to request features such as new mailbox cabinets and electrical power clocks after the designs had been approved, thus triggering expensive change orders.[25]

The division's poor reputation in construction had reverberated all the way to the Greater Houston Partnership, an independent group of powerful local business leaders with broad influence over public works in the city of Houston. So when Superintendent Paige approached the group for help as the HISD faced major deferred maintenance problems and a bond referendum had failed, the partnership refused unless he turned the Facilities Division around.[26]

In 1999 Paige recruited Richard Lindsay of Texas A&M University to head the division. Essentially agreeing to turn the division into a self-sustaining M-Form unit, Paige promised to clear away red tape and give Lindsay autonomy in return for measurable results: Lindsay was to build a certain number of schools over a certain period of time within a certain budget. He was to report his results to the superintendent and meet quarterly with an eight-member external oversight committee for construction and with the central lay school board. If he were to fail, he would likely be replaced.

The first bureaucratic rule Paige waived was the one dictating that administrators' salaries be governed by seniority. This allowed him to offer Lindsay a competitive salary. Then Paige took a series of crucial steps to give Lindsay the authority he needed to run the division. The first step was in the area of personnel. Paige swept aside rigid hiring and job advertising procedures to let Lindsay pick the employees he wanted to keep, dismiss the rest, and hire his own people.

Second, Paige fought to give Lindsay broad discretion over the selection of architects and contractors. The ability to hire quality architects is critical to controlling costs and quality and meeting deadlines in the construction industry because low-quality architects tend to make mistakes in design that trigger delays and costly change orders later on. So Paige ended the central school board's alleged tradition of patronage over architects. The board accepted a request-for-proposal qualification process for architects that put Lindsay firmly in charge of determining what types of firms were hired.

In addition, Lindsay took advantage of a 1993 Texas law that allowed the HISD to award contracts on the basis not just of cost (the lowest bidder) but also of quality. He wrote detailed bidding criteria that put a premium on quality. As a result, top companies that did not bid in the past because they assumed that other, inferior companies would have under-bid them began to compete for school construction work.

But to enable Lindsay to attract and keep top firms working for the HISD, Paige had to make the district as business friendly as possible. So Paige let Lindsay remove from the HISD contract for architects a host of rigid "gotcha" provisions that were intended to stop corruption and save every penny for the district but that in effect scared away good architects and created red tape.

Along the same lines, Lindsay speeded up the time it took the HISD to pay architects from six months to ten days. The central Budget Office still operated under the premise that it had to question virtually every ex-pense on every bill to save the district money. Knowing that no quality ar-chitect would put up with this, Lindsay, with Paige's backing, went to the budget division and told administrators that if they could not pay the ar-chitects within thirty days of receiving their bills, he would hire a private contractor to process their payments. To give his threat bite, he had lined up a private contractor. But budget officials not only met his challenge; they beat it, processing most payments within about ten days.

The reforms' success so far is impressive. In November 1998, when Lindsay first came on board, a three-year, $678-million bond proposal had passed to renovate sixty-nine schools and build ten new ones. Not only did Lindsay complete all the construction and renovation within the three years, but he also came in $100 million under budget. In April 2001, he received permission from the school board to use the leftover money to renovate an additional nine schools and build an eleventh. As of the sum-mer of 2002, he was planning to ask for an additional $808-million pro-gram for further construction and renovation.

As for the corruption and abuse that used to affect the division, a Lexis/Nexis search reveals no media reports of fraud and abuse—in marked contrast to a search of the media earlier in the 1990s. As for au-dits, they are most telling. The main problem auditors appear to be find-ing now is that facilities administrators are not questioning every possible discrepancy and enforcing exceptions in contractors' bills.[27] One audit, for instance, informed facilities personnel that they could technically seek liquidated damages from a contractor who had taken too long to com-plete one project, even though the district had not suffered any actual damage due to the delay.

But that is the whole point. By moving away from the nitpicky, input-oriented mentality to one driven by results and trust, Lindsay was able to nurture good relationships with quality contractors. Because he was ac-countable for results, he had the incentive to weigh the costs versus the benefits of enforcing small liquidated damages clauses. The bottom line is that while Lindsay may have lost the district a few hundred dollars by not seeking exceptions, he essentially saved the children $100 million and built them more schools than the district had hoped for.

HOW ADMINISTRATORS MIGHT REACT

NEW YORK CITY'S STREAMLINED PROCUREMENT SYSTEM

What should we expect of administrators who are suddenly able to operate under loosened regulations? New York City's new streamlined procurement rules may give us an inkling.

In March 1995, in the wake of investigations into theft from the main warehouse, the chancellor assigned Louis "Lou" Benevento, a thirty-two-year Board of Education veteran to revamp the rules.[28] Benevento's first step was to close the warehouse. The following year he began drastically cutting back on anticorruption procurement procedures[29] and established "fast track," a paperless electronic purchasing system, and a local purchasing option that allowed principals and district office managers to buy directly from vendors.

With fast track, principals and local managers no longer had to leaf through voluminous catalogues and telephone a hard-to-reach central administrator to verify whether it was up to date. They could simply turn on their computers to view whether an item was available through the school system and, if so, its price and specifications. Ordering is as simple as entering the item number and quantity in the computer and pressing a button. The result: delivery takes from three to seven weeks from the time a purchase order is submitted (compared to six months to one year under the previous system), while oversight is vastly improved as a result of computerized order tracking.

The local purchasing option allowed principals and district office managers to buy instructional goods directly from vendors so long as they were cheaper or provided better terms than those available through the school system.[30] Principals and local managers, moreover, were not restricted to items on the school system's master list. They could buy almost anything, whether macaroni or microwave ovens, so long as they could justify the item as instructional. (This local option does not apply to computer equipment and photocopiers, which must be ordered centrally.)

These changes were implemented in the schools in 1996 and in the remainder of the system in 1997. Since then Benevento has made many further improvements, including streamlining professional services, introducing on a limited basis a procurement card for small purchases, establishing a new office supplies contract with Staples that includes an internet ordering feature, and establishing a check distribution system for the Teacher's Choice Program.

What is noteworthy is that people are not using their newfound purchasing freedom for illegitimate purposes. A Lexis/Nexis search revealed no cases of anyone abusing the local purchasing option since 1998. The new Special Commissioner of Investigation, Richard Condon, reported that he knew of no cases of local purchasing fraud since the rules were revamped.[31] The acting deputy commissioner, who has been working at the SCI since 1992, reported that the number of corroborated procurement fraud cases involving credit pools has gone down dramatically since procurement was revamped.[32] Further, the SCI's database showed that none of the fraud cases investigated between 2000 and 2001 involved procurement credit cards handed out to select administrators and local managers.[33] As for conspiracies between vendors and employees to circumvent purchasing rules, not a single case has been reported since 1997.

A LAST WORD

As I finish this book, some revolutionary reforms for New York City schools are on the horizon. Mayor Michael Bloomberg, an eminently successful businessman with a communications empire to his name, has courageously persuaded the state legislature to give him the reins to the most complex school system in the nation, ending nearly thirty years of scandal-marred community school decentralization. He has repeatedly expressed the conviction that schools should be the primary unit of improvement and that the central office should be revamped. He has selected as chancellor Joel Klein, an attorney whose resume and professional experience prosecuting Microsoft for antitrust violations suggest an understanding of what it takes to break up a big bureaucracy. The mayor has also recruited a group of world-renowned business leaders to head a new Leadership Academy for school principals.

So far, however, it is hard to tell if principals will be given the tools and freedom they need to actually lead. Amid the euphoria over the prospect of real change, there are also some causes for concern. The organizational structure proposed appears to be one of the most radically recentralized plans for the New York City schools since 1871, when Boss William Marcy Tweed took them over. The mayor now picks the chancellor, who picks all the superintendents without the need for any local input. The mayor now controls the central lay board as well as the school inspector general, which has gone from being one of the most independent offices of its kind in the nation to essentially reporting to the same person who runs the school system. The mayor has moved to abolish what was left of the local community school boards and replace them with Parent Engagement Boards. In light of some of the school system's historical problems with graft, the absence of real external checks and monitors is somewhat alarming. It will be important for New Yorkers in the coming years to restore a greater degree of independence to the office of the Special Commissioner of Investigation and introduce checks by parents.

At the same time, however, precisely because the top now has the power and a mandate for reform, there is a tremendous opportunity to push discretion down to principals and local managers. To realize his vision of the school as the system's most important unit, Bloomberg has to cut through many union rules and central mandates. As an immensely successful businessman, and because he did not rely on organized labor to get elected, Bloomberg has a real opportunity to negotiate a deal that will put principals in charge.

By letting past fears of decentralization, union rules, and interest groups continue to dictate how schools are organized, we risk wasting this window of opportunity. A number of school officials in districts from New York City to Los Angeles have heard about the successes of radically decentralized districts such as Edmonton and Houston. I hope this book has helped show that these new decentralized ways of doing business can work in large districts, if the proper safeguards are in place, and will likely reduce waste and abuse or at least not increase them. Of course, no structural organization, including the one advocated in this book, can answer every problem. But given the crisis our city children face, it is time to change the status quo, stop providing incentives for abuse and waste, and give teachers, principals, and local managers the authority and responsibility to do what so many of them desperately want to do: help children and improve learning.

INTRODUCTION: CORRUPTION AND THE FUTURE OF AMERICA'S GREAT CITY SCHOOLS

1. International Assessment, *Second International Assessment of Educational Progress: 1990–91* (Washington, D.C.: Congressional Budget Office, 1993); U.S. Department of Education, "The Third International Mathematics and Science Study (TIMSS) and Third International Mathematics and Science Study—Repeat (TIMSS-R)," by Cynthia A. Tananis, Steven J. Chrostowski, Nancy R. Bunt, Marcia M. Seeley, and Louis Tamler, Southwest Pennsylvania Regional Benchmarking Report, TIMSS, 1999; "Eighth Grade Mathematics and Science: Achievement for a Workforce Region in a National and International Context," International Study Center, Lynch School of Education, Boston College; available at http://nces.ed.gov/timss.

2. Lester C. Thurow, *Head to Head: The Coming Economic Battle among Japan, America, and Europe* (New York: William Morrow, 1992); Paul E. Peterson, *Our Schools and Our Future: Are We Still at Risk?* (Stanford, Calif.: Hoover Institution, 2003); Louis Gerstner Jr. and Tommy Thompson, "The Problem Isn't the Kids" (op-ed), *New York Times*, December 8, 2000, p. A39.

3. U.S. Department of Education, *supra.*

4. See, for example, Paul Shin, "U.S. Students Fail to Make the Grade," *New York Daily News*, December 6, 2000, p. 8 (in 2000, 77 percent of New York City eighth graders failed to meet the state math standards); Louise Mirrer, executive vice chancellor, City University of New York, testimony before the New York City Council's Higher Education Committee, October 25, 2002.

5. See, for example, Raymond Domanico, "State of the New York City Public Schools 2002," Civic Report no. 26, March 2002.

6. Emanuel Tobier, "New York City's Public Schools: The Facts about Spending and Performance," *Civic Bulletin* 26 (May 2001).

7. Carl Campanile, "Schools Revamping: New Bid to Whip Worst into Shape," *New York Post*, October 15, 2002, p. 12.

8. Carl Campanile and Leah Hanes, "School Halls of Shame," *New York Post*, October 14, 2002, p. 8.

9. I interviewed the architect in Los Angeles in the summer of 2001. To protect his privacy, I have changed his name.

10. Little Hoover Commission, "Teach Our Children Well," September 5, 2001, p. xii.

11. Terry Pristin, "In Survey, Business Leaders Criticize New York Schools: City Said to Turn Out Poor Job Candidates," *New York Times*, September 28, 1998, p. A24, Northeast edition.

12. Coopers and Lybrand L.L.P., "Resource Allocations in the New York City Public Schools," Report for Mayor Rudolph Giuliani and Herman Badillo, special counsel for fiscal oversight of education, October 4, 1994; Abby Goodnough, "Trial Begins in Suit Challenging New York State's Formula for School Funds," *New York Times*, October 13, 1999.

13. Edward Wyatt, "Success of City School Pupils Isn't Simply a Money Matter," *New York Times,* June 14, 2000, p. A1.

14. Tobier, *supra.*

15. *Id.;* Manhattan Institute, *supra.*

16. Diane Ravitch, *Left Back: A Century of Battles of School Reform* (New York: Simon and Schuster, 2001).

17. Ravitch, "Bust the Monopoly" (op-ed), *New York Daily News,* October 12, 2002; Larry Cuban, "Reforming Again, Again, and Again," *Educational Researcher* 19 (1990): 3–13; Richard Elmore and Milbrey McLaughlin, *Steady Work: Policy, Practice, and the Reform of American Education* (Santa Monica, Calif.: Rand Corporation, 1990).

18. Joseph Viteritti, *Across the River: Politics and Education in the City* (New York: Holmes and Meier, 1983).

19. See, for example, Jeffrey R. Henig, Richard C. Hula, Marion Orr, and Desiree S. Pedescleaux, *Color of School Reform: Race, Politics, and the Challenge of Urban Education* (Princeton, N.J.: Princeton University Press, 1999).

20. Rosalind Rossi, "Finance Official Urges Overhaul for Schools: Teachers Would Lose Job Guarantee under Plan," *Chicago Sun-Times,* April 23, 1995, p. 7.

21. Mary Mitchell, "Ex-School Aide Sentenced for Extortion," *Chicago Sun-Times,* May 18, 1996, p. 4.

22. See, generally, John Noonan, *Bribes* (New York: Macmillan, 1984).

23. Peter M. Blau and R. A. Schoenherr, *The Structure of Organizations* (New York: Basic Books, 1971); W. Richard Scott, *Organizations: Rational, Natural, and Open Systems,* 4th ed. (Upper Saddle River, N.J.: Prentice-Hall, 1998).

CHAPTER ONE: PUBLIC EDUCATION AS BIG BUSINESS

1. See, for example, James William Coleman, "The Theory of White-Collar Crime: From Sutherland to the 1990s," in *White-Collar Crime Reconsidered,* ed. Kip Schlegel and David Weisburd (Boston: Northeastern University Press, 1992), 53–77. Coleman argues that "the efforts of a religious organization to 'save souls' or a welfare agency to help the poor seem far less likely to encourage crime than the demand that a private corporation turn a profit or cease to exist" (p. 65).

2. Diane Ravitch, *The Great School Wars: New York City, 1805–1973* (New York: Basic Books, 1974).

3. David Tyack and Elisabeth Hansot, *Managers of Virtue: Public School Leadership in America, 1820–1980* (New York: Basic Books, 1982).

4. Los Angeles, like most cities west of the Mississippi River, did not have this kind of problem in the mid-1800s because its school system did not begin to grow in earnest until the late 1800s.

5. Ravitch, 1974, *supra* at pp. 85–88.

6. *Id.*

7. Charles Nicodemus, "3 Other School Officials Faced Recent Trouble," *Chicago Sun-Times,* June 22, 1995, p. 6.

8. David Tyack and Larry Cuban, *Tinkering toward Utopia: A Century of Public School Reform* (Cambridge, Mass.: Harvard University Press, 1995).

9. John E. Chubb, "The System," in *A Primer on America's Schools,* ed. Terry M. Moe (Stanford, Calif.: Hoover Institution, 2001).

10. National Center for Education Statistics, "Characteristics of the 100 Largest Public

Elementary and Secondary School Districts in the United States: 2000–02," U.S. Department of Education, Office of Educational Research, p. 2.

11. William Ouchi with Lydia Segal, *Making Schools Work* (Simon and Schuster, forthcoming 2003).

12. *Id.*

13. Wyatt, "Success of City School Pupils," *supra*.

14. Erik Hanuschek, Michael Rebell, and Emanuel Tobier (panelists), "New York City's Public Schools: The Facts about Spending and Performance," Center for Civic Innovation, Manhattan Institute, May 2, 2000. The New York City schools' operating budget, moreover, does not include legal judgments and claims and most pensions. The city contributes to pension systems for all employees except those in reimbursable programs, which the Department of Education covers. The city also pays for heat, light, and power to city schools on the basis of cost allocation formulas developed by city agencies.

15. Anemona Hartocollis, "After 4 Years of Crew, Still No Final Grade," *New York Times*, October 14, 1999, p. B1.

16. Michael Burke, director of leasing, Division of School Facilities, New York City Board of Education. Interview by Lydia Segal, April 5, 2002, Long Island City, N.Y.

17. The Board of Education must also serve meals to a number of parochial and private school students.

18. John Sullivan, "School Vendors Charged with Price Fixing," *New York Times*, June 2, 2000, p. B3.

19. National Center for Education Statistics, *supra* at p. 4.

20. Ouchi with Segal, *supra*.

21. Saul Bruckner, principal, Edward R. Murrow High School, New York City Board of Education. Interview by Lydia Segal, May 3, 2002.

22. Edward Wyatt, "School Board to Turn to Outside Advisers," *New York Times*, September 26, 2000, p. B3.

23. Burke, *supra*.

24. If Chicago, another city where the mayor took over the schools, is any indication, however, the new chancellor will have to devote time and personnel to "politicking," regardless of who is in charge.

25. Burke, *supra*.

26. Los Angeles Unified School District, Office of the Inspector General, SR 00-01, "Report of Audit: Pupil Transportation," November 14, 2000.

27. Solomon Moore, "Romer Backs Team to Finish Belmont," *Los Angeles Times*, February 27, 2002, p. B4.

28. Susan Edelman, "Unions Hijack Reform: Critics," *New York Post*, February 13, 2000, p. 18.

29. Selwyn Raab, "Contractor Known for Work on Schools," *New York Times*, May 20, 1994, p. 2, col. 1.

30. Los Angeles Unified School District, Office of the Inspector General, "Annual Report to the Board of Education: Fiscal Year 2001"; Los Angeles Unified School District, Audit OA 00-32.

31. Chicago School Reform Board of Trustees, Office of the Inspector General, "Interim Annual Report: July 1, 1998, to April 30, 1999," Maribeth Vander Weele, inspector general.

32. Raab, *supra*.

33. Los Angeles Unified School District, Internal Audit and Special Investigations Unit, "Annual Report to the Board of Education: Fiscal Year 1999," OIA 99-1; Los Angeles Unified School District, Audit SP 128-99.

34. Chicago School Reform Board of Trustees, Office of Inspector General, "Second Annual Report," December 28, 1995, p. 32.

35. Chris Sheridan, "It Matters How Schools Are Run," *The Plain Dealer,* March 9, 1997, p. 2E; Chicago OIG, "Second Annual Report," 1995, *supra.*

36. See, for example, Raab, *supra.*

37. Sam Dillon, "18 Named in Graft Tied to Projects for School Board," *New York Times,* May 20, 1994, p. A1, col. 4.

38. Eddie Dunne, "Who Killed Dan Conlin?" *Brooklyn Bridge* 2, no. 10 (June 1997): 30–37.

39. Patrice O'Shaughnessy, *New York Daily News,* March 5, 1995, p. 4.

40. Maria Newman, "Bodies' Discovery Revives 6-Year-Old Murder Case," *New York Times,* February 18, 1995, p. 25, col. 5.

41. Sylvia Moreno, "Stein Asks for Criminal Probe of Bronx School District Chief," *New York Newsday,* August 6, 1991, p. 8.

42. *Id.;* Special Commissioner of Investigation for the New York City School District, Edward Stancik, "A System Like No Other: Fraud and Misconduct by New York City School Custodians," November 1992.

43. Special Commissioner of Investigation for the New York City School District, Edward Stancik, "Power, Politics, and Patronage: Education in Community School District 12," April 1993.

44. Selwyn Raab, "School Chief, Now Dead, Is Accused of Stealing," *New York Times,* January 28, 1993, p. B1; Joe Calderone, "3 Charged in $180,000 Fed Scam; South Bronx Antipoverty Money Spent," *New York Newsday,* January 28, 1993, p. 6.

45. Gerry Mullany, " 'It's Just a Mystery'—School District Looking for $1.2 Million," *New York Times,* December 1, 1988, p. B1.

46. Rossi, *supra.*

47. State of New York, "Report and Recommendations of the Joint Legislative Committee to Investigate the Affairs of the City of New York on the Board of Education," February 15, 1922, p. 30.

48. Henig et al., *supra.*

CHAPTER TWO: CHARTING CORRUPTION, WASTE, AND ABUSE

1. Chapter 15 discusses school inspectors general in depth.

2. Since the mayor assumed control over the New York City schools in the summer of 2002, New York City's school inspector general, whose head is indirectly selected by the mayor, has accordingly, for most practical purposes, lost its independence from school management.

3. Chicago's school Office of Inspector General was authorized by 105 ILCS 5/34-201.1, effective November 14, 1993. It was first affiliated with the Chicago School Finance Authority, a body entrusted to oversee the Chicago school system's finances. After the Finance Authority was dismantled in 1995, the OIG started reporting to the then-new Chicago School Board of Trustees by the Amendatory Act (1995) to the Illinois School Code.

4. New York's Special Commissioner of Investigation reports only on its most important cases.

5. See Stanton Wheeler and Mitchell Rothman, "The Organization as Weapon in White-Collar Crime," *Michigan Law Review* 80 (1982): 1403–26.

6. LAUSD IASI, OIA 99-1, *supra.*

7. Some degree of low-level abuse, what Anthony Downs calls "leakage," is inevitable in every bureaucracy; see Anthony Downs, *Bureaucracy* (Boston: Little, Brown and Co., 1967) and Michael C. Jensen, *Foundations of Organizational Strategy* (Cambridge, Mass.: Harvard University Press, 1998). However, this book is concerned with abuse that is sustained and systemic and that harms the agency's mission.

8. William Stanbury and Fred Thompson, "Toward a Political Economy of Government Waste: First Step, Definitions," *Public Administration Review* 55, no. 5 (September/October 1995): 418–27.

9. Although abuse involves deliberate or reckless harm to an agency and gross waste involves grossly negligent harm, distinguishing between the two can be hard. It is difficult to determine whether an employee knew that there was a grave risk that harm would result from his conduct (recklessness) or whether he should have known that grave harm would have resulted (gross negligence). The problem is illuminated by thinkers such as Oliver Wendell Holmes, *The Common Law* (Boston: Little, Brown, and Co., 1963); see also Paul H. Robinson and Jane A. Grall, "Element Analysis in Defining Criminal Liability," *Stanford Law Review* 35 (1983): 681–762, esp. 691–705; Model Penal Code and Commentaries, § 2.02 (General Requirements of Criminal Liability), American Law Institute.

10. The contract is rife with abuses, as described in Chapters 13 and 14.

11. New York City Board of Education, "Memorandum of Understanding between the Board of Education of the City School District of the City of New York and Local 891," 1994.

12. New York City Comptroller, "Board of Education Financial and Operating Practices Pertaining to Custodial Services," 1975, p. 3.

13. Shaila Dewan, "Janitorial Rules Leave Teachers Holding a Mop," *New York Times,* May 28, 2001, p. A1.

14. NYC BOE, "Memorandum of Understanding," *supra.*

15. Dewan, *supra.*

16. Los Angeles Unified School District, Office of Inspector General, "Report of Audit: Payroll Overtime," OA 01-61, June 29, 2001, p. 8.

17. *Id.*

18. "Internal Investigation Alleges Fraud in LA School District's Payroll Division," Associated Press, State and Local Wire, November 26, 1999; "Developments in Los Angeles County: Payroll Fraud Rampant, District Auditor Reports" (news summary), *Los Angeles Times,* November 27, 1999, p. B6.

19. Chicago OIG, 1995, *supra* at pp. 14, 15, 39.

20. *Id.* at p. 14.

21. Although principals may persuade them to carry out their wishes, these employees are hired, fired, assigned, transferred, promoted, and paid by central or regional offices and are accountable to supervisors in those offices.

22. M. David Ermann and Richard Lundman, eds., *Corporate and Governmental Deviance* (New York: Oxford University Press, 1978).

23. New York City Department of Investigation, William Herlands, commissioner of investigation, "Purchase of School Supplies in New York City: Survey of Bureau of Supplies, Board of Education," Report to Hon. Fiorello La Guardia, mayor of the City of New York, December 31, 1942, p. 16.

24. New York City, Commissioner of Accounts, 1917, pp. 5, 6.

25. *Id.* at p. 137.

26. *Id.* at p. 31.

27. New York City Department of Investigation, Patrick McGinley, commissioner, "The Board of Education of the City of New York: A Review of Management Controls, Conclusions, and Recommendations," no. 350/84D, September 1984, p. 12.

28. Marcia Chambers, "School Official Told to Hold Back Data from Goldin," *New York Times,* March 13, 1978, p. A19.

29. NYC DOI, 1984, *supra* at p. 12.

30. *Id.*

31. *Id.* at p. 11.

32. Newman, *supra.*

33. Rossi, *supra.*

34. Better Government Association (Chicago), "Report," May 17, 1995, pp. 8–9.

35. *Id.* at p. 13.

36. See, for example, New York City Mayoral Committee Appointed to Make a Survey of the Bureau of Construction and Maintenance, Department of Education, "Report to Hon. James J. Walker, Mayor of the City of New York," January 3, 1928, pp. 4, 14. The overpayments exposed were for architectural plans.

37. *Id.*

38. Marcia Chambers, "Goldin Finds 'Serious Weaknesses' in Procedures on Schools Supplies," *New York Times,* January 30, 1978, p. A19.

39. Jim Dwyer, "A Textbook Case of Waste," *New York Newsday,* October 10, 1994, p. A2.

40. *Id.* at p. 12.

41. Edward Ranzal, "Handling of School Funds Assailed in Goldin Report," *New York Times,* August 9, 1976, p. 26.

42. NYC DOI, 1942, *supra.*

43. *Id.* at p. 68.

44. "Goldin Assails Board of Education over Awarding of Bus Contracts," *New York Times,* February 18, 1978, p. 40.

45. NYC DOI, 1942, *supra* at p. 57.

46. Richard Perez-Pena, "In School Bus Dispute, Focus Shifts from the Drivers to the Companies," *New York Times,* April 23, 1995, sec. 1, p. 39.

47. Selwyn Raab, "School Bus Pacts Go to Companies with Ties to Mob: No Competitive Bidding," *New York Times,* December 26, 1990, p. A1; Raab, "Officials Say Bus Concerns Cheat School Board on Fees," *New York Times,* December 27, 1990.

48. Los Angeles Unified School District, Office of Inspector General, BE-013, Investigation, 2001.

49. LAUSD OIG, "Annual Report," 2000, *supra.*

50. Los Angeles Unified School District, Office of Inspector General, MF-027, Investigation, 2000; Los Angeles Unified School District, Office of Inspector General, MF-028, Investigation, 2000.

51. The assistant superintendent was placed on a limited contract and subsequently retired. The others implicated, however, continue working in the system although they no longer have overtime assignments.

CHAPTER THREE: WHERE THE MONEY GOES

1. Patricia Hurtado, "Inspectors Guilty of Kickbacks," *Newsday,* April 5, 1989, p. 6; Hurtado, "DA: Inspectors' Bribery Ring Was Systematic," *Newsday,* March 22, 1989, p. 4.

2. *People v. John Manfredi,* 560 N.Y.S. 2d 679 (1990) (Supreme Court of New York, Appellate Division, Second Department).

3. *Id.*

4. "What's Up at the Docks?" (editorial), *New York Daily News,* December 13, 2001, p. 56.

5. "School Custodians Swept into Court in Bribe Scam," *New York Daily News*, February 10, 2003.

6. Leonard Buder, "School Aide Got Job for His Wife," *New York Times*, January 30, 1975. The superintendent had been a consultant for the company in a previous school job in another school district.

7. Laurie Johnston, "Ex-School Aide Tells of Collecting $400,000 as Co-Author of Tests," *New York Times*, April 19, 1977, p. 73.

8. Iver Peterson, "Friend Who Got a School Post Gave Monserrat $3,000 Loan," *New York Times*, October 30, 1975, p. 42; Gene Maeroff, "Monserrat Plans to Leave Post at Board for 6 Months," *New York Times*, June 21, 1975, p. 31.

9. New York State Commission of Investigation, "An Investigation of Certain Contracting Practices and Procedures of the New York City Board of Education and Related Matters," The Temporary Commission of Investigation of the State of New York, David W. Brown, chairman, October 31, 1975; Leonard Buder, "20 Admit Gifts from Concern Doing School Business," *New York Times*, March 16, 1975.

10. Leonard Buder, "2 Ex-Judges to Investigate School Aides' Outside Ties," *New York Times*, December 3, 1974, p. 45.

11. *Id.*

12. Buder, "20 Admit Gifts from Concern Doing School Business," 1975.

13. NY State Commission of Investigation, *supra.*

14. News reports at the time of Stancik's death claimed that the case about the former board member would be released; Kirsten Danis and Carl Campanile, "Ed Stancik, Schools Prober, Dies at 47" (editorial), *New York Post*, March 13, 2002. However, the SCI decided to close the case.

15. New York City Board of Education, Office of Inspector General, Draft Audit Report, "Compliance Audit of: Contingency Account Budget Code 0944, Object Code 403: for Fiscal Years 1990, 1991, 1992 and 1993," by Romeo Rancio, Madlyn Korman, and Stephen Obeng, May 10, 1995.

16. NYC DOI, 1984, *supra* at p. 10.

17. Ralph Blumenthal, "Gold Is Entering Inquiry on Monserrat; May Coordinate with Federal Attorney," *New York Times*, November 29, 1974, p. 43.

18. Max Seigel, "2 Are Indicted in Scheme to Get Pay for Teachers Who Had No-Show Jobs," *New York Times*, January 11, 1978, p. 35.

19. NYC DOI, 1984, *supra.*

20. *Id.* at p. 8.

21. New York City Comptroller, "Audit Report on The New York City Board of Education Controls over Custodial Employees' Work Hours," by Alan Hevesi, March 14, 1996.

22. See, for example, LAUSD, OIG, "Annual Report to the Board of Education," 2000, SP 138–99.

23. See, for example, LAUSD OIG, "Annual Report," 2001, *supra* at p. 47.

24. Chicago OIG, 1995, *supra* at pp. 31, 32; Chicago OIG, 1998–99, *supra.*

25. Chicago OIG, 1995, *supra* at p. 10.

CHAPTER FOUR: THE TOLL ON EDUCATION

1. Robert K. Merton, *Social Theory and Social Structure* (New York: Free Press, 1968); Michael Johnston, *Political Corruption and Public Policy in America* (Monterey, Calif.: Cole, 1982).

2. Michael Johnston, "Comparing Corruption: Participation, Institutions, and Development," paper presented at the conference "Corruption: Public and Private," John Jay

College of Criminal Justice, City University of New York, September 13–14, 2001; Robert Klitgaard, *Controlling Corruption* (Berkeley: University of California Press, 1988).

3. Matthew Purdy and Maria Newman, "Where Patronage Thrives, Students Lag in Districts," *New York Times,* May 13, 1996, p. A1, col. 1. The evidence shows that, on average, school performance in districts where investigators have identified wrongdoing is worse than in other city schools.

4. SCI, "Power, Politics, and Patronage," *supra.*

5. Purdy and Newman, *supra.*

6. Massachusetts Department of State Auditor, "State Auditor's Report on Certain Activities of the Lawrence Public School System: July 1, 1993 through March 31, 1997," 97-6003-9, June 12, 1997.

7. Kate Zernike, "DeNucci Orders Audit of Schools in Lawrence," *Boston Globe,* January 7, 1997, p. A1.

8. New Jersey State Education Department, "Comprehensive Compliance Investigation Report for the Jersey City School District", May 1988; New Jersey State Education Department, "Comprehensive Compliance Investigation Report for the Paterson School District," April 19, 1991; New Jersey State Education Department, "Comprehensive Compliance Investigation Report for the Newark School District," July 1994.

9. NJ SED, 1988, *supra.*

10. *Id.* at p. 4.

11. *Id.;* Victoria Irwin, "Jersey Maps Takeover of School District," *The Christian Science Monitor,* May 25, 1988, p. 3; Ezra Bowen, "When Schools Become Jungles: New Jersey Moves to Take Over a Failing Urban System," *Time,* June 7, 1988, p. 70; Neil MacFarquhar, "Better Finances, But Not Better Test Scores: State Takeover of Schools Has Not Improved Student Performance," *New York Times,* July 9, 1995, p. 29.

12. NJ SED, 1988, *supra* at p. 6.

13. NJ SED, 1994, *supra* at pp. 0010, 0014.

14. *Id.* at p. 0014.

15. *Id.* at p. 0015.

16. *Id.* at p. 0011.

17. *Id.* at p. 0014.

18. NJ SED, 1991, *supra.*

19. See, for example, Thomas Kellaghan, Kathryn Sloane, and Benjamin Alvarez, *The Home Environment and School Learning: Promoting Parental Involvement in the Education of Children* (San Francisco: Jossey-Bass, 1993).

20. James S. Coleman, E. Q. Campbell, C. J. Hobson, J. McPartland, A. M. Mood, F. D. Weinfeld, and R. L. York, *Equality of Educational Opportunity* (Washington, D.C.: U.S. Government Printing Office, 1966); Eric Hanushek, *Making Schools Work: Improving Performance and Controlling Costs* (Washington, D.C.: Brookings Institution, 1994); Gary Burtless, ed., *Does Money Matter? The Effect of School Resources on Student Achievement and Adult Success* (Washington, D.C.: Brookings Institution, 1996).

21. See, for example, Rob Greenwald, Larry V. Hedges, and Richard D. Laine, "The Effect of School Resources on Student Achievement," *Review of Educational Research* 66, no. 3 (fall 1996): 361; B. D. Spencer and D. E. Wiley, "The Sense and the Nonsense of School Effectiveness," *Journal of Policy Analysis and Management* 1 (1981): 43–52.

22. Coopers and Lybrand L.L.P., *supra.*

23. NJ SED, 1994, *supra* at p. 0014.

24. Leonard Buder, "School Suspends 3 in Lunches Inquiry," *New York Times,* September 2, 1976, p. 1; Buder, "School Aide Getting $250,000 Fine," *New York Times,* February 2, 1977, p. B2.

25. State of New York Moreland Act Commission on New York City Schools, "Building Better Schools: A Critical Examination of How New York City Builds and Maintains Its Public Schools," Roslynn R. Mauskopf, chair, August 2002; Los Angeles Unified School District, Office of the Inspector General, "Report of Findings: Proposition BB Bond Program," IG 00-21, March 28, 2000.

26. Murray Weiss, "Ex-Queens School Boss Targeted in Kickback Probe," *New York Post,* September 28, 2000, p. 4.

27. Murray Weiss, "5 Rosedale Homes Focus of Probe," *New York Post,* September 28, 2000, p. 4.

28. Weiss, "Ex-Queens School Boss Targeted," 2000, *supra.*

29. Regina Loughran, acting commissioner, Special Commissioner of Investigation for the New York City School District, telephone interview by Lydia Segal, May 21, 2002, New York City.

30. Sarah Kershaw, "In Decade, Queens School District Slips from Desirable to Troubled," *New York Times,* November 9, 2000, p. D1; "Test Scores Show Dist. 29 Needs a Super," *New York Newsday,* October 25, 2001, p. A42.

31. See, for example, "What's Up at the Docks," *New York Daily News, supra.*

32. Ronald F. Ferguson, "Paying for Public Education: New Evidence on How and Why Money Matters," *Harvard Journal on Legislation* 28 (summer 1991): 465–98.

33. See, for example, Maureen Edwards, "Building Condition: Parental Involvement and Student Achievement in the D.C. Public School System," Washington, D.C., 1992; Carol Cash, "A Study of the Relationship between School Building Condition and Student Achievement and Behavior," Blacksburg, Va., 1993; Eric Hines, "Building Condition and Student Achievement and Behavior," Blacksburg, Va.

34. Edwards, *supra.*

35. SCI, "Power, Politics, and Patronage," *supra.*

36. New York City Joint Commission on Integrity in the Public Schools, Kevin Gill, chairman, "The New Tammany Hall," April 1990.

37. Purdy and Newman, *supra.*

38. NJ SED, 1988, *supra.*

39. *Id.*

40. Sam Dillon, "Testing Power, Cortines Will Seize 6 Bad Schools," *New York Times,* April 29, 1994, p. A1, col. 2; Liz Willen, "Ultimatum on Principal," *Newsday,* July 29, 1994, p. A26.

41. SCI, "Power, Politics, and Patronage," *supra.*

42. *Id.*

43. *Rutan v. Republican Party of Illinois,* 110 S. Ct. 2729, 497 U.S. 62 (1990).

44. Klitgaard, *supra* at p. 33 (italics removed).

45. Henig et al., *supra.*

46. Larry Rother, "Teacher Given a Promotion Says She Gave Chief a Loan," *New York Times,* February 19, 1986, p. B1.

47. Los Angeles Unified School District, Office of the Inspector General, "Annual Report to the Board of Education," Fiscal Year 2002.

48. *Id.* at pp. 19–21; LAUSD OIG, "Annual Report," 2001, p. 29.

49. Chicago OIG, 1995, *supra* at p. 36.

50. Chicago OIG, 1997, *supra.*

51. SCI, "Power, Politics, and Patronage," *supra.*

52. Peg Tyre, "Officials Indicted in Bribe Probe," *Newsday,* May 20, 1994, p. A7.

53. Chicago OIG, 1995, *supra* at p. 39.

54. Built-in waste is not the hidden cost associated with achieving legitimate, reasonable goals such as honoring employee due process and democratic procedures. Rather, it occurs when regulatory procedures, the decision-making process, and entitlements become unreasonable and unnecessary and cost more than they save or protect.

CHAPTER FIVE: THE QUEST FOR ACCOUNTABILITY

1. Michael C. Jensen and William H. Meckling, "The Nature of Man," *Journal of Applied Corporate Finance* 7, no. 2 (summer 1994): 4–19; Travis Hirschi and M. Gottfredson, "Causes of White-Collar Crime," *Criminology* 25 (1987): 949–74.

2. See, for example, Lawrence Cohen and Marcus Felson, "Social Change and Crime Rate Trends: A Routine Activities Approach," *American Sociological Review* 44 (1979): 588–608; James Q. Wilson, *Thinking about Crime,* rev. ed. (New York: Vintage Books, 1983); Derek Cornish and Ronald Clarke, eds., *The Reasoning Criminal: Rational Choice Perspectives on Offending* (New York: Springer Verlag, 1986).

3. George B. Vold and Thomas J. Bernard, *Theoretical Criminology,* 3d ed. (New York: Oxford University Press, 1986); David O. Friedrichs, *Trusted Criminals: White-Collar Crime in Contemporary Society* (Belmont, Calif.: Wadsworth, 1996); R. Paternoster and S. Simpson, "A Rational Choice Theory of Corporate Crime," in *Routine Activity and Rational Choice,* ed. R. V. Clarke and M. Felson (New Brunswick, N.J.: Transaction, 1993), 37–58.

4. M. Spence and R. Zeckhouser, "Insurance, Information, and Individual Action," *American Economic Review* 61, no. 2 (May 1971): 380–87; S. A. Ross, "The Economic Theory of Agency: The Principal's Problems," *American Economic Review* 63, no. 2 (May 1973): 134–39.

5. Jensen, 1998; Armen A. Alchian and Harold Demsetz, "Production, Information Costs, and Economic Organization," *American Economic Review* 62, no. 5 (1972): 777–95.

6. Paul C. Light, *Monitoring Government: Inspectors General and the Search for Accountability* (Washington, D.C.: Brookings Institution, 1993); Lydia Segal, "Corruption Moves to the Center: An Analysis of New York's 1996 School Governance Law," *Harvard Journal on Legislation* 36, no. 2 (summer 1999): 323–67.

7. Michael Barzelay with Babak Armajani, *Breaking through Bureaucracy: A New Vision of Management in Government* (Berkeley: University of California Press, 1992).

8. There are, of course, other forms of accountability. See, generally, Barbara S. Romzek and Melvin J. Dubnick, "Accountability in the Public Sector: Lessons from the Challenger Tragedy," *Public Administration Review* 47, no. 3 (May/June 1987): 227–38.

9. Oliver Williamson, *Corporate Control and Business Behavior: An Inquiry into the Effects of Organization Form on Enterprise Behavior* (Englewood Cliffs, N.J.: Prentice-Hall, 1970), p. 131.

10. Dennis F. Thompson, *Ethics in Congress* (Washington, D.C.: Brookings Institution, 1995).

11. William Clark, director, Financial and Administrative Services, Chicago Public Schools, Department of Procurement and Contracts. Interview by Lydia Segal as part of the School Design Project, October 23, 2001.

12. Jacqueline Goldwyn Kingon, "A View from the Trenches," *New York Times,* Education Life (sec. 4A), April 8, 2001, p. 30.

13. A 1995 Illinois law gave Chicago's mayor the authority to appoint all seven members of the central board. By law, the central board was to consist of five members until 1999, when it was to expand to seven.

14. A 2002 state law allowed New York City's mayor to select eight of its central board's thirteen members, including the chancellor, who serves on the board. The remaining five members are chosen by each of the city's five borough presidents, as before the 2002 law.

15. Lawrence A. Cremin, *The Transformation of the School: Progressivism in American Education, 1876–1957* (New York: Knopf, 1961).

16. Ravitch, 1974, *supra* at pp. 403–4.

17. LAUSD OIG, "Annual Report," 2001, *supra*.

18. See, for example, Chicago OIG, 1995, *supra* at p. 28; Chicago OIG, 1998–99; LAUSD OIG, "Annual Report," 2001, *supra* at pp. 39–40.

19. I interviewed this official on October 22, 2002, at his office in the Chicago Public School headquarters for the School Design Project. I am keeping his name confidential.

20. The Chicago Public School headquarters are located in a high-rise on an entire block at 125 South Clark Street.

21. The LAUSD superintendent receives direct reports from approximately twenty-seven offices, some quite specialized, ranging from the division of Chandra Smith, to the Division of Environmental Health and Safety and the Division of Facilities (Central Support System Chart, Los Angeles Unified School District, Multiple District Plan, October 30, 2001).

22. Chicago is in the process of further decentralizing its six regions. Each region will be further subdivided into four instructional areas: three areas for elementary schools and one for high schools. Each elementary school subunit will have three people in it.

23. These include two rarely mentioned districts: the Chancellor's High School District (District 74) and the Charter Schools District (District 84).

24. The exception was Community School District 2 in Manhattan, which oversaw six high schools in addition to elementary and middle schools.

25. Jacques Steinberg, "Crew Seeks to Overhaul New York City School Bureaucracy," *New York Times*, March 5, 1996, p. B2.

26. I interviewed this local district superintendent, whose name I am keeping confidential, on July 5, 2001. For an in-depth discussion of school district resistance to decentralization, see Paul Hill, "A Public Education System for the New Metropolis," *Education and Urban Society* 29 (August 1997): 490–508.

CHAPTER SIX: THE CENTRALIZATION MESS

1. Minutes of the Board of Education meeting of November 22, 1854, in *Journal of the BOE of the City of New York* (New York: William C. Bryant and Co., 1854).

2. *Id.*

3. Minutes of BOE meeting of January 18, 1854, *Journal of the BOE, supra* at pp. 13–15.

4. Minutes of BOE meeting of March 1, 1854, *Journal of the BOE, supra* at pp. 37–44, 48.

5. Frank Anechiarico and James B. Jacobs, *The Pursuit of Absolute Integrity: How the Anti-Corruption Project Makes Government Inefficient* (Chicago: Chicago University Press, 1996).

6. Ravitch, 1974, *supra* at pp. 71, 84–88.

7. Lincoln Steffins, *Shame of Cities* (New York: Peter Smith, 1948); Lydia Segal, "Can We Fight the New Tammany Hall? Difficulties of Prosecuting Political Patronage and Suggestions for Reform," *Rutgers Law Review* 50, no. 2 (February 1998): 507–62.

8. Richard Hofstadter, *Age of Reform* (New York: Vintage Books, 1955); Frederick Taylor, *The Main Beliefs of Scientific Management* (New York: Harper and Brothers, 1911).

9. Tyack and Hansot, 1982, *supra* at p. 157.

10. *Id.*

11. Segal, 1999, *supra.*

12. The source for this information was an upper-level official in the New York City Schools Division of Financial Operations. I interviewed him on April 8, 2002, and have changed his name to Mr. Rossi.

13. Today schools that have a concentration of more than 50 percent poor children can apply for a waiver to use Title I funds for schoolwide improvement, so long as it services poor children.

14. Judith Rosenberg Raftry, *Land of Fair Promise: Politics and Reform in Los Angeles Schools, 1885–1941* (Stanford, Calif.: Stanford University Press, 1992).

15. New York City Board of Education, "Report of the Chancellor's Commission on the Capital Plan," Peter M. Lehrer, chair, 2002.

16. New York City Board of Education, "A Source Document on Custodians and Custodial Helpers," January 1977; New York City Board of Education, "Memorandum of Understanding," 1987, *supra.*

17. It is difficult to compare the incidence of corruption over time, even within the same organization, because rules, laws, and societal expectations and definitions of wrongdoing may change, as may the intensity and degree of scrutiny and law enforcement activity. However, the only realistic way to estimate the incidence of corruption in an organization is by analyzing the number and severity of publicly released investigations, arrests, indictments, and convictions. This analysis is based on such numbers.

18. New York City Board of Education, "Procurement of Essential Professional Services in Standard Operating Procedures Manual," Office of Purchasing Management, 2002, 65–77.

19. *Id.* at pp. 25–30, under "What Must I Know about Contracts, Bids and Non-list Items?"

20. NYC DOI, 1942, *supra.*

21. Ranzal, "Schools Accused on Contract Bids," *New York Times,* August 1, 1976.

22. NYC DOI, 1984, *supra* at p. 12.

23. Doug Smith, "Judge Dismisses Charges against School Contractors," *Los Angeles Times,* May 12, 1994, p. B4.

24. NYC DOI, 1984, *supra.*

25. Ranzal, 1976, *supra.*

26. NYC DOI, 1984, *supra.* See also NYC BOA, "Standard Operating Procedures Manual," pp. 25–30. In response to such scandals, the BOE now requires that, if expenditures associated with the same vendor exceed $5,000 in a fiscal year, officials must solicit three written bids for additional purchases from that vendor. But since audits are sporadic and post factum, officials can take a chance on being audited after the fact.

27. Ranzal, 1976, *supra.*

28. "Ex-L.A. Unified Employee Pleads Guilty in Bribe Case" (news summary), *Los Angeles Times,* June 28, 2000, p. B4.

29. Doug Smith, "Judge Dismisses Charges against School Contractors," *Los Angeles Times,* May 12, 1999, p. B4.

30. Los Angeles Unified School District, Internal Audit and Special Investigations Unit, "Annual Report to the Board of Education," Fiscal Year 1999, OSI 99–1.

31. See, for example, Chicago OIG, "Interim Annual Report: July 1, 1998 to April 30, 1999," *supra.*

32. Better Government Association (Chicago), "Report," May 17, 1995.

CHAPTER SEVEN: TOWARD A THEORY OF SCHOOL WASTE AND FRAUD

1. Susan Rose-Ackerman, *Corruption: A Study in Political Economy* (New York: Academic Press, 1978); Klitgaard, *supra.* I do not address microlevel theories about individual psychological traits and propensities toward corruption because I do not have enough data to draw conclusions about them.

2. See, for example, James Q. Wilson, "Corruption: The Shame of the States," *Public Interest* 2 (1966): 28–38; Ronald Wraith and Edgar Simpkins, *Corruption in Developing Countries* (New York: W. W. Norton, 1963).

3. Richard Griswold del Castillo, *The Los Angeles Barrio, 1850–1890: A Social History* (Berkeley: University of California Press, 1979).

4. Allan N. Kornblum, *The Moral Hazards: Strategies for Honesty and Ethical Behavior* (Lexington, Mass.: Lexington Books, 1976).

5. Solomon Gross, "Bureaucracy and Decision-making Viewed from a Patrol Precinct Level," *Police Chief* 42 (January 1975): 59–64.

6. Anechiarico and Jacobs, *supra.*

7. See, for example, Commission to Investigate Allegations of Police Corruption and the City's Anti-Corruption Procedures (Knapp Commission), 1973; Ralph E. Anderson, "Police Integrity: Accent on the Positive," *Police Chief* 40 (December 1973): 38ff.; "Report of the Special Counsel on the Los Angeles Sheriff's Department" (Kolts Commission), James G. Kolts, chairman, 1992; Warren Independent Commission on the Los Angeles Police Department (Christopher Commission), Warren Christopher, chairman, 1991; J. E. Conklin, *Illegal but Not Criminal: Business Crime in America* (Englewood Cliffs, N.J.: Prentice-Hall, 1977); M. Dowie, "Pinto Madness," in *Crisis in American Institutions,* ed. J. Skolnick and E. Currie, 4th ed. (Boston: Little, Brown and Co., 1979); M. B. Clinard and P. C. Yeager, *Corporate Crime* (New York: Free Press, 1980).

8. Edward Gross, "Organizational Structure and Organizational Crime," in *White-Collar Crime: Theory and Research,* ed. G. Geis and E. Stotland (Beverly Hills, Calif.: Sage Publications, 1980), 52–77.

9. Blau and Schoenherr, *supra.*

10. Williamson, 1970, *supra.*

11. Jerald Hage and Michael Aiken, "Program Change and Organizational Properties: A Comparative Analysis," *American Journal of Sociology* 72, no. 3 (1967): 503–19; Oliver Williamson, *Markets and Hierarchy: Analysis and Antitrust Implications* (New York: Free Press, 1975).

12. Williamson, 1970, *supra;* Gordon Tullock, *The Politics of Bureaucracy* (Washington, D.C.: Public Affairs Press, 1965); Downs, *supra;* Jensen, 1998, *supra;* Terry M. Moe, "The New Economics of Organization," *American Journal of Political Science* 28 (November 1984): 739–77; Jay B. Barney and William Ouchi, eds., *Organizational Economics: Toward a New Paradigm for Understanding and Studying Organizations* (San Francisco: Jossey-Bass, 1986), 187–204.

13. Technology can raise the threshold at which oversight starts to break down, but it cannot make bounded rationality disappear.

14. Little Hoover Commission, "Recommendations for Improving the School Facilities Program in the Los Angeles Unified School District," November 3, 1999 (available on the Web at little.hoover@lhc.ca.gov).

15. Sylvia Moreno, "District 4's Money Man Gets the Ax," *New York Newsday,* October 31, 1989, p. 4.

16. Little Hoover Commission, 1999, *supra* at p. 12.

17. See, for example, Robert E. Lane, *The Regulation of Businessmen: Social Conditions of Government Control* (New Haven, Conn.: Yale University Press, 1954), p. 98.

18. See, for example, Clinard and Yeager, *supra* at p. 130; Marshall Schminke, "Considering the Business in Business Ethics: An Exploratory Study of the Influence of Organizational Size and Structure on Individual Ethical Predispositions (Part II)," *Journal of Business Ethics* 30, no. 4 (April 2001): 375–90.

19. J. W. Frederickson, "The Comprehensiveness of Strategic Decision Processes: Extension, Observations, Future Directions," *Academy of Management Journal* 27 (1984): 445–66; S. Wally and J. R. Baum, "Personal and Structural Determinants of the Pace of Strategic Decision Making," *Academy of Management Journal* 37 (1994): 932–56.

20. David Tyack, *The One Best System: A History of American Urban Education* (Cambridge, Mass.: Harvard University Press, 1974).

21. James Allen Jr., commissioner of education, State of New York, "Report on New York City School Reorganization," by Mark C. Schinnerer, consultant on New York City Reorganization, State Education Department, December 26, 1961. This report recommended decentralizing certain aspects of administration so that top officials' time would not be so consumed with detail work that they would not have time to deal adequately with difficult problems of far-reaching significance (see p. 19).

22. *Id.* at p. 22.

23. James Q. Wilson, *Bureaucracy: What Government Agencies Do and Why They Do It* (New York: Basic Books, 1989).

24. Susan Sachs, "As New York Immigration Thrives, Diversity Widens," *New York Times,* November 8, 1999, p. A24, Northeast edition.

25. For the inability of overworked executives to oversee operations, see generally John Kleinig, *Ethics of Policing Cambridge* (Cambridge, England: Cambridge University Press, 1996), especially p. 211; Dennis F. Thompson, *Political Ethics and Public Choice* (Cambridge, Mass.: Harvard University Press, 1987), chpt. 2.

26. Williamson, 1970, *supra;* Barney and Ouchi, *supra.*

27. Williamson, 1970, *supra* at p. 25; Tullock, *supra* at pp. 142–93; Downs, *supra* at p. 143; Jensen, 1998, *supra* at p. 117.

28. See, generally, Richard H. Hall, *Organizations: Structure and Process* (Englewood Cliffs, N.J.: Prentice-Hall, 1982), especially chpt. 9. Hall points out that when many subordinates have high levels of expertise, upward communication is inhibited.

29. New York City Office of the Comptroller, Bureau of Management Audit EDP Audit Division, "Data Integrity and Reliability of Board of Education Personnel/Payroll Computer Records," Audit 7A95-108, by Alan Hevesi, June 24, 1996.

30. *Id.*

31. Institute for Education and Social Policy, "Second Annual Report: Evaluation of the Performance Driven Budgeting Initiative of the New York City Board of Education," September 1998–August 1999, by Dorothy Siegel, Erica Zurer, and Norm Fruchter, May 2000, p. 101.

32. Los Angeles County Civil Grand Jury, "Final Report," June 2001, p. 81.

33. *Id.* at p. 81.

34. *Id.* at p. 75.

35. Rose-Ackerman, who describes four catch-all bureaucratic models, would probably categorize this as a fragmented or sequential bureaucratic model, because each bureaucrat has his or her own particular powers that are, for most purposes, unreviewable by others. Each functions as an independent, specialized expert. See Rose-Ackerman, chpt. 9.

36. Los Angeles Unified School District, Internal Audit and Special Investigations Unit, Belmont Part II, "Report of Findings: Part II: Belmont Learning Complex," OSI 99-20, December 13, 1999; California State Auditor/Bureau of State Audits, "Los Angeles Unified School District: Its School Site Selection Process Fails to Provide Information Necessary for Decision Making and to Effectively Engage the Community," Report no. 99123, December 1999.

37. Los Angeles Unified School District, Office of the Inspector General, "Annual Report to the Board of Education," OSI 99-20, Fiscal Year 2000.

38. LAUSD IASI, "Belmont," 1999, *supra* at p. 4.

39. LAUSD OIG, "Annual Report," 2000, *supra* at p. 13.

40. Little Hoover Commission, 2000, *supra* at p. vii; Little Hoover Commission, 1999, *supra*.

CHAPTER EIGHT: WATCHING THE PENNIES

1. I interviewed this LAUSD official, whose name I am keeping confidential as a protection of privacy, in Los Angeles on July 6, 2001.

2. Tyack and Hansot, *supra* at p. 157.

3. Peter F. Drucker, *Management Challenges for the Twenty-first Century* (New York: Harper Business, 1999).

4. Anechiarico and Jacobs, *supra*.

5. Aaron Wildavsky, *The Politics of the Budgetary Process* (Boston: Little, Brown, 1974), p. 3.

6. I interviewed this officer by telephone on December 18, 2002. To protect his privacy, I am keeping his name confidential.

7. LAUSD OIG, "Annual Report," 2001, *supra* at p. 11.

8. Klitgaard, *supra* at pp. 24–25.

9. *Id.* at p. 26, fig. 1.

10. Current school districts appear to be pursuing the goal, at least on paper, of absolute moral integrity, although this seems to be due not to any philosophical belief but to inertia.

11. Even from a moral standpoint, not all corruption and waste are equally blameworthy and not all crimes are equally serious. Negligent wrongs are less culpable than intentional ones. Some crimes are inherently and universally evil, known in the law as *mala in se*. Others are crimes simply because a law prohibits them at a particular time in a particular society; these are known as *mala prohibita*.

12. Little Hoover Commission, 1999, *supra*.

13. I interviewed these officials on July 2, 2001, in Santa Monica, California, as part of the School Design Project. I am keeping their names confidential to protect their privacy.

14. Little Hoover Commission, 1999, *supra*.

15. Ann Berger. I have changed this teacher's real name to protect her privacy. I interviewed her by telephone on April 27, 2002, and in person at her school in Manhattan in May 2002.

16. W. Edwards Deming, "Improvement of Quality and Productivity through Action by Management," *National Productivity Review* (winter 1981–82): 12–22.

17. Moss Kanter points out that in "segmented" organizations, where employees work on parts of problems in isolated divisions, people gradually lose awareness of how their work

fits in the whole. See Rosabeth Moss Kanter, *The Change Masters* (New York: Simon and Schuster, 1983), pp. 28, 29.

18. New York City Council, "School Maintenance Operations," October 1993.

19. I interviewed this architect at his office on July 2, 2001, as part of the School Design Project. I am keeping his name confidential to protect his privacy.

20. Institute of Education and Social Policy, "Focus on Learning: A Report on Reorganizing General and Special Education in New York City," by Norm Fruchter, Robert Berne, Ann Marcus, Mark Alter, and Jay Gottlieb, October 1995, New York University, p. 32.

21. Kathleen M. Dunn, "TQM at George Westinghouse Vocational High School: A Model for Quality in New York City Public Education," paper for MGGB 7621, Dr. Martha Mooney, Fordham University, Winter 1994.

22. I have changed the principal's real name to Mr. Alexander to safeguard his privacy. I interviewed him on May 3, 2002, at his school in New York City.

23. LAUSD OIG, "Proposition BB Bond Program," IG 00-21, 2000, *supra* at p. 91.

24. *Id.*

25. I interviewed Mr. Rossi in his office on April 8, 2002. I have changed his name to try to protect his privacy. Note that the cost of $125 was in 2001; it can be expected to be higher today.

26. BOE reimbursement rules do not have a minimum expenditure. So long as it is a legitimate business expense, officials are entitled to get their money back.

27. Rossi, 2002.

28. *Id.*

29. LAUSD OIG, "Proposition BB Bond Program," IG 00-21, 2000, *supra.*

30. *Id.* at pp. 113, 142. The scope and design of the work was so vague that contractors "were never sure what the scope of their work was."

31. *Id.* at p. 130.

32. *Id.* at p. 133.

33. *Id.* at p. 126.

34. *Id.* at p. 114.

35. LAUSD OIG, "Annual Report," 2001, *supra.*

36. LAUSD OIG, "Accounts Payable Process," OA 01-60, 2001, *supra* at p. 20.

37. *Id.* at pp. 8–9.

38. *Id.* at pp. 13, 22.

39. *Id.* at p. 18.

40. *Id.* at p. 122.

41. *Id.* at p. 108.

42. *Id.* at p. 125.

43. See, for example, LAUSD OIG, "Accounts Payable Process," OA 01-60, 2001, *supra* at p. 114.

44. See, for example, LAUSD OIG, "Proposition BB Bond Program," IG 00-21, 2000, *supra.*

45. I interviewed this architect over the telephone on September 25, 2001. I am keeping his name confidential to protect his privacy.

46. I interviewed this principal on July 6, 2001, as part of the School Design Project. I am keeping her name confidential to protect her privacy.

47. Don Mullinax, inspector general, Los Angeles Unified School District. Interview by William Ouchi and Lydia Segal, July 6, 2001, Los Angeles, for the School Design Project.

48. "Anker Set to Run District in Bronx," *New York Times,* November 28, 1974.

49. New York City Commissioner of Accounts, "Bureau of Supplies, Department of Education, City of New York: Examination of Its Accounts and Methods," by Leonard Wallstein, 1917, p. 5.

50. I interviewed this Los Angeles neighborhood leader over the telephone on September 25, 2001. I am keeping his name confidential to protect his privacy.

51. State of New York Moreland Act Commission, 2002, *supra.*

52. *Id.*

53. Don Mullinax, inspector general, Los Angeles Unified School District. Interview by Lydia Segal, April 2, 2003.

54. Frank Anechiarico, paper presented for the conference "Corruption: Public and Private," John Jay College of Criminal Justice, City University of New York, September 13–14, 2002.

CHAPTER NINE: THE COST OF MANAGERIAL PARALYSIS

1. Friedrich Hayek, "The Use of Knowledge in Society," *American Economic Review* 35, no. 3 (1945): 519–30, especially p. 524; Wilson, 1989, *supra;* Jensen, 1998, *supra;* Michael C. Jensen and William H. Meckling, "Specific and General Knowledge and Organizational Structure," in *Contract Economics,* ed. Lars Werin and Hans Wijkander (Oxford, England: Blackwell, 1992).

2. Hayek, *supra* at p. 524.

3. Wilson, 1989, *supra.*

4. Samuel Casey Carter, *No Excuses* (Washington, D.C.: Heritage Foundation, 1999).

5. John Chubb and Terry Moe, *Politics, Markets, and America's Schools* (Washington, D.C.: Brookings Institution, 1990).

6. Public Agenda, "Trying to Stay Ahead of the Game: Superintendents and Principals Talk about School Leadership," New York City, November 2001.

7. James Traub, "In Theory: A School of Your Own," *New York Times,* April 4, 1999, sec. 4A, p. 30, col. 1.

8. Alexander, *supra.*

9. The money discussed here is noncategorical and not pre-earmarked by an outside agency for a particular purpose.

10. The federal government, for instance, earmarks "categorical funds" for specific purposes, such as helping destitute children in poor schools; states may earmark certain funds for purposes such as buying textbooks; and cities may earmark funds for various programs on which local politicians want to leave their mark, such as art classes or technology.

11. This money is referred to as "tax levy" in New York City.

12. Some programs, such as drug prevention, come with very strict conditions to make sure the money goes only to the targeted group. Other programs allow for more flexibility, particularly if they are not bound by class size mandates.

13. Ouchi with Segal, *supra.*

14. Alexander, *supra.*

15. Mary Walton, *The Deming Management Methods* (New York: Perigee Books, 1986); Deming, *supra* at pp. 12–22.

16. William Triant, "Autonomy and Innovation: How Do Massachusetts Charter Schools

Principals Use Their Freedom?" Thomas B. Fordham Foundation, December 2001, p. 1 (available at http://www.edexcellence.net/cgi-bin/search/search.cgi?terms=triant).

17. See, generally, Dale Ballou, "The New York City Teachers' Union Contract: Shackling Principals' Leadership," *Civic* 6 (June 1999): 1–29.

18. I interviewed this principal, Mr. Alberts, on May 3, 2002, at his school in New York City. I have changed his name to protect his privacy.

19. Anemona Hartocollis, "Teacher Hiring Plan Is More Than a Matter of Decree," *New York Times,* September 2, 2000, p. B1.

20. Although the Chicago Public Schools' central office can influence teacher hiring by screening candidates and defining what certificates are required for what subjects, principals there have greater discretion in hiring teachers than do their counterparts in New York City and Los Angeles.

21. Ca. Ed. Code 44660–44665.

22. Ballou, *supra.*

23. Maribeth Vander Weele catalogues the difficulties in firing underperforming principals in Chicago; see Vander Weele, *Reclaiming Our Schools: The Struggle for Chicago School Reform* (Chicago: Loyola University Press, 1994).

24. Alberts, *supra.*

25. Pamela A. Riley with Rosemarie Fusano, Larae Munk, and Ruben Peterson, "Contract for Failure: The Impact of Teacher Union Contracts on the Quality of California Schools," Pacific Research Institute for Public Policy, September 2001.

26. Alberts, *supra.*

27. *Id.*

28. Alexander, *supra.*

29. "Exempt" refers to employees who do not have to take a test to get their job.

30. "Little Hoover Commission Report," *Daily News of Los Angeles,* November 14, 1999, p. V1; Little Hoover Commission, 1999, *supra.*

31. The number of exempt employees in New York would increase slightly, however, if it included noncentral personnel, such as high school and community school district superintendents.

32. Hall, *supra;* Robert Denhardt and Janet Denhardt, "Leadership for Change: Case Studies in American Local Government," Report for the PricewaterhouseCoopers Endowment for the Business of Government, September 1999; Charles A. O'Reilly and Karlene H. Roberts, "Information Filtration in Organizations: Three Experiments," *Organizational Behavior and Human Performance* 11, no. 2 (April 1974): 253–65.

33. See, generally, O'Reilly and Roberts, *supra.*

34. This figure includes acting chancellors.

35. LAUSD OIG, "Annual Report," 2001, *supra* at p. 15.

36. I interviewed this former New York City school official on October 19, 2001, in New York City. I am keeping the name confidential.

37. I interviewed this former chancellor as part of the School Design Project on July 6, 2001. I am keeping his name confidential to protect his privacy.

38. California State Auditor/Bureau of State Audits, "Summary of Report Number 99123, Los Angeles Unified School District," December 1999; LAUSD OIG, "Annual Report," 2000, *supra;* Little Hoover Commission, 1999, *supra.*

39. Duke Helfand, "School Repairs Face $600-Million Shortfall," *Los Angeles Times,* November 29, 2001.

40. Recently there has been discussion of possibly finishing the project for an additional $68 million to $88 million; see Moore, *supra.*

CHAPTER TEN: CREATIVE NONCOMPLIANCE

1. See, for example, Gil Geis, "White-Collar Crime: The Heavy Electrical Equipment Antitrust Cases of 1961," in *Criminal Behavior Systems: A Typology,* ed. M. Clinard and R. Quinney (New York: Holt, Rinehart and Winston, 1967), 139–51 (in Geis's study of the heavy electrical equipment industry from the 1930s to the 1950s, for instance, manufacturers encouraged illegal price fixing by employees as a response to market pressures); Harvey Farberman, "A Criminogenic Market Structure: The Automobile Industry," *Sociological Quarterly* 16: 438–57; William Leonard and Marvin Weber, "Automakers and Dealers: A Study of Criminogenic Market Forces," *Law and Society Review* 4: 407–10; John Braithwaite, "Criminological Theory and Organizational Crime," *Justice Quarterly* 6 (1989): 333–58; R. A. Kagan and J. T. Scholz, "The Criminology of the Corporation and Regulatory Enforcement Strategies," in *Enforcing Regulation,* ed. K. Hawkinds and J. M. Thomas (Boston: Kluwer-Nijhoff, 1984), 67–96.

2. See, for example, Peter DeLeon, *Thinking about Political Corruption* (Armonk, N.Y.: M. E. Sharpe, 1993), and Rose-Ackerman, *supra.*

3. DeLeon, *supra;* Klitgaard, *supra;* R. C. Kramer, "Corporate Crime: An Organizational Perspective," in *White-Collar and Economic Crime,* ed. P. Wickman and T. Dailey (Lexington, Mass.: Lexington Books, 1982), 75–94.

4. "Finding What Really Works in Education" (panel discussion), *Chief Executive* 94 (May 1994): 48; Seymour Fliegel with James McGuire, *Miracle in East Harlem: The Fight for Choice in Public Education* (New York: Times Books, 1993).

5. I interviewed the CPS school inspector general in Chicago on October 22, 2001, for the School Design Project. She has since stepped down from that post.

6. I interviewed this official on April 18, 2002, in his Community School District office. I am keeping his name confidential to protect his privacy.

7. *Id.*

8. Sanchez, 2001. I interviewed this former principal in Los Angeles on July 6, 2001, as part of the School Design Project. I changed her name to protect her privacy.

9. Special Commissioner of Investigation for the New York City School District, "An Investigation into the Sex Crime Conviction of Former Personnel Administrator Jerry Olshaker and the Concealment of the Conviction by the Division of Personnel," October 1991.

10. Moss Kanter, *supra* at p. 24.

11. Tullock, *supra.*

12. See Chapter 7 for a discussion of U-Form organizations.

13. I interviewed this official by telephone on August 29, 2002, and in the Department of Education on May 7, 2002, as part of the School Design Project. I am keeping her name confidential to protect her privacy.

14. PCEN, the New York State program discussed in Chapter 6, which funds student support, will pay for reading and math teachers but only if they are supplemental to the classroom. It will not fund school aides or regular teachers, even if they teach largely disadvantaged students. PCEN may fund coordinators in certain situations but generally will not fund principals and assistant principals unless the school has a schoolwide PCEN program and the person knows how to write a funding plan to use PCEN to pay for a principal or assistant principal.

15. John W. Meyer, W. Richard Scott, and David Strang, "Centralization, Fragmentation, and School District Complexity," *Administrative Science Quarterly* 32 (1987): 186–201; Scott and Meyer, "Environmental Linkages and Organizational Complexity: Public and Private Schools," in *Comparing Public and Private Schools,* vol. 1, ed. Thomas James and Henry M. Levin (New York: Falmer Press, 1988), 128–60.

16. Kevin B. Smith and Kenneth J. Meier, "Politics, Bureaucrats, and Schools," *Public Administration Review* 54, no. 6 (November–December 1994): 551.

17. Rossi, 2002, *supra*. Rossi, as noted earlier, is not the official's real name.

18. *Id.*

19. I interviewed this upper-level official at the Board of Education on April 8, 2002. For reasons of privacy, I am keeping the official's name confidential.

20. LAUSD OIG, "Accounts Payable Process," OA 01-60, 2001.

21. *Id.* at p. 13.

22. Jeff Simmons, "In the Name of Cleanup, Ed Bd Sweeps out Secretary," *New York Daily News,* July 18, 1996, p. 12; Jacques Steinberg, "School Board to Remove Its Secretary, a Bane to Chancellors," *New York Times,* July 17, 1996, p. B1; Robert Polner and Liz Willen, "Power Play Brewing at Ed Board," *New York Newsday,* July 14, 1996, p. A4; Willen, "School Aide's Suite Deal: Crew's Former Spokesman Stayed Free at Swanky Hotel," *New York Newsday,* June 14, 1996, p. A2.

23. Steinberg, "School Board to Remove Its Secretary," 1996, *supra*.

24. Willen, 1996, *supra*.

25. Harold O. Levy, chancellor of the New York City School System, speech for the Center for Educational Innovation, March 16, 2000, Roosevelt Hotel, New York City.

26. Polner and Willen, *supra*.

27. *Id.*

28. *Id.*

29. Steinberg, "School Board to Remove Its Secretary," 1996, *supra*.

30. Simmons, *supra*.

CHAPTER ELEVEN: WHEN ANTICORRUPTION MACHINERY BREEDS CORRUPTION

1. For a discussion of occupational corruption, see, generally, Ermann and Lundman, eds., *Corporate and Governmental Deviance, supra;* James William Coleman, *The Criminal Elite* (New York: St. Martin's Press, 1989), pp. 8–10; Herbert Edelhertz, *The Nature, Impact, and Prosecution of White-Collar Crime* (Washington, D.C.: U.S. Government Printing Office, 1970), pp. 19–20.

2. Fliegel and McGuire, *supra*.

3. Edward B. Fiske, "Lessons," *New York Times,* November 1, 1989, p. B8.

4. Ralph Blumenthal, "Supplemental Pay Involved in Alvarado Inquiry Is Widely Used in Schools," *New York Times,* March 9, 1984, p. B2.

5. NYC DOI, 1984, *supra* at p. 8.

6. As Alvarado later explained to investigators, he interpreted per session to encompass any work beyond the normal workday, regardless of whether it was similar to tasks done during the regular day; see Blumenthal, 1984, *supra*.

7. James C. McKinley Jr., "Former City Aide Guilty of School Repair Bribery," *New York Times,* July 26, 1995, p. B3, col. 5; Katherine Pushkar, "The School House Follies," *The Village Voice,* Education Supplement, April 16, 1996, p. 10; Dillon, "18 Named in Graft," 1994, *supra;* "Prosecutor Charges City School Contractors," *Engineering News-Record* 232, no. 22 (May 30, 1994): 11.

8. Raab, 1994, *supra*.

9. Tyre, *supra*.

10. Raab, 1994, *supra*.

11. Tyre, *supra*.

12. Dillon, "18 Named in Graft," 1994, *supra*.

13. See, for example, LAUSD OIG, "Accounts Payable Process," OA 01-60, 2001, *supra*.

14. Special Commissioner of Investigation for the New York City School District, "Paper, Pencils, and Planes to the Caribbean: Corruption in the Purchasing of School and Office Supplies," October 1994, p. 51.

15. *Id.* at p. 9.

16. *Id.* at pp. 4–5, 7.

17. *Id.* at p. 9.

18. *Id.* at p. 9.

19. *Id.* at p. 44.

20. *Id.* at pp. 24, 25, 27, 28.

21. *Id.* at p. 44.

22. *Id.* at pp. 38–39.

23. *Id.* at p. 41.

24. *Id.* at p. 29.

25. At least eighteen of twenty-five current and former BOE employees engaged in fraudulent purchasing schemes with the vendor but did not attempt to enrich themselves financially (*id.* at pp. 14–15).

26. *Id.* at pp. 16–18 and 19–21.

27. *Id.* at p. 39.

28. *Id.* at p. 11.

29. *Id.* at p. 12.

30. Deloitte and Touche LLP, "Procurement Reorganization Feasibility Study," commissioned by the LAUSD, December 16, 1999.

31. Los Angeles Unified School District, Office of the Inspector General, "Annual Report to the Board of Education," Fiscal Year 2002, p. 38.

CHAPTER TWELVE: LESSONS FROM LOCAL POLITICAL SCHOOL CONTROL

1. A portion of this chapter is adapted from Lydia Segal, "The Pitfalls of Political Decentralization and Proposals for Reform: The Case of the New York City Schools," *Public Administration Review* 57, no. 2 (March/April 1997): 141–49.

2. NY Ed. Law at 2590ff.

3. Mario Fantini and Marilyn Gittell, *Decentralization: Achieving Reform* (New York: Praeger, 1973).

4. David Rogers and Norman H. Chung, *110 Livingston Street Revisited: Decentralization in Action* (New York: New York University Press, 1983); Viteritti, *supra*.

5. Ravitch, 1974, *supra* at pp. 295–98.

6. *Id.*

7. Rogers and Chung, *supra* at pp. 2–3.

8. Alan A. Altshuler, *Community Control: The Black Demand for Participation in Large American Cities* (New York: Pegasus, 1970).

9. Segal, 1997, *supra*.

10. New York City Joint Commission on Integrity in the Public Schools, "The New Tammany Hall?" 1990, *supra* at p. 9.

11. *Id.* at p. 41.

12. "Second School District 9 Board Member Pleads Guilty," United Press International, July 11, 1989.

13. "Districts at a Glance," *New York Times,* April 24, 1989, p. B4.

14. "Second School District 9 Board Member Pleads Guilty," *supra.*

15. Mullany, *supra.*

16. Nina Bernstein, Manuel Perez-Rivas, et al., "S. Bronx Teacher Arrested on Drug-Buying Charges," *New York Newsday,* December 14, 1988, p. 3.

17. New York City Bronx District Attorney's Office, Grand Jury Report, "Politics in Our School System: A Corrupting Influence," 1986.

18. SCI, "Power, Politics, and Patronage," 1993, *supra* at p. 54.

19. *Id.* at p. 7.

20. *Id.* at p. 16.

21. *Id.* at p. 55.

22. *Id.* at p. 57.

23. *Id.* at pp. 4–5.

24. Lane, *supra.*

25. Raymond E. Wolfinger, "Why Political Machines Have Not Withered Away and Other Revisionist Thoughts," *Journal of Politics* 34 (1972): 365.

26. Segal, 1999, *supra.*

27. *Id.*

28. New York City Council, Report, "Frequent Flyers and Big Spenders: Community School Board Spending on Travel, Conference, and Meals," February 10, 1994.

29. SCI, "Power, Politics, and Patronage," 1993, *supra* at p. 71.

30. William J. Cook Jr., "Corruption and Racketeering in the New York City School Boards," in *Handbook of Organized Crime in the United States,* ed. Robert J. Kelly, Ko-Lin Chin, and Rufus Schatzberg (Westport, Conn.: Greenwood Press, 1994), 269–88.

31. SCI, "Power, Politics, and Patronage," 1993, *supra* at pp. 42–47.

32. Joseph Berger with Elizabeth Kolbert, "Schools and Politics: Channels of Power—A Special Report: New York Schools and Patronage—Experience Teaches Hard Lessons," *New York Times,* December 11, 1989, pp. A1, col. 3.

33. SCI, "Power, Politics, and Patronage," 1993, *supra.*

34. *Id.* at p. 74.

35. Neil A. Lewis and Ralph Blumenthal, "Powerbase vs. Schools in Brooklyn District," *New York Times,* February 10, 1989, p. A1.

36. SCI, "Power, Politics, and Patronage," 1993, *supra* at pp. 83–88.

37. *Id.* at pp. 94–109.

38. SCI, "From Chaos to Corruption: An Investigation into the 1993 Community School Board Election," December 1993, pp. 57–59.

39. SCI, "Power, Politics, and Patronage," 1993, *supra* at p. 78.

40. *Id.* at p. 79.

41. *Id.* at p. 75.

42. *Id.* at p. 89.

43. SCI, "From Chaos to Corruption," 1993, *supra.*

44. SCI, "Power, Politics, and Patronage," 1993, *supra* at p. 87.

45. New York City Joint Commission on Integrity in the Public Schools, "The New Tammany Hall," 1990, *supra* at p. 7.

46. *Id.*

47. *Id.* at p. 4.

48. *Id.* at p. 61.

49. SCI, "Power, Politics, and Patronage," 1993, *supra* at p. 36.

50. *Id.*

51. Segal, 1999, *supra.*

52. New York City Charter at 2604(b)(9)b and 2604(b)(11)a.

53. 18 U.S.C. 1951(b).

54. *McCormick v. U.S.* (1991).

55. Segal, 1999, *supra.*

56. Daniel H. Lowenstein, "Political Bribery and the Intermediate Theory of Politics," *UCLA Law Review* 32 (1985): 784; Segal, "Corruption Moves to the Center," 1999, *supra.*

57. *Rutan v. Republican Party of Illinois* (1990).

58. Anne Freedman, "Doing Battle with the Patronage Army: Politics, Courts and Personnel Administration in Chicago," *Public Administration Review* 48 (September/October 1988): 847–59.

59. NYC Joint Commission on Integrity in the Public Schools, "The New Tammany Hall," 1990, *supra* at p. 97.

60. *Id.* at p. 38.

61. Berger with Kolbert, 1989, *supra.*

62. SCI, "Power, Politics, and Patronage," 1993, *supra* at p. 99.

63. Segal, 1999, *supra.*

64. NY Ed. Law, Title II, Article 52-A, at 2590 (1997).

65. Richard Condon, commissioner, Special Commissioner of Investigation for the New York City School District, telephone interview, January 8, 2003.

66. Owen Moritz, "Levy Threatens Campaign Funds Probe," *New York Daily News,* July 14, 2002, p. 16.

67. Nicole Bode, "2 Hopefuls Vie for Job in District," *New York Daily News,* May 1, 2002.

68. Bill Egbert, "School Tie in Politics," *New York Daily News,* July 13, 2001, p. 2.

CHAPTER THIRTEEN: LESSONS FROM BUREAUCRATIC AUTONOMY

1. This chapter is adapted from Lydia Segal, "Roadblocks in Reforming Corrupt Agencies: The Case of the New York City School Custodians," *Public Administration Review* 62 (July/August 2002): 445–60.

2. Harold Levy, "Report of the Commission on School Facilities and Maintenance Reform," June 1995, New York State, p. 5.

3. NYC BOE, "A Source Document on Custodians and Custodial Helpers," 1977, *supra.*

4. New York State Comptroller, "Custodial Service at a Certain High School—New York City Board of Education," NYC-4-77, January 28, 1977.

5. *Beck v. New York City Board of Education,* 52 N.Y.S.2d 712 (1945).

6. New York State Comptroller, "Custodial Service at a Certain High School," 1977, *supra* at p. 28.

7. Joseph Michalak, "Custodians' Pay Still in Top Bracket," *New York Herald Tribune,* October 19, 1964.

8. New York City Board of Education, "Rules and Regulations for the Custodial Workforce," 1903.

9. New York City Board of Education, "Rules and Regulations for the Custodial Force in the Public Schools of New York City," 1977.

10. New York City Board of Education, "Memorandum of Understanding," 1987.

11. SCI, "A System Like No Other," 1992, *supra* at pp. 64–65.

12. *Id.* at pp. 11–15, 77, 88. The literature shows that supervisors tend not to give low evaluation ratings anyway; see James L. Medoff and Katherine G. Abraham, "Experience, Performance, and Earnings," *Quarterly Journal of Economics* 95 (December 1980): 705–36. Fear of retaliation can only make this tendency worse, however.

13. Kathy Maire, "A Triple Tax on Toilets?" *New York Newsday,* June 20, 1991, p. 60.

14. New York City Joint Commission on Integrity in the Public Schools (Kevin Gill, chairman), "Investigating the Investigators," March 1990; Special Commissioner of Investigation for the New York City School District, "Cheating the Children: Educator Misconduct on Standardized Tests," December 1999.

15. Special Commissioner of Investigation for the New York City School District, Case no. 97-0520 re Irwin Crespi, January 28, 1999.

16. SCI, "A System Like No Other," 1992, *supra.*

17. SCI, re Irwin Crespi, 1999, *supra.*

18. SCI, "A System Like No Other," 1992, *supra.*

19. New York City Office of Administrative Trials and Hearings, In *re Luther Drakeford,* 1995–96.

20. John Fager, ". . . And I'll Turn on the Heat When I'm Done Cleaning My Yacht," *Washington Monthly,* July 24, 1994.

21. Suzanne Daley, "Custodian vs. Principal: Stacked Deck," *New York Times,* February 25, 1988, p. B1.

22. SCI, "A System Like No Other," 1992, *supra* at p. 10.

23. *Id.* at p. 21.

24. *Id.* at p. 22.

25. *Id.* at p. 30.

26. *Id.* at pp. 30, 39.

27. *Id.* at pp. 22–23.

28. Ravitch, 1974, *supra.*

29. SCI, "A System Like No Other," 1992, *supra* at pp. 56, 62, 63.

30. New York State Comptroller, "Financial and Operating Practices, Bureau of Plant Operations—Custodial Services, New York City Board of Education: July 1, 1974 to January 31, 1977," NYC-64-77, 1977, p. 2.

31. *Id.*

32. NYC Comptroller, "New York City Board of Education Controls over Custodial Employees' Work Hours," 1996, *supra.*

33. SCI, "A System Like No Other," 1992, *supra* at pp. 63–64.

34. Hay Group, "Preliminary Report of Findings and Recommendations for the New York City Public School System Plant Operations Study," November 1990, p. 63.

35. SCI, "A System Like No Other," 1992, *supra* at pp. 17–18.

36. *Id.* at pp. 25–27.

37. *Id.* at p. 12.

38. *Id.* at p. 14.

CHAPTER FOURTEEN: LESSONS FROM RESISTANCE TO REFORM

1. Part of this chapter has been adapted from Lydia Segal, "Roadblocks in Reforming Corrupt Agencies: The Case of the New York City School Custodians," *Public Administration Review* 62 (July/August 2002): 445–60.

2. New York City Board of Education, School Survey Committee, "Report: Survey of the Public School System, City of New York," 1929.

3. NYC BOE, "A Source Document on Custodians and Custodial Helpers," 1977, *supra* at p. 9.

4. New York State Comptroller, 1981.

5. See, for example, SCI, "*re Irwin Crespi,*" 1999; NYC Comptroller, "The School Custodians' Contract," 1989, *supra.*

6. New York Ed. Law § 2590-h26.

7. Special Commission of Investigation, "Taking Their Time: An Investigation into BOE Custodial Employee Time Abuse," March 1996.

8. NYC Comptroller, "Controls over Custodial Employees' Work Hours," 1996, *supra* at p. 7.

9. New York City Comptroller, "Audit Report on the New York City Board of Education Controls over Custodial Hiring Practices and Use of Separate Bank Accounts," June 27, 1996.

10. Advocates for Children of New York, "Neglected Buildings, Damaged Health: A Snapshot of New York City Public School Environmental Conditions," October 1999.

11. NYC BOE, "Rules and Regulations for the Custodial Workforce," 1903.

12. Marshall W. Meyer and Lynne G. Zucker, *Permanently Failing Organizations* (Newbury Park, Calif.: Sage Publications, 1989), p. 23; Max Weber, "Bureaucracy," in *From Max Weber: Essays in Sociology,* ed. H. H. Gerth and C. W. Mills (New York: Oxford University Press, 1946), 196–244.

13. Richard Matland, "Synthesizing the Implementation Literature: The Ambiguity-Conflict Model of Policy Implementation," *Journal of Public Administration Research and Theory* 5, no. 2 (April 1995): 145–74.

14. Theodore Lowi, *The End of Liberalism* (New York: W. W. Norton, 1969).

15. Jeffrey Pressman and Aaron Wildavsky, *Implementation* (Berkeley: University of California Press, 1973).

16. D. S. Van Meter and C. E. Van Horn, "The Policy Implementation Process: A Conceptual Framework," *Administration and Society* 6, no. 4 (1975): 445–87.

17. New York City Comptroller, "Board of Education Financial and Operating Practices Pertaining to Custodial Services," 1975, p. 7.

18. Robert K. Merton, *Social Theory and Social Structure* (New York: Free Press, 1968).

19. W. Lawrence Sherman, *Scandal and Reform: Controlling Police Corruption* (Berkeley: University of California Press, 1978).

20. Blau and Schoenherr, *supra.*

21. Segal, 1999, *supra.*

22. William A. Niskanen, *Bureaucracy and Representative Government* (Chicago: Aldine-Atherton, 1971).

23. Viteritti, *supra.*

24. L. 1967, ch. 392, 2 (codified as amended at N.Y. Civ. Serv. Law 200-214).

25. See, for example, Dunne, *supra,* for a custodian who went from being union vice president to deputy director of the Division of School Facilities to a private contractor doing lucrative work at some of the city's largest schools.

26. New York City Comptroller, "The School Custodians' Contract: An Evalutaion of the Reforms of 1985 and 1988," December 1989, *supra;* D. D. Guttenplan, "School Custodians Willing to Let Other Unions Take Lead," *New York Newsday,* October 22, 1990.

27. Levy, *supra.*

28. New York City Comptroller, "Report on the Financial and Operating Practices of the Board of Education Pertaining to Custodial Services for the Calendar Year 1975," January 19, 1977, p. 14.

29. NYC Comptroller, 1975, *supra* at p. 13.

30. John Fager, "About Education: Getting Tough with Custodians," *New York Newsday,* July 6, 1990, p. 60.

31. NYC Comptroller, 1975, *supra* at p. 11.

32. SCI, "A System Like No Other," 1992, *supra* at p. 74.

33. NYC BOE, "Memorandum of Understanding," 1994.

34. Education Priorities Panel, "New York City School Custodial and Maintenance Costs," New York City, July 20, 1976.

35. New York State Comptroller, "Bureau of Plant Operations—Custodial Services Follow-up New York City Board of Education," NYC-21-81, October 9, 1981, pp. 10, 11.

36. NYC Comptroller, 1989, *supra.*

37. New York State Comptroller, 1981, *supra.*

38. New York State Comptroller, "Tentative Draft Audit Report, Bureau of Plant Operation Contracted Custodial Services," June 29, 1976, p. 2.

39. Hal Rainey and Paula Steinbauer, "Galloping Elephants: Developing Elements of a Theory of Effective Government Organizations," *Journal of Public Administration Research and Theory* (January 1999): 1–32.

40. New York State Comptroller, "Custodial Service at a Certain High School," 1977, *supra* at p. 85.

41. SCI, "A System Like No Other," 1992, *supra* at p. 20.

42. *Id.* at pp. 22–23.

43. Kevin Sack, "Cuomo Signs Bill on Control of School Custodians," *New York Times,* November 27, 1993, sec. 1, p. 25.

44. James Lonergan, "Custodial Contract between BOE and Local 891: An Analysis" (master's thesis, Queens College, City University of New York, 1998), 37–40.

45. Fager, "Study on School Custodians Doesn't Even Scratch the Surface" (letter), *New York Times,* April 9, 1991, p. A24.

46. SCI, "A System Like No Other," 1992, *supra* at pp. 60, 75.

47. Yvonne P. Kong, "A System Like No Other—School Custodians" (master's thesis, City University of New York, 1995).

48. James G. March and Johan P. Olsen, *Ambiguity and Choice in Organizations* (Bergen, Norway: Universitetsforlaget, 1976).

49. G. Yukl, *Leadership in Organizations* (Upper Saddle River, N.J.: Prentice-Hall, 1998); R. D. Behn, *Leadership Counts* (Cambridge, Mass.: Harvard University Press, 1991).

50. Sherman, *supra.*

51. "Fall Guys for the BOE" (editorial), *New York Newsday,* November 30, 1993.

52. NYC BOE, "Memorandum of Understanding," 1987, *supra* at p. 102.

53. NYC Comptroller, "The School Custodians' Contract," 1989, *supra* at p. 34.

54. Jim Lonergan, Division of School Facilities, New York City Department of Education, interview by Lydia Segal for the School Design Project, April 5, 2002.

55. American Arbitration Association, "In the Matter of the Arbitration between the NYC BOE and Local 891," Case 130 39000709 96, December 18, 1996, p. 10.

56. Anechiarico and Jacobs, *supra.*

57. Segal, 1998, *supra.*

CHAPTER FIFTEEN: ESTABLISHING INDEPENDENT INSPECTORS GENERAL

1. Denis P. McGowan, "The Offices of Inspector General," *The Badge* (spring 1995): 21–29.

2. The first inspector general in a civilian agency was established in 1962 in the U.S. Department of Agriculture; the second, in 1972, in the U.S. Department of Housing and Urban Development; see McGowan, *supra*.

3. The Inspector General Act Amendments (1988) created thirty-four additional federal inspector general offices, but the heads of these offices were appointed by management; see Public Law 100-504.

4. Joint Commission on Integrity in the Public Schools, "Investigating the Investigators," March 1990.

5. The internal unit was known as the Office of Inspector General.

6. Doug Smith, "L.A. Schools' Fiscal Watchdog Faces Dismissal," *Los Angeles Times*, August 13, 1998, p. B1.

7. *Id.;* Doug Smith, "Study of L.A. District Finds Widespread Weaknesses in Auditing," *Los Angeles Times*, October 16, 1998, p. B3.

8. Doug Smith, "L.A. Schools' Fiscal Watchdog Faces Dismissal," 1998, *supra*.

9. LAUSD OIG, "Annual Report," 2001, *supra*.

10. City of New York, Office of the Mayor, Executive Order no. 11, June 28, 1990. This office was initially called the Deputy Commissioner of Investigation.

11. The late Edward Stancik, former deputy chief of the Rackets Bureau in the Manhattan District Attorney's Office, led the office from its inception until his death in 2002. Richard Condon, former commissioner of the New York City Police Department from 1989 to 1999 who also led investigations into police corruption for the Knapp Commission, is now at the helm of the Special Commissioner of Investigation.

12. The board called the new office the Internal Audit and Special Investigations Unit and recruited an experienced investigator, Don Mullinax, then chief investigator for the U.S. Senate Permanent Subcommittee on Investigations, to head it.

13. California Education Code, sections 35400 and 35401.

14. "Don't Muzzle School's Watchdog" (editorial), *New York Daily News*, December 10, 1997, p. 28.

15. Charles Hurt, "Detroit School Reform Stalls: Officials Afraid of Losing Power Are Fighting Overhaul That Will Revive City, Advocates Say," *Detroit News*, February 17, 1998, p. 1.

16. Margaret Gates and Mark Moore, *Inspectors-General: Junkyard Dogs or Man's Best Friend? Social Research Perspectives* (New York: Russell Sage Foundation, 1986).

17. Marilyn Gittell, *Participants and Participation: A Study of School Policy in New York City* (New York: Center for Urban Education, 1967), p. 24; Michael Katz, *Class, Bureaucracy, and the School* (New York: Praeger, 1971).

18. Marcia Chambers, "School Official Told to Hold Back Data from Goldin," *New York Times*, March 13, 1978, p. A19.

19. In fact, auditors from the Comptroller's Office complained that while principals and teachers wanted to cooperate with them, central office bureaucrats prevented them from doing so.

20. Edward F. Stancik, guest lecture at John Jay College of Criminal Justice, City University of New York, March 8, 2001.

21. *Id.*

22. *Id.*

23. Doug Smith and Amy Pyle, "Zacarias Considering Defamation Lawsuit," *Los Angeles Times,* September 23, 1999, p. B1.

24. Sonia Giordani, "LAUSD Watchdog Role Eyed," *Los Angeles Daily News,* April 7, 2002. Mullinax won both those battles.

25. Los Angeles Unified School District, Internal Audit and Special Investigations Unit, "Report of Findings: Belmont Learning Complex," OSI 99-12, September 13, 1999, p. 157.

26. Stancik, *supra.*

27. Peter Schmidt, "Throwing Light on Dark Corners of N.Y.C.'s Bureaucracy," *Education Week on the Web,* September 29, 1993.

28. Paul Light has made similar points about inspectors general at the federal level—those who get press get most of the attention. See Light, *supra* at p. 216.

29. SCI, "Paper, Pencils, and Planes to the Caribbean," 1994, *supra* at p. 17.

30. *Id.* at p. 32.

31. Jensen, 1998, *supra.*

32. For the multiple and sometimes conflicting goals of inspectors general, see Gates and Moore, *supra.* Note that the need to evaluate a school district's infrastructure does not mean ignoring fraud. On the contrary, as a district decentralizes and puts a greater premium on performance, the inspector general should be on the lookout for schemes to fraudulently inflate achievement, such as on student test scores.

33. Light, *supra.*

34. Los Angeles Unified School District, Office of Inspector General, "Budget Request—Fiscal Year 2004," March 19, 2003.

CHAPTER SIXTEEN: REMOVING THE DOMINANT COALITION

1. Part of this chapter has been adapted from Lydia Segal, "Roadblocks in Reforming Corrupt Agencies: The Case of the New York City School Custodians," *Public Administration Review* 62 (July/August 2002): 445–60.

2. Vander Weele, *Reclaiming Our Schools,* 1994, *supra;* Rossi, "School Board Tightens Purchasing Procedure," 1994, *supra* at p. 12.

3. Rossi, "School Engineers Get Warning," *supra* at p. 4; Mary Mitchell, "Ex-School Aide Sentenced for Extortion," *Chicago Sun-Times,* May 18, 1996, p. 4.

4. This information came from an upper-level CPS official who was crucial to the reforms under Vallas. I am keeping his name confidential to protect his privacy.

5. Rossi, "School Engineers Get Warning," 1996, *supra.*

6. Mary A. Johnson, "Structure and Leadership: Question of Who Is Boss Still Debated," *Chicago Sun-Times,* March 28, 1993, p. 24.

7. Vander Weele, 1995, *supra.*

8. Matt O'Connor, "Ex-School Bureaucrat Took Bribe," *Chicago Tribune,* March 1, 1996, N3.

9. Better Government Association (Chicago), p. 21.

10. Maribeth Vander Weele, "Schools Feel OT Pinch: Private Custodial Pacts Studied," Schools in Ruins Series, *Chicago Sun-Times,* April 29, 1991, p. 1.

11. Casey Banas and Jean Davidson, "City Schools Back in Business: 2-Year Teacher Contract Links State Aid, Raises," *Chicago Tribune,* September 5, 1985, p. C1.

12. "School Councils Can Meet More Often," *Chicago Tribune,* January 26, 1990, p. C3.

13. Meribeth Vander Weele, "Overtime for Maintenance Staff at City Schools Tops $6 Million," *Chicago Sun-Times,* September 11, 1991, p. 35.

14. Vander Weele, 1993, *supra*.

15. Vander Weele, "Schools Feel OT Pinch," 1991, *supra*.

16. The Office of Inspector General was authorized by 105 ILCS 5/34-201.1, effective November 14, 1993. The OIG was first created for the Finance Authority, a group entrusted with overseeing the CPS's finances. But when the Finance Authority was dismantled in 1995, the OIG started reporting to the then-new Chicago School Board of Trustees in accordance with the Amendatory Act to the Illinois School Code (1995).

17. See, for example, Fran Spielman and Rosalind Rossi, "Ex-Reporter Appointed Top School Investigator," *Chicago Sun-Times*, September 3, 1998, p. 18.

18. Michael B. Katz, Michelle Fine, and Elaine Simon, "Poking Around: Outsiders View Chicago School Reform," Teachers College Record, Teachers College, Columbia University, October 11, 1997.

19. Vander Weele, 1995, *supra*.

20. *Id.*

21. Chicago OIG, "Second Annual Report," *supra* at p. 38.

22. Rossi, "School Board Tightens Purchasing Procedure," 1994, *supra*.

23. Katz, Fine, and Simon, *supra* at p. 117.

24. Vander Weele, *Reclaiming Our Schools*, 1994, *supra*.

25. Rosalind Rossi, "Schools Put 40 Vendors on Notice: Vallas to Bar 8 Contractors Suspected of Overcharges," *Chicago Sun-Times*, May 29, 1996, p. 6.

26. Rosalind Rossi, "Special Unit to Probe School Fraud: Service 'Bought' from State's Attorney," *Chicago Sun-Times*, September 25, 1997, p. 12.

27. Rosalind Rossi, "Schools Target 32 for Firing: Biggest Crackdown Ever, Officials Say," *Chicago Sun-Times*, January 23, 1996, p. 1.

28. *Id.*

29. Sheridan, *supra*.

30. Mitchell, *supra*.

31. Rossi, 1995, *supra*.

32. Sheridan, *supra*.

33. Chicago OIG, 1995, *supra* at p. 39.

34. This anecdote was repeated to me by two CPS officers whom I interviewed separately in October 2002. To protect their privacy, I am not revealing their names.

35. *Id.;* Sheridan, *supra;* Michael Martinez, "Schools, Janitors Reach Accord: Building Engineers' Jobs Safe for Now," *Chicago Tribune*, July 22, 1996, p. N3.

36. Rossi, "School Engineers Get Warning," 1996, *supra*.

37. Martinez, *supra;* Rossi, "School Engineers Get Warning," 1996, *supra*.

38. Martinez, *supra*.

39. Steven R. Strahler, "So Long, Pershing Road," *Crains Chicago Business*, August 7, 1995, p. 1.

40. § 105 ILCS 5/34-8.1.

41. This description was given to me by an upper-level CPS officer in the facilities division. I am not revealing the officer's name for reasons of privacy.

42. Segal, 1997, *supra*.

43. Jorge Oclander, "School Billing Racket: Firms, Employees Still Scam System," *Chicago Sun-Times*, May 22, 1996, p. 1.

44. Rossi, 1995, *supra*.

45. Steve Neal, "Chicago Needs a Lesson on Sharing Spotlight," *Chicago Sun-Times*, May 7, 1999, p. 8.

46. Benjamin Marrison, "Hard Lobbying for School Plan; Legislators Beseeched to Give Mayoral Control of District a Chance," *The Plain Dealer*, March 13, 1997, p. 1A.

CHAPTER SEVENTEEN: RESTRUCTURING SCHOOL DISTRICTS

1. See, for example, Commission to Investigate Allegations of Police Corruption (Mollen Commission), Milton Mollen, chairman, "Report of the New York City Commission to Investigate Allegations of Police Corruption and the Anti-Corruption Procedures of the Police Department," July 7, 1994.

2. Hayek, *supra.*

3. Williamson, 1970, *supra* at p. 113, citing Alfred Chandler Jr., *Strategy and Structure* (New York: Doubleday, Anchor Books, 1966).

4. See Williamson, 1970, *supra* at p. 127.

5. Because M-Forms put a premium on performance, their biggest corruption risk will be from overstating performance. See, generally, Segal, 1999, *supra.*

6. Oliver Williamson, "Transaction Cost Economics and Organization Theory," in *The Handbook of Economic Sociology,* ed. Neil J. Smelser and Richard Swedberg (Princeton, N.J.: Princeton University Press and Russell Sage Foundation, 1994), 77–107; Ouchi, 1977, *supra.*

7. Williamson, 1970, *supra* at p. 132.

8. William G. Ouchi, "Markets, Bureaucracies, and Clans," *Administrative Science Quarterly* 25 (1980): 129–41.

9. This incentive is called *variable performance budget.* Jensen, 1998, *supra* at p. 120.

10. *Id.*

11. Segal, 1998, *supra.*

12. Williamson, 1970, *supra* at p. 129.

13. See Chapter 18 for an analysis of how the Edmonton Public Schools have accomplished this.

14. A number of school-based governance decentralization reforms, such as New York City's school leadership teams, would be perfectly compatible with the structural decentralization proposed here. From the standpoint of corruption, the important feature of any such reform is that parents are allowed to make actual hiring and spending decisions, they be held accountable for these decisions.

15. See U.S. Government Accounting Office, "Performance Budgeting: Initial Experiences under the Results Act in Linking Plans with Budgets," GAO/AIMD/GGD-99-67, April 12, 1999.

16. See Nick Chiles, "Raspberries for BlackBerries? Devices' Cost a School Sore Point," *New York Newsday,* April 3, 2002, p. A2.

17. Administrators' response to the media may, if Larry Sabato is right, encourage journalists even more because they relish the prospect of influencing public institutions; see Larry Sabato, *Feeding Frenzy: How Attack Journalism Has Transformed American Politics* (New York: Free Press, 1991).

18. Johanna Neuman, *Lights, Camera, War: Is Media Technology Driving International Politics?* (New York: St. Martin's Press, 1996).

CHAPTER EIGHTEEN: THE MODEL OF EDMONTON, CANADA

1. Betty Malen, Rodney Ogawa, and J. Kranz, "What Do We Know about School-based Management? A Case Study of the Literature—A Call for Research," in *Choice and Control in American Education,* vol. 2, *The Practice of Choice, Decentralization, and School Restructuring,* ed. William H. Clune and John F. Witte (London: Falmer Press, 1990), 289–342.

2. Kenneth Leithwood and Teresa Menzies, "Forms and Effects of School-based Management: A Review," *Educational Policy* 12, no. 3 (1998): 325-46.

3. See, for example, Joseph Murphy, "Restructuring in Kentucky: The Changing Role of the Superintendent and the District Office," in *Effective School District Leadership: Transforming Politics into Education,* ed. Kenneth Leithwood (Albany: State University of New York Press, 1995); Priscilla Wohlstetter and Karen McCurdy, "The Link between School Decentralization and School Politics," *Urban Education* 25, no. 4 (1991): 391-414.

4. For a discussion of the charter school movement, see Joe Nathan, *Charter Schools* (San Francisco: Jossey-Bass, 1996).

5. The material for this chapter is part of what I researched for the School Design Project.

6. I interviewed this officer for the School Design Project on October 17, 2001. I am keeping her name confidential.

7. Daniel J. Brown, *Decentralization and School-based Management* (Bristol, Penn.: Falmer Press, 1990).

8. Ouchi with Segal, 2003, *supra.*

9. Brian Barkley, director of purchasing and finance, Edmonton Public Schools, interview by Lydia Segal for the School Design Project, October 15, 2001.

10. Avi Habinski, director of information technology, Edmonton Public Schools, interview by Lydia Segal for the School Design Project, October 16, 2001.

11. This is in consonance with theories of Hayek, Jensen, Meckling, Wilson, Ouchi, and many others that decision makers must be held accountable for their decisions.

12. Albert O. Hirschman, *Exit, Voice, and Loyalty* (Cambridge, Mass.: Harvard University Press, 1970).

13. Hirschman, *supra.*

14. Randall Denley, "Where Parents Call the Shots: The Future of Education Can Be Found in Alberta's Public Schools," *The Ottawa Citizen,* April 15, 1999, p. D4.

15. Edmonton Public School Policies, 2001, Alberta, Canada.

16. Noel Gareau, internal auditor, Edmonton Public School District, telephone interview by Lydia Segal for the School Design Project, October 12, 2001.

17. Deming, *supra* at pp. 12-22.

18. Barkley, *supra.*

19. *Id.*

CHAPTER NINETEEN: LOOSENED TOP-DOWN CONTROLS AND TRUST

1. Ouchi with Segal, *supra.*

2. *Id.*

3. I collected these data for the School Design Project.

4. As discussed in Chapter 7, culture may trump structure if the culture is extremely honest or extremely crooked. In Edmonton, it appears, most people are very honest, so structure may be less important than in other districts in explaining the incidence and prevalence of corruption.

5. In New York City, the most common allegations regarding principals appear to be helping children cheat on standardized tests and false inflation of enrollment to get more money. However, both of these problems can be curbed with independent outside monitors.

6. LAUSD OIG, "Annual Report," 2001, *supra.*

7. *Id.* at p. 47.

8. *Id.* at p. 45.

9. *Id.* at p. 49.

10. Correspondence from Richard J. Condon, Special Commissioner of Investigation for the New York City School District, to Lydia Segal, January 27, 2003.

11. See Chapter 3.

12. Note that this does not include fraud by cafeteria workers or custodians. Although these employees work at schools, they report to and are accountable to the central office, not the principal.

13. LAUSD OIG, "Annual Report," 2001, *supra.*

14. These data, good as of the summer of 2002, come from the School Design Project.

15. LAUSD OIG, "Annual Report," 2001, *supra* at p. 8.

16. Donald McAdams, "Fighting to Save Our Urban Schools . . . and Winning," Teachers College, Columbia University, 2000.

17. See, for example, Rebecca Trounson and Melanie Markley, "Prosecutors Criticize Cost, Quality of HISD Theft Probe," *Houston Chronicle,* April 3, 1992, p. A1; Markley, "HISD Lawyers Deny They Mismanaged Theft Probe: Call Prosecutors' Complaints Unwarranted," *Houston Chronicle,* April 4, 1992, p. A25; Julie Mason and Eric Hanson, "HISD Suspects Cover-up in Break-in," *Houston Chronicle,* February 26, 1992, p. A13.

18. Mason and Hanson, *supra.*

19. Melanie Markley, "HISD Digging Up Long Pattern of Misuse of Funds by Workers," *Houston Chronicle,* April 2, 1992, p. A1.

20. Jim Zook, "6 Ex-HISD Workers Fired in Theft Probe Sue District," *Houston Chronicle,* June 11, 1992, p. A34.

21. Markley, "HISD Digging Up Long Pattern of Misuse of Funds by Workers," 1992, *supra;* Houston Independent School District, "Consultant's Report: Audit of Project Renewal Procedures and Internal Control," November 2, 1991.

22. Houston Independent School District, Internal Auditing Department, "Audit of Wesley Elementary School Renovation/Addition Project," Audit no. 93-22, November 10, 1993.

23. *Id.* at p. 30.

24. *Id.* at p. 26.

25. *Id.* at p. 31.

26. Richard Lindsay, senior project executive, Houston Independent School District Rebuild 2002, interview by Lydia Segal for the School Design Project, October 8, 2001.

27. Houston Independent School District, Internal Auditing Department, "Roofing Audit for Forty-Seven Schools," January 4, 1999; Houston Independent School District, Internal Auditing Department, "Audit Report in Davis H.S. Athletic Facility," Audit no. 2000-11, February 8, 2001.

28. Louis Benevento, e-mail to Lydia Segal in response to questions, January 6, 2003. Benevento is currently executive director of the Division of Financial Operations, New York City Department of Education (as the New York City Board of Education is now called).

29. New York's 1996 school governance law prodded reforms by suggesting that procurement be made less onerous. NY Ed. Law, Title II, Article 52-A, at 2590-h(36) (1997).

30. This local purchasing option was prescribed by New York's 1996 school governance law, *supra.*

31. Condon, *supra.*

32. Loughran, *supra.*

33. Correspondence from Condon to Segal, *supra.*

Advocates for Children of New York, Inc. "Neglected Buildings, Damaged Health: A Snapshot of New York City Public School Environmental Conditions." New York City, October 1999.

Alchian, Armen A., and Harold Demsetz. "Production, Information Costs, and Economic Organization." *American Economic Review* 62, no. 5 (1972): 777–95.

Alexander (pseudonym for a New York City public school principal). Interview at his school by Lydia Segal for the School Design Project. May 3, 2002.

Allen, James, Jr., commissioner of education, State of New York. "Report on New York City School Reorganization," by Mark C. Schinnerer, consultant on New York City Reorganization, State Education Department, Albany, December 26, 1961.

Altshuler, Alan A. *Community Control: The Black Demand for Participation in Large American Cities.* New York: Pegasus, 1970.

American Arbitration Association. "In the Matter of the Arbitration between the NYC BOE and Local 891." Case 130 39000709 96, New York City, December 18, 1996.

Anderson, Ralph E. "Police Integrity: Accent on the Positive." *Police Chief* 40 (December 1973): 38ff.

Anechiarico, Frank, and James B. Jacobs. *The Pursuit of Absolute Integrity: How the Anti-Corruption Project Makes Government Inefficient.* Chicago: Chicago University Press, 1996.

"Anker Set to Run District in Bronx." *New York Times,* November 28, 1974.

Ballou, Dale. "The New York City Teachers' Union Contract: Shackling Principals' Leadership." *Civic* 6 (June 1999): 1–29.

Banas, Casey, and Jean Davidson. "City Schools Back in Business: 2-Year Teacher Contract Links State Aid, Raises." *Chicago Tribune,* September 5, 1985, p. C1.

Barkley, Brian, director of Purchasing and Finance, Edmonton Public Schools. Telephone interview by Lydia Segal for the School Design Project. October 15, 2001.

Barney, Jay B., and William G. Ouchi, eds. *Organizational Economics: Toward a New Paradigm for Understanding and Studying Organizations,* 187–204. San Francisco: Jossey-Bass, 1986.

Barzelay, Michael, with Babak Armajani. *Breaking through Bureaucracy: A New Vision of Management in Government.* Berkeley: University of California Press, 1992.

Behn, Robert D. *Leadership Counts.* Cambridge, Mass.: Harvard University Press, 1991.

Benevento, Louis, executive director of the Division of Financial Operations, New York City Department of Education. Interview by Lydia Segal for the School Design Project. April 8, 2002.

———. E-mail to Lydia Segal in response to questions. January 6, 2003.

Berger, Joseph. "School Boards Said to Pad Their Payrolls." *New York Times*, March 14, 1990, p. B1, col. 5.

Berger, Joseph, with Elizabeth Kolbert. "Schools and Politics: Channels of Power— A Special Report: New York Schools and Patronage—Experience Teaches Hard Lessons." *New York Times*, December 11, 1989, p. A1, col. 3.

Bernstein, Nina. "DA Investigating New Allegations against Alvarado." *New York Newsday*, April 21, 1989, p. 6.

Bernstein, Nina, Manuel Perez-Rivas, et al. "Bronx Teacher Arrested on Drug-Buying Charges." *New York Newsday*, December 14, 1988, p. 3.

Better Government Association Report, Chicago, May 17, 1995.

Blau, Peter M., and R. A. Schoenherr. *The Structure of Organizations*. New York: Basic Books, 1971.

Blumenthal, Ralph. "Gold Is Entering Inquiry on Monserrat; May Coordinate with Federal Attorney." *New York Times*, November 29, 1974, p. 43.

———. "Vidata Program Recruited School-System Employees." *New York Times*, December 12, 1974, p. 47.

———. "Supplemental Pay Involved in Alvarado Inquiry Is Widely Used in Schools." *New York Times*, March 9, 1984, p. B2.

Bode, Nicole. "2 Hopefuls Vie for Job in District." *New York Daily News*, May 1, 2002.

Bowen, Ezra. "When Schools Become Jungles: New Jersey Moves to Take Over a Failing Urban System." *Time*, June 7, 1988, p. 70.

Braithwaite, John. "Criminological Theory and Organizational Crime." *Justice Quarterly* 6 (1989): 333–58.

Brown, Daniel J. *Decentralization and School-based Management*. Bristol, Penn.: Falmer Press, 1990.

Buder, Leonard. "Inquiry Begun on Concern That Employed Monserrat." *New York Times*, November 23, 1974, p. 35.

———. "2 Ex-Judges to Investigate School Aides' Outside Ties." *New York Times*, December 3, 1974, p. 45.

———. "School Aide Got Job for His Wife." *New York Times*, January 30, 1975.

———. "20 Admit Gifts from Concern Doing School Business." *New York Times*, March 16, 1975.

———. "School Suspends 3 in Lunches Inquiry." *New York Times*, September 2, 1976, p. 1.

———. "School Aide Getting $250,000 Fine." *New York Times*, February 2, 1977, p. B2.

Buffa, Denise. "Bribe Teacher Is Still on Payroll." *New York Post*, February 8, 1997, p. A4.

Burke, Michael, director of leasing, Division of School Facilities, New York City Board of Education. Interview by Lydia Segal. Long Island City, N.Y. April 5, 2002.

Burtless, Gary, ed. *Does Money Matter? The Effect of School Resources on Student Achievement and Adult Success*. Washington, D.C.: Brookings Institution, 1996.

Calderone, Joe. "3 Charged in $180,000 Fed Scam; South Bronx Antipoverty Money Spent." *New York Newsday*, January 28, 1993, p. 6.

California State Auditor, Bureau of State Audits. "Summary of Report Number 99123, Los Angeles Unified School District." December 1999.

———. "Summary of Report Number 99123, Los Angeles Unified School District." 1999.

————. "Summary of Report Number 2000-125, Los Angeles Unified School District." July 2001.

Campanile, Carl. "Ed. Board Blowing $2.4M to Rent Crumbling Schools." *New York Post*, May 22, 2001.

————. "Levy Aide Caught in Ethics Outrage." *New York Post*, March 22, 2002, p. 25.

————. "School Cop Wants to Teach 'Lawless' Faculty a Lesson." *New York Post*, August 12, 2002.

————. "Schools Revamping: New Bid to Whip Worst into Shape." *New York Post*, October 15, 2002, p. 12.

Campanile, Carl, and Leah Hanes. "School Halls of Shame." *New York Post*, October 14, 2002, p. 8.

Campbell, Michelle, Michael Sneed, and Rosalind Rossi. "Clemente Audited; Accountant Assigned as Finance Manager." *Chicago Sun-Times*, February 7, 1997, p. 6.

Casey Carter, Samuel. *No Excuses*. Washington, D.C.: Heritage Foundation, 1999.

Cash, Carol. "A Study of the Relationship between School Building Condition and Student Achievement and Behavior." Blacksburg, Va., 1993.

Chambers, Marcia. "Goldin Is Pressing a Major Audit of the New York School System." *New York Times*, May 8, 1977, p. 1.

————. "Goldin Finds 'Serious Weaknesses' in Procedures on Schools Supplies." *New York Times*, January 30, 1978, p. A19.

————. "School Official Told to Hold Back Data from Goldin." *New York Times*, March 13, 1978, p. A19.

Chandler, Alfred, Jr. *Strategy and Structure*. New York: Doubleday, Anchor Books, 1966.

Chicago School Reform Board of Trustees, Office of Inspector General. "Second Annual Report." December 28, 1995.

————. "Fourth Annual Report." Kenneth K. Holt, inspector general. December 30, 1997.

————. "Interim Annual Report: July 1, 1998, to April 30, 1999." Maribeth Vander Weele, inspector general.

Chiles, Nick. "Raspberries for BlackBerries? Devices' Cost a School Sore Point." *New York Newsday*, April 3, 2002, p. A2.

Chubb, John E. "The System." In *A Primer on America's Schools*, edited by Terry M. Moe. Stanford, Calif.: Hoover Institution, 2001.

Clark, William, director, Financial and Administrative Services, Chicago Public Schools, Department of Procurement and Contracts. Interview by Lydia Segal for the School Design Project. October 23, 2001.

————. Telephone interview by Lydia Segal for the School Design Project. August 8, 2002.

Clinard, Marshall B., and Peter C. Yeager. *Corporate Crime*. New York: Free Press, 1980.

Cohen, Elizabeth, John Meyer, Richard Scott, and Terrence Deal. "Technology and Teaming in the Elementary School." *Sociology of Education* 52 (January 1979): 20–33.

Cohen, Lawrence, and Marcus Felson. "Social Change and Crime Rate Trends: A Routine Activities Approach." *American Sociological Review* 44 (1979): 588–608.

Coleman, James S., E. Q. Campbell, C. J. Hobson, J. McPartland, A. M. Mood, F. D. Weinfeld, and R. L. York. *Equality of Educational Opportunity*. Washington, D.C.: U.S. Government Printing Office, 1966.

Coleman, James William. *The Criminal Elite*. New York: St. Martin's Press, 1989.
————. "The Theory of White Collar Crime: From Sutherland to the 1990s." In *White-Collar Crime Reconsidered*, edited by Kip Schlegel and David Weisburd, 53–77. Boston: Northeastern University Press, 1992.
Commission to Investigate Allegations of Police Corruption (Mollen Commission), Milton Mollen, chairman. "Report of the New York City Commission to Investigate Allegations of Police Corruption and the Anti-Corruption Procedures of the New York City Police Department." July 7, 1994.
Commission to Investigate Allegations of Police Corruption and the City's Anti-Corruption Procedures (Knapp Commission), Whitman Knapp, chairman. "Report of the Commission to Investigate Allegations of Police Corruption and the City's Anticorruption Procedures." 1972.
Condon, Richard, Special Commissioner of Investigation for the New York City School District. Telephone interview. January 8, 2003.
————. Correspondence to Lydia Segal, January 27, 2003.
Conklin, J. E. *Illegal but Not Criminal: Business Crime in America*. Englewood Cliffs, N.J.: Prentice-Hall, 1977.
Cook, William J., Jr. "Corruption and Racketeering in the New York City School Boards." In *Handbook of Organized Crime in the United States*, edited by Robert J. Kelly, Ko-Lin Chin, and Rufus Schatzberg, 269–88. Westport, Conn.: Greenwood Press, 1994.
Cooper, Bruce S., et al. "From Transactional to Transformational Accounting." *School Business Affairs* 64, no. 10 (October 1998): 4–16.
Coopers and Lybrand L.L.P. "Resource Allocations in the New York City Public Schools." Report for Mayor Rudolph Giuliani and Herman Badillo, special counsel for fiscal oversight of education. October 4, 1994.
Cornish, Derek, and Ronald Clarke, eds. *The Reasoning Criminal: Rational Choice Perspectives on Offending*. New York: Springer Verlag, 1986.
Cremin, Lawrence A. *The Transformation of the School: Progressivism in American Education, 1876–1957*. New York: Knopf, 1961.
Crowley, Kieran. "Ex-adviser Ripped Off Schools: DA." *New York Post*, November 10, 2000, p. 13.
Cuban, Larry. "Reforming Again, Again, and Again." *Educational Researcher* 19 (1990): 3–13.
Daley, Suzanne. "Custodian vs. Principal: Stacked Deck." *New York Times*, February 25, 1988, p. B1.
Danis, Kirsten, and Carl Campanile. "Ed Stancik, Schools Prober, Dies at 47" (editorial). *New York Post*, March 13, 2002.
Del Castillo, Richard Griswold. *The Los Angeles Barrio, 1850–1890: A Social History*. Berkeley: University of California Press, 1979.
DeLeon, Peter. *Thinking about Political Corruption*. Armonk, N.Y.: M. E. Sharpe, 1993.
Deloitte and Touche LLP. "Procurement Reorganization Feasibility Study." Study commissioned by the Los Angeles Unified School District. December 16, 1999.
Deming, W. Edwards. "Improvement of Quality and Productivity through Action by Management." *National Productivity Review* (winter 1981–82): 12–22.
Denhardt, Robert, and Janet Denhardt. "Leadership for Change: Case Studies in American Local Government." Report for the PricewaterhouseCoopers Endowment for the Business of Government. September 1999.

Denley, Randall. "Where Parents Call the Shots: The Future of Education Can Be Found in Alberta's Public Schools." *The Ottawa Citizen*, April 15, 1999, p. D4.

"Developments in Los Angeles County: Payroll Fraud Rampant, District Auditor Reports" (news summary). *Los Angeles Times*, November 27, 1999, p. B6.

Dewan, Shaila. "Janitorial Rules Leave Teachers Holding a Mop." *New York Times*, May 28, 2001, p. A1.

Dezin, Norman K. "Notes on the Criminogenic Hypothesis: A Case Study of the American Liquor Industry." *American Sociological Review* 42 (1977): 905–20.

Dillon, Sam. "Testing Power, Cortines Will Seize 6 Bad Schools." *New York Times*, April 29, 1994, p. A1, col. 2.

———. "18 Named in Graft Tied to Projects for School Board." *New York Times*, May 20, 1994, p. A1, col. 4.

"Districts at a Glance." *New York Times*, April 24, 1989, p. B4.

Dowie, M. "Pinto Madness." In *Crisis in American Institutions*, edited by J. Skolnick and E. Currie. 4th ed. Boston: Little, Brown and Company, 1979.

Downs, Anthony. *Bureaucracy*. Boston: Little, Brown and Company, 1967.

Drucker, Peter F. *Management Challenges for the Twenty-first Century*. New York: Harper Business, 1999.

Dunn, Kathleen M. "TQM at George Westinghouse Vocational High School: A Model for Quality in New York City Public Education." Paper for MGGB 7621, Dr. Martha Mooney, Fordham University. Winter 1994.

Dunne, Eddie. "Who Killed Dan Conlin?" *Brooklyn Bridge* 2, no. 10 (June 1997): 30–37.

Dwyer, Jim. "A Textbook Case of Waste." *New York Newsday*, October 10, 1994, p. A2.

Edelhertz, Herbert. *The Nature, Impact, and Prosecution of White-Collar Crime*. Washington, D.C.: Government Printing Office, 1970.

Edelman, Susan. "Unions Hijack Reform: Critics." *New York Post*, February 13, 2000, p. 18.

Education Priorities Panel. "New York City School Custodial and Maintenance Costs." New York City, July 20, 1976.

Edwards, Maureen. "Building Condition: Parental Involvement and Student Achievement in the D.C. Public School System." Washington, D.C., 1992.

Egbert, Bill. "School Tie in Politics." *New York Daily News*, July 13, 2001, p. 2.

Elmore, Richard, and Milbrey McLaughlin. *Steady Work: Policy, Practice, and the Reform of American Education*. Santa Monica, Calif.: Rand, 1990.

Ermann, M. David, and Richard Lundman, eds. *Corporate and Governmental Deviance*. New York: Oxford University Press, 1978.

"Ex-L.A. Unified Employee Pleads Guilty in Bribe Case" (news summary). *Los Angeles Times*, June 28, 2000, p. B4.

Fager, John. "About Education: Getting Tough with Custodians." *New York Newsday*, July 6, 1990, p. 60.

———. "Study on School Custodians Doesn't Even Scratch the Surface" (letter). *New York Times*, April 9, 1991, p. A24.

———. ". . . And I'll Turn On the Heat When I'm Done Cleaning My Yacht." *Washington Monthly*, July 24, 1994.

"Fall Guys for the BOE" (editorial). *New York Newsday*, November 30, 1993.

Fantini, Mario, and Marilyn Gittell. *Decentralization: Achieving Reform*. New York: Praeger, 1973.

Farberman, Harvey. "A Criminogenic Market Structure: The Automobile Industry." *Sociological Quarterly* 16 (1975): 438–57.

Ferguson, Ronald F. "Paying for Public Education: New Evidence on How and Why Money Matters." *Harvard Journal on Legislation* 28 (summer 1991): 465–98.

"Finding What Really Works in Education" (panel discussion). *Chief Executive* 94 (May 1994): 48.

Fiske, Edward B. "Lessons." *New York Times,* November 1, 1989, p. B8.

Fliegel, Seymour, and James McGuire. *Miracle in East Harlem: The Fight for Choice in Public Education.* New York: Times Books, 1993.

Frederickson, J. W. "The Comprehensiveness of Strategic Decision Processes: Extension, Observations, Future Directions." *Academy of Management Journal* 2 7 (1984): 445–66.

Freedman, Anne. "Doing Battle with the Patronage Army: Politics, Courts and Personnel Administration in Chicago." *Public Administration Review* 48 (September/October 1988): 847–59.

Friedrichs, David O. *Trusted Criminals: White-Collar Crime in Contemporary Society.* Belmont, Calif.: Wadsworth, 1996.

Gamble, Richard H. "High Tech Meets Low Tech, on the Purchasing Playing Field." *Controller Magazine,* April 1998, p. 33.

Gareau, Noel, internal auditor, Edmonton Public School District. Telephone interview by Lydia Segal for the School Design Project. October 12, 2001.

Gates, Margaret, and Mark Moore. *Inspectors-General: Junkyard Dogs or Man's Best Friend? Social Research Perspectives.* New York: Russell Sage Foundation, 1986.

Geis, Gil. "White-Collar Crime: The Heavy Electrical Equipment Antitrust Cases of 1961." In *Criminal Behavior Systems: A Typology,* edited by M. Clinard and R. Quinney, 139–51. N.Y.: Holt, Rinehart and Winston, 1967.

Gerstner, Louis, Jr., and Tommy Thompson. "The Problem Isn't the Kids" (op-ed). *New York Times,* December 8, 2000, p. A39.

Giordani, Sonia. "LAUSD Watchdog Role Eyed." *Los Angeles Daily News,* April 7, 2002.

Gittell, Marilyn. *Participants and Participation: A Study of School Policy in New York City.* New York: Center for Urban Education, 1967.

"Goldin Assails Board of Education over Awarding of Bus Contracts." *New York Times,* February 18, 1978, p. 40.

Goldwyn Kingon, Jacqueline. "A View from the Trenches." *New York Times,* Education Life, April 8, 2001, sec. 4A, p. 30.

Goodnough, Abby. "Trial Begins in Suit Challenging New York State's Formula for School Funds." *New York Times,* October 13, 1999.

Greenwald, Rob, Larry V. Hedges, and Richard D. Laine. "The Effect of School Resources on Student Achievement." *Review of Educational Research* 66, no. 3 (fall 1996): 361.

Gross, Edward. "Organization Structure and Organizational Crime." In *White-Collar Crime: Theory and Research,* edited by Gilbert Geis and Ezra Scotland, 52–76. Beverly Hills, Calif.: Sage Publications, 1980.

Gross, Solomon. "Bureaucracy and Decision-making Viewed from a Patrol Precinct Level." *Police Chief* 42 (January 1975): 59–64.

Guttenplan, D. D. "School Custodians Willing to Let Other Unions Take Lead." *New York Newsday,* October 22, 1990.

Habinski, Avi, director of information technology, Edmonton Public Schools. Telephone interview by Lydia Segal for the School Design Project. October 16, 2001.

Hage, Jerald, and Michael Aiken. "Program Change and Organizational Properties: A Comparative Analysis." *American Journal of Sociology* 72, no. 3 (1967): 503–19.

Hall, Richard H. *Organizations: Structure and Process.* Englewood Cliffs, N.J.: Prentice-Hall, 1982.

Hansen, Phil, chief accountability officer, Office of Accountability, Chicago Public Schools. Interview by Lydia Segal for the School Design Project. October 22, 2001.

Hanushek, Eric A., et al. *Making Schools Work: Improving Performance and Controlling Costs.* Washington, D.C.: Brookings Institution, 1994.

Hanushek, Eric A., Michael Rebell, and Emanuel Tobier (panelists). "New York City's Public Schools: The Facts about Spending and Performance." Center for Civic Innovation, Manhattan Institute, May 2, 2000.

Hartocollis, Anemona. "After 4 Years of Crew, Still No Final Grade." *New York Times,* October 14, 1999, p. B1.

———. "9 Educators Accused of Encouraging Students to Cheat." *New York Times,* May 3, 2000, p. B4.

———. "Teacher Hiring Plan Is More Than a Matter of Decree." *New York Times,* September 2, 2000, p. B1.

Hay Group. "Preliminary Report of Findings and Recommendations for the New York City Public School System Plant Operations Study." November 1990.

Hayek, Friedrich. "The Use of Knowledge in Society." *American Economic Review* 35, no. 3 (1945): 519–30.

Haynes, V. Dion, and David Jackson. "New Schools Not Impossible; Other Big Cities Make the Grade When New Facilities Are Needed." Lesson in Waste series. *Chicago Tribune,* May 23, 1995.

Helfand, Duke. "Purchase of Classrooms Broke Law, Audit Says." *Los Angeles Times,* July 9, 1999, p. B1.

———. "School Repairs Face $600-Million Shortfall." *Los Angeles Times,* November 29, 2001.

Henig, Jeffrey R., Richard C. Hula, Marion Orr, and Desiree S. Pedescleaux. *The Color of School Reform: Race, Politics, and the Challenge of Urban Education.* Princeton, N.J.: Princeton University Press, 1999.

Hess, G. Alfred, Jr. *Restructuring Urban Schools: A Chicago Experience.* New York: Teachers' College Press, 1995.

Hill, Paul. "A Public Education System for the Metropolis." *Education and Urban Society* 29, no. 4 (1997): 490–508.

Hines, Eric. "Building Condition and Student Achievement and Behavior." Blacksburg, Va., 1996.

Hirschi, Travis, and M. Gottfredson. "Causes of White-Collar Crime." *Criminology* 25 (1987): 949–74.

Hirschman, Albert O. *Exit, Voice, and Loyalty.* Cambridge, Mass.: Harvard University Press, 1970.

Hofstadter, Richard. *The Age of Reform.* New York: Vintage Books, 1955.

Holmes, Oliver Wendell. *The Common Law.* Boston: Little, Brown and Co., 1963.

Houston Independent School District. "Consultant's Report: Audit of Project Renewal Procedures and Internal Control." November 2, 1991.

Houston Independent School District, Internal Auditing Department. "Audit of Wesley Elementary School Renovation/Addition Project." Audit no. 93-22. November 10, 1993.

————. "Roofing Audit for Forty-Seven Schools." January 4, 1999.

————. "Audit Report in Davis H. S. Athletic Facility." Audit no. 2000-11. February 8, 2001.

Hurt, Charles. "Detroit School Reform Stalls: Officials Afraid of Losing Power Are Fighting Overhaul That Will Revive City, Advocates Say." *Detroit News*, February 17, 1998, p. 1.

Hurtado, Patricia. "DA: Inspectors' Bribery Ring Was Systematic." *Newsday*, March 22, 1989, p. 4.

————. "Inspectors Guilty of Kickbacks." *Newsday*, April 5, 1989, p. 6.

Illinois Legislature Report. *Special Committee on Roberto Clemente Community Academy in Chicago and State Chapter 1 Educational Funding: Final Report*, Edgar Lopez, chairman, House of Representatives, January 1999.

Independent Commission on the Los Angeles Police Department (Christopher Commission), Warren Christopher, chairman, 1991.

Institute of Education and Social Policy. "Focus on Learning: A Report on Reorganizing General and Special Education in New York City," by Norm Fruchter, Robert Berne, Ann Marcus, Mark Alter, and Jay Gottlieb, New York University, October 1995.

————. "Second Annual Report: Evaluation of the Performance Driven Budgeting Initiative of the New York City Board of Education," May 2000.

"Internal Investigation Alleges Fraud in LA School District's Payroll Division." The Associated Press, State and Local Wire, November 26, 1999.

International Assessment. *Second International Assessment of Educational Progress: 1990–91*. Washington, D.C.: Congressional Budget Office, 1993.

Irwin, Victoria. "Jersey Maps Takeover of School District." *The Christian Science Monitor*, May 25, 1988, p. 3.

Jensen, Michael C., *Foundations of Organizational Strategy*. Cambridge, Mass.: Harvard University Press, 1998.

Jensen, Michael C. and William H. Meckling. "Specific and General Knowledge and Organizational Structure." In *Contract Economics*, edited by Lars Werin and Hans Wijkander. Oxford, England: Blackwell, 1992.

————. "The Nature of Man." *Journal of Applied Corporate Finance* 7, no. 2 (summer 1994): 4–19.

Johnson, Mary A. "Structure and Leadership: Question of Who Is Boss Still Debated." *Chicago Sun-Times*, March 28, 1993, p. 24.

Johnston, Laurie. "Ex-School Aide Tells of Collecting $400,000 as Co-Author of Tests." *New York Times*, April 19, 1977, p. 73.

Johnston, Michael. *Political Corruption and Public Policy in America*. Monterey, Calif.: Cole, 1982.

————. "Comparing Corruption: Participation, Institutions, and Development." Paper presented for seminar "Corruption: Public and Private," John Jay College of Criminal Justice, City University of New York, September 13–14, 2001.

Journal of the BOE of the City of New York. New York: William C. Bryant and Co., 1854.

Kagan, R. A., and J. T. Scholz. "The Criminology of the Corporation and Regulatory Enforcement Strategies." In *Enforcing Regulation*, edited by K. Hawkinds and J. M. Thomas, 67–96. Boston: Kluwer-Nijhoff, 1984.

Katz, Michael. *Class, Bureaucracy, and the School*. New York: Praeger, 1971.

Katz, Michael B., Michelle Fine, and Elaine Simon. "Poking Around: Outsiders

View Chicago School Reform." Teachers College Record, Columbia University, Teachers College, October 11, 1997.

Kellaghan, Thomas, Kathryn Sloanc, and Benjamin Alvarez. *The Home Environment and School Learning: Promoting Parental Involvement in the Education of Children.* San Francisco: Jossey-Bass, 1993.

Kershaw, Sarah. "In Decade, Queens School District Slips from Desirable to Troubled." *New York Times,* November 9, 2000, p. D1.

Ketchum, Stuart. Interview by William Ouchi and Lydia Segal. Beverly Hills, Calif. July 2, 2001.

Kleinig, John. *Ethics of Policing.* Cambridge, England: Cambridge University Press, 1996.

Klitgaard, Robert. *Controlling Corruption.* Berkeley: University of California Press, 1988.

Kong, Yvonne P. "A System Like No Other: School Custodians." Master's thesis, City University of New York, 1995.

Kornblum, Allan N. *The Moral Hazards: Strategies for Honesty and Ethical Behavior.* Lexington, Mass.: Lexington Books, 1976.

Kramer, R. C. "Corporate Crime: An Organizational Perspective." In *White-collar and Economic Crime,* edited by P. Wickman and T. Dailey, 75–94. Lexington, Mass.: Lexington Books, 1982.

Lane, Robert E. *The Regulation of Businessmen: Social Conditions of Government Control.* New Haven, Conn.: Yale University Press, 1954.

———. *Political Life: Why and How People Get Involved in Politics.* New York: Free Press, 1959.

Lehrer, Peter M. "Report of the Chancellor's Commission on the Capital Plan." New York City: Board of Education, 2002.

Leithwood, Kenneth, and Teresa Menzies. "Forms and Effects of School-based Management: A Review." *Educational Policy* 12, no. 3 (1998): 325–46.

Leonard, William, and Marvin Weber. "Automakers and Dealers: A Study of Criminogenic Market Forces." *Law and Society Review* 4 (1970): 407–10.

Levy, Harold. "Report of the Commission on School Facilities and Maintenance Reform." June 1995.

———. Speech given for The Center for Educational Innovation, Roosevelt Hotel, New York City. March 16, 2000.

———. "Principals Union Is Anything But." (op-ed.) *New York Post,* January 2, 2003.

Lewis, Neil A., and Ralph Blumenthal. "Powerbase vs. Schools in Brooklyn District." *New York Times,* February 10, 1989, p. A1.

Light, Paul C. *Monitoring Government: Inspectors General and the Search for Accountability.* Washington, D.C.: Brookings Institution, 1993.

Lindsay, Richard, senior project executive, Houston Independent School District Rebuild 2002. Interview by Lydia Segal for the School Design Project. October 8, 2001.

Little Hoover Commission. "Recommendations for Improving the School Facilities Program in the Los Angeles Unified School District." November 3, 1999. Available on the Web at little.hoover@lhc.ca.gov.

———. "To Build a Better School." February 8, 2000.

———. "Teach Our Children Well." September 5, 2001.

"Little Hoover Commission Report." *Daily News of Los Angeles,* November 14, 1999.

Lonergan, James. "Custodial Contract between BOE and Local 891: An Analysis." Master's thesis, Queens College, City University of New York, 1998.

Lonergan, James, director of building services, Division of School Facilities, New York City Department of Education. Interview by Lydia Segal for School Design Project, April 5, 2002.

Los Angeles County Civil Grand Jury. "Final Report." June 2001.

Los Angeles Unified School District, Internal Audit and Special Investigations Unit. "Annual Report to the Board of Education." OIA 99-1. Fiscal Year 1999.

———. "Report of Findings: Belmont Learning Complex." OSI 99-12. September 13, 1999.

———. "Report of Findings Part II: Belmont Learning Complex." OSI 99-20. December 13, 1999.

Los Angeles Unified School District, Office of the Inspector General. "Report of Audit: Pupil Transportation." SR 00-01. November 14, 2000.

———. "Report of Audit: Proposition BB Bond Change Order Process." OA 01-42. February 14, 2001.

———. "Report of Findings: Proposition BB Bond Program." IG 00-21. March 28, 2000.

———. "Report of Audit: Accounts Payable Process." OA 01-60. June 27, 2001.

———. "Annual Report to the Board of Education." OSI 99-20. Fiscal Year 2000.

———. "Report of Audit: Payroll Overtime." OA 01-61. June 29, 2001.

———. "Budget Request—Fiscal Year 2004." March 19, 2003.

———. Investigation. BE-013. 2001.

———. Investigation. MF-027. 2000.

———. Investigation. MF-028. 2000.

———. "Annual Report to the Board of Education." Fiscal Year 2001.

———. "Annual Report to the Board of Education." Fiscal Year 2002.

Loughran, Regina, acting commissioner, Special Commissioner of Investigation. Telephone interview by Lydia Segal. May 16, 2002.

———. Telephone interview by Lydia Segal. May 21, 2002.

———. E-mail to Lydia Segal. July 9, 2002.

Lowenstein, Daniel H. "Political Bribery and the Intermediate Theory of Politics." *UCLA Law Review* 32 (1985): 784.

Lowi, Theodore. *The End of Liberalism*. New York: W. W. Norton, 1969.

MacFarquhar, Neil. "Better Finances, But Not Better Test Scores: State Takeover of Schools Has Not Improved Student Performance." *New York Times*, July 9, 1995, p. 29.

Maeroff, Gene. "Monserrat Plans to Leave Post at Board for 6 Months." *New York Times*, June 21, 1975, p. 31.

Maire, Kathy. "A Triple Tax on Toilets?" *New York Newsday*, June 20, 1991, p. 60.

Malen, Betty, Rodney Ogawa, and J. Kranz. "What Do We Know about School-based Management? A Case Study of the Literature—A Call for Research." In *Choice and Control in American Education*, vol. 2, *The Practice of Choice, Decentralization, and School Restructuring*, edited by William H. Clune and John F. Witte, 289–342. London: Falmer, 1990.

Mangan, Patricia. *New York Daily News*, July 14, 1995, p. 5.

Manhattan Institute. "State of the New York City Public Schools 2002," by Raymond Domanico. Civic Report no. 26. March 2002.

March, James G., and Johan P. Olsen. *Ambiguity and Choice in Organizations*. Bergen, Norway: Universitetsforlaget, 1976.

―――. "What Administrative Reorganizations Tell Us About Governing." *American Political Science Review* 72 (June 1983): 281.

Markley, Melanie. "HISD Digging Up Long Pattern of Misuse of Funds by Workers." *Houston Chronicle,* April 2, 1992, p. A1.

―――. "HISD Lawyers Deny They Mismanaged Theft Probe: Call Prosecutors' Complaints Unwarranted." *Houston Chronicle,* April 4, 1992, p. A25.

Marrison, Benjamin. "Hard Lobbying for School Plan; Legislators Beseeched to Give Mayoral Control of District a Chance." *The Plain Dealer,* March 13, 1997, p. 1A.

Martinez, Michael. "Schools, Janitors Reach Accord: Building Engineers' Jobs Safe for Now." *Chicago Tribune,* July 22, 1996, p. N3.

Mason, Julie, and Eric Hanson. "HISD Suspects Cover-up in Break-in." *Houston Chronicle,* February 26, 1992, p. A13.

Massachusetts Department of State Auditor. "State Auditor's Report on Certain Activities of the Lawrence Public School System: July 1, 1993 through March 31, 1997." 97-6003-9. June 12, 1997.

Matland, Richard. "Synthesizing the Implementation Literature: The Ambiguity-Conflict Model of Policy Implementation." *Journal of Public Administration Research and Theory* 5, no. 2 (April 1995): 145–74.

McAdams, Donald "Fighting to Save Our Urban Schools ... and Winning." Teachers College, Columbia University, New York City, 2000.

McCabe, Paula, director, Department of Operations, Board of Education, Chicago Public Schools. Interview. November 3, 2000.

McGowan, Denis P. "The Offices of Inspector General." *The Badge* (spring 1995): 21–29.

McKinley, James C., Jr. "Former City Aide Guilty of School Repair Bribery." *New York Times,* July 26, 1995, p. B3, col. 5.

McLaughlin, Milbrey. "Implementation as Mutual Adaptation." In *Social Program Implementation,* edited by Walter Williams and Richard Elmore, 167–80. New York: Academic Press, 1976.

Medoff, James L., and Katherine G. Abraham. "Experience, Performance, and Earnings." *Quarterly Journal of Economics* 95 (December 1980): 705–36.

Mendieta, Ana. "More Oversight Urged for School Councils." *Chicago Sun-Times,* January 8, 1999, p. 20.

Merton, Robert K. *Social Theory and Social Structure.* New York: Free Press, 1968.

Meyer, John W., and Brian Rowan. "Institutionalized Organizations: Formal Structure as Myth and Ceremony." *American Journal of Sociology* 83 (1977): 340–63.

Meyer, John W., W. Richard Scott, and Terrence E. Deal. "Institutional and Technical Sources of Organizational Structure: Explaining the Structure of Educational Organizations." In *Organization and the Human Services,* edited by Herman D. Stein, 151–79. Philadelphia: Temple University Press, 1981.

Meyer, John W., W. Richard Scott, and David Strang. "Centralization, Fragmentation, and School District Complexity." *Administrative Science Quarterly* 32 (1987): 186–201.

Meyer, Marshall W., and Lynne G. Zucker. *Permanently Failing Organizations.* Newbury Park, Calif.: Sage Publications, 1989.

Michalak, Joseph. "Custodians' Pay Still in Top Bracket." *New York Herald Tribune,* October 19, 1964.

Mills, C. Wright. *The Power Elite.* New York: Oxford University Press, 1959.

Mirrer, Louise, executive vice chancellor, City University of New York. Testimony before the New York City Council's Higher Education Committee. October 25, 2002.

Mitchell, Mary. "Ex-School Aide Sentenced for Extortion." *Chicago Sun-Times,* May 18, 1996, p. 4.

Model Penal Code. American Law Institute, Model Penal Code and Commentaries, § 2.02 (General Requirements of Criminal Liability).

Moe, Terry M. "The New Economics of Organization." *American Journal of Political Science* 28 (November 1984): 739–77.

Moore, Solomon. "Romer Backs Team to Finish Belmont." *Los Angeles Times,* February 27, 2002, p. B4.

Moreno, Sylvia. "New School Scam: Dial-a-Dirt: District Workers Rang Up Huge 'Personal' Phone Bills." *New York Newsday,* October 26, 1989, p. 5.

———. "District 4's Money Man Gets the Ax." *New York Newsday,* October 31, 1989, p. 4.

———. "Stein Asks for Criminal Probe of Bronx School District Chief." *New York Newsday,* August 6, 1991, p. 8.

Moritz, Owen. "Levy Threatens Campaign Funds Probe." *New York Daily News,* July 14, 2002, p. 16.

Moss Kanter, Rosabeth. *The Change Masters.* New York: Simon and Schuster, 1983.

Mullany, Gerry. " 'It's Just a Mystery'—School District Looking for $1.2 Million." *New York Times,* December 1, 1988.

Mullinax, Don, inspector general, Los Angeles Unified School District; Jerry Thornton, assistant inspector general for investigations; Robert Kasper, assistant inspector general for audits. Interview by William Ouchi and Lydia Segal for the School Design Project. Los Angeles. July 6, 2001.

Mullinax, Don, inspector general, Los Angeles Unified School District. Interview by Lydia Segal. April 2, 2003.

Murphy, Joseph. "Restructuring in Kentucky: The Changing Role of the Superintendent and the District Office." In *Effective School District Leadership: Transforming Politics into Education,* edited by Kenneth Leithwood. Albany: State University of New York Press, 1995.

Nathan, Joe. *Charter Schools.* San Francisco: Jossey-Bass, 1996.

National Center for Education Statistics. "Characteristics of the 100 Largest Public Elementary and Secondary School Districts in the United States: 2000–02." U.S. Department of Education, Office of Educational Research, 2002.

National Commission of Excellence in Education. *A Nation at Risk: The Imperative for Educational Reform.* Washington, D.C.: U.S. Government Printing Office, 1983.

Neal, Steve. "Chicago Needs a Lesson on Sharing Spotlight." *Chicago Sun-Times,* May 7, 1999, p. 8.

Needleman, M. L., and C. Needleman. "Organizational Crime: Two Models of Criminogenesis." *The Sociological Quarterly* 20 (1979): 517–28.

Neuman, Johanna. *Lights, Camera, War: Is Media Technology Driving International Politics?* New York: St. Martin's Press, 1996.

New Jersey State Education Department. "Comprehensive Compliance Investigation Report for the Jersey City School District." May 1988.

———. "Comprehensive Compliance Investigation Report for the Paterson School District." April 19, 1991.

———. "Comprehensive Compliance Investigation Report for the Newark School District." July 1994.

New York City Board of Education. "Rules and Regulations for the Custodial Workforce." 1903.
———. School Survey Committee. "Report: Survey of the Public School System." 1929.
———. "Rules and Regulations for the Custodial Force in the Public Schools of New York City." 1977.
———. "A Source Document on Custodians and Custodial Helpers." January 1977.
———. "Memorandum of Understanding between the Board of Education of the City School District of the City of New York and Local 891." 1987.
———. "Memorandum of Understanding between the Board of Education of the City School District of the City of New York and Local 891." 1994.
———. "Procurement of Essential Professional Services in Standard Operating Procedure Manual." Office of Purchasing Management. 2002.
New York City Bronx District Attorney's Office. "Politics in Our School System: A Corrupting Influence." Grand Jury Report. 1986.
New York City Commissioner of Accounts. "Bureau of Supplies, Department of Education, City of New York: Examination of Its Accounts and Methods," by Leonard Wallstein. 1917.
New York City Comptroller. "Board of Education Financial and Operating Practices Pertaining to Custodial Services." 1975.
———. "Report on the Financial and Operating Practices of the Board of Education Pertaining to Custodial Services for the Calendar Year 1975." January 19, 1977.
———. "The School Custodians' Contract: An Evaluation of the Reforms of 1985 and 1988." December 1989.
———. "Audit Report on the New York City Board of Education Controls over Custodial Employees' Work Hours," by Alan Hevesi. March 14, 1996.
———. Office of the Comptroller, Bureau of Management Audit EDP Audit Division. "Data Integrity and Reliability of Board of Education Personnel/Payroll Computer Records." Audit 7A95-108, by Alan Hevesi. June 24, 1996.
———. "Audit Report on the New York City Board of Education Controls over Custodial Hiring Practices and Use of Separate Bank Accounts." June 27, 1996.
New York City Council. "School Maintenance Operations." October 1993.
———. "Frequent Flyers and Big Spenders: Community School Board Spending on Travel, Conference, and Meals." Finance Committee Report. February 10, 1994.
New York City Department of Investigation. William Herlands, commissioner of investigation. "Purchase of School Supplies in New York City: Survey of Bureau of Supplies, Board of Education." Report to Hon. Fiorello La Guardia, mayor of the City of New York, December 31, 1942.
———. Patrick McGinley, commissioner. "The Board of Education of the City of New York: A Review of Management Controls, Conclusions and Recommendations." No. 350/84D. September 1984.
New York City Joint Commission on Integrity in the Public Schools. "Investigating the Investigators." March 1990.
———. Kevin Gill, chairman. "The New Tammany Hall." April 1990.
New York City Mayoral Committee Appointed to Make a Survey of the Bureau of

Construction and Maintenance, Department of Education. "Report to Hon. James J. Walker, Mayor of the City of New York." January 3, 1928.

New York City Office of Administrative Trials and Hearings. In *re Luther Drakeford*. 1995–96.

New York City Office of the Inspector General. BOE Draft Audit Report by Romeo Rancio, Madlyn Korman, and Stephen Obeng. "Compliance Audit of: Contingency Account Budget Code 0944, Object Code 403: for Fiscal Years 1990, 1991, 1992 and 1993." May 10, 1995.

New York City Office of the Mayor. Executive Order no. 11, June 28, 1990.

New York State Commission of Investigation. "An Investigation of Certain Contracting Practices and Procedures of the New York City Board of Education and Related Matters." The Temporary Commission of Investigation of the State of New York, David W. Brown, chairman. October 31, 1975.

New York State Comptroller. "Tentative Draft Audit Report, Bureau of Plant Operation Contracted Custodial Services." June 29, 1976.

———. "Custodial Service at a Certain High School—New York City Board of Education." NYC-4-77. January 28, 1977.

———. "Financial and Operating Practices, Bureau of Plant Operations—Custodial Services, New York City Board of Education: July 1, 1974 to January 31, 1977." NYC-64-77. 1977.

———. "Bureau of Plant Operations—Custodial Services Follow-up New York City Board of Education." NYC-21-81. October 9, 1981.

New York State Education Department. "Findings and Recommendations Based on an Investigation of the Roosevelt Junior/Senior High Schools," by Daniel A. Domenech, superintendent of the Western Suffolk Bureau of Cooperative Educational Services. May 1995.

New York State Education Law, Title II, Article 52-A, at 2590 (1997).

New York State Joint Legislative Committee. "Report and Recommendations of the Joint Legislative Committee to Investigate the Affairs of the City of New York on the Board of Education." February 15, 1922.

Newman, Maria. "Bodies' Discovery Revives 6-Year-Old Murder Case." *New York Times*, February 18, 1995, p. 25, col. 5.

Nicodemus, Charles. "3 Other School Officials Faced Recent Trouble." *Chicago Sun-Times*, June 22, 1995, p. 6.

Niskanen, William A. *Bureaucracy and Representative Government*. Chicago: Aldine-Atherton, 1971.

Noonan, John. *Bribes*. New York: Macmillan, 1984.

Oclander, Jorge. "School Billing Racket: Firms, Employees Still Scam System." *Chicago Sun-Times*, May 22, 1996, p. 1.

O'Connor, Matt. "Ex-School Bureaucrat Took Bribes: He Admits Trading Contracts for Favors." *Chicago Tribune*, March 1, 1996, p. N3.

Okrzesik, Daryl, deputy comptroller, Department of Finance, Chicago Public School System. Telephone interview by Lydia Segal for the School Design Project. August 9, 2002.

O'Reilly, Charles A., and Karlene H. Roberts. "Information Filtration in Organizations: Three Experiments." *Organizational Behavior and Human Performance* 11, no. 2 (April 1974): 253–65.

O'Shaughnessy, Patrice. *New York Daily News*, March 5, 1995, p. 4.

Ouchi, William G. "The Relationship between Organizational Structure and Organizational Control." *Administrative Science Quarterly* 22 (1977): 95–113.

————. "Markets, Bureaucracies, Clans." *Administrative Science Quarterly* 25 (1980): 129–41.

————. *Theory Z: How American Management Can Meet the Japanese Challenge.* New York: Addison-Wesley Publishing, 1981.

Ouchi, William G., with Lydia Segal. *Making Schools Work: A Revolutionary Plan to Get Your Children the Education They Need.* New York: Simon and Schuster, forthcoming 2003.

Parker, Faye, director of planning, Edmonton Public Schools. Telephone interview by Lydia Segal for the School Design Project. October 17, 2001.

Paternoster, R., and S. Simpson. "A Rational Choice Theory of Corporate Crime." In *Routine Activity and Rational Choice*, edited by R. V. Clarke and M. Felsen, 37–58. New Brunswick, N.J.: Transaction, 1993.

People v. John Manfredi, 166 A.D.2d 460; 560 N.Y.S.2d 679 (1990), Supreme Court of New York, Appellate Division, Second Department.

People v. Olin Darby, 114 Cal. App. 2d 412 (1952).

Perez-Pena, Richard. "In School Bus Dispute, Focus Shifts from the Drivers to the Companies." *New York Times,* April 23, 1995, sec. 1, p. 39.

Peterson, Iver. "Friend Who Got a School Post Gave Monserrat $3,000 Loan." *New York Times,* October 30, 1975. p. 42.

Peterson, Paul E., editor. *Our Schools and Our Future: Are We Still at Risk?* (An assessment by the Koret task force on K-12 education). Stanford, Calif.: Hoover Institution Press.

Pike, Rayner. "NYC School Phone Bill Lists Porn, Party Line Calls." The Associated Press, October 26, 1989.

Polner, Robert, and Liz Willen. "Power Play Brewing at Ed Board." *New York Newsday,* July 14, 1996, p. A4.

Pressman, Jeffrey, and Aaron Wildavsky. *Implementation.* Berkeley: University of California Press, 1973.

Pristin, Terry. "In Survey, Business Leaders Criticize New York Schools: City Said to Turn Out Poor Job Candidates." *New York Times,* September 28, 1998, Northeast edition, p. A24.

"Prosecutor Charges City School Contractors." *Engineering News-Record* 232, no. 22 (May 30, 1994): 11.

Public Agenda. "Trying to Stay Ahead of the Game: Superintendents and Principals Talk about School Leadership." New York City, November 2001.

Purdy, Matthew, and Maria Newman. "Where Patronage Thrives, Students Lag in Districts." *New York Times,* May 13, 1996, p. A1, col. 1.

Pushkar, Katherine. "The School House Follies." *The Village Voice,* Education Supplement, April 16, 1996, p. 10.

Raab, Selwyn. "School Bus Pacts Go to Companies with Ties to Mob: No Competitive Bidding." *New York Times,* December 26, 1990, p. A1.

————. "Officials Say Bus Concerns Cheat School Board on Fees." *New York Times,* December 27, 1990, p. 3.

————. "School Chief, Now Dead, Is Accused of Stealing." *New York Times,* January 28, 1993, p. B1.

————. "Alfredo Mathew Jr." *New York Times,* January 28, 1993, p. B1, col. 2.

————. "Contractor Known for Work on Schools." *New York Times,* May 20, 1994, p. 2, col. 1.

Raftery, Judith Rosenberg. *Land of Fair Promise: Politics and Reform in Los Angeles Schools, 1885–1941.* Stanford, Calif.: Stanford University Press, 1992.

Rainey, Hal, and Paula Steinbauer. "Galloping Elephants: Developing Elements of a Theory of Effective Government Organizations." *Journal of Public Administration Research and Theory* 9, no. 1 (January 1999): 1–32.

Ranzal, Edward. "Schools Accused on Contract Bids." *New York Times*, August 1, 1976, p. 26.

———. "Handling of School Funds Assailed in Goldin Report." *New York Times*, August 9, 1976, p. 26.

Ravitch, Diane. *The Great School Wars: New York City, 1805–1973.* New York: Basic Books, 1974.

———. *Left Back: A Century of Battles of School Reform.* New York: Simon and Schuster, 2001.

———. "Bust the Monopoly" (op-ed). *New York Daily News*, October 12, 2002.

"Report of the Special Counsel on the Los Angeles Sheriff's Department" (Kolts Commission Report). James G. Kolts, chairman, 1992.

Riley, Pamela A., with Rosemarie Fusano, Larae Munk, and Ruben Peterson. "Contract for Failure: The Impact of Teacher Union Contracts on the Quality of California Schools." Pacific Research Institute for Public Policy, San Francisco. September 2001.

Robbins, Tom, Kevin Flynn, and Joe Calderone. "Ed Board Gets Help on Leases." *New York Daily News*, April 25, 1996, p. 2.

Robinson, Paul H., and Jane A. Grall. "Element Analysis in Defining Criminal Liability." *Stanford Law Review* 35 (1983): 681–762.

Rogers, David, and Norman H. Chung. *110 Livingston Street Revisited: Decentralization in Action.* New York: New York University Press, 1983.

Romzek, Barbara S., and Melvin J. Dubnick. "Accountability in the Public Sector: Lessons from the Challenger Tragedy." *Public Administration Review* 47, no. 3 (May/June 1987): 227–38.

Rose-Ackerman, Susan. *Corruption: A Study in Political Economy.* New York: Academic Press, 1978.

Ross, S. A. "The Economic Theory of Agency: The Principal's Problems." *American Economic Review* 62 1 (May 1973): 134–39.

Rossi, Rosalind. "School Board Tightens Purchasing Procedure." *Chicago Sun-Times,* July 19, 1994, p. 12.

———. "Finance Official Urges Overhaul for Schools: Teachers Would Lose Job Guarantee under Plan." *Chicago Sun-Times,* April 23, 1995, p. 7.

———. "Schools Target 32 for Firing: Biggest Crackdown Ever, Officials Say." *Chicago Sun-Times,* January 23, 1996, p. 1.

———. "Schools Put 40 Vendors on Notice: Vallas to Bar 8 Contractors Suspected of Overcharges." *Chicago Sun-Times,* May 23, 1996, p. 6.

———. "School Engineers Get Warning." *Chicago Sun-Times,* May 25, 1996, p. 4.

———. "Special Unit to Probe School Fraud: Service Bought from State's Attorney." *Chicago Sun-Times,* September 25, 1997, p. 12.

Rossi, Rosalind, and Jorge Oclander. "Scandals' Task Measured in Scandals." *Chicago Sun-Times,* December 3, 1995, p. 13.

Rother, Larry. "Teacher Given a Promotion Says She Gave Chief a Loan." *New York Times,* February 19, 1986, p. B1.

Sabato, Larry. *Feeding Frenzy: How Attack Journalism Has Transformed American Politics.* New York: Free Press, 1991.

Sachs, Susan. "As New York Immigration Thrives, Diversity Widens." *New York Times,* November 8, 1999, Northeast edition, p. A24.

Sack, Kevin. "Cuomo Signs Bill on Control of School Custodians." *New York Times,* November 27, 1993, sec. 1, p. 25.

Schmidt, David. "Planning the P-Card Change." *Controller Magazine,* August 1997, p. 23.

Schmidt, Peter. "Throwing Light on Dark Corners of N.Y.C.'s Bureaucracy." *Education Week on the Web.* September 29, 1993.

Schminke, Marshall. "Considering the Business in Business Ethics: An Exploratory Study of the Influence of Organizational Size and Structure on Individual Ethical Predispositions." *Journal of Business Ethics* 30, no. 4 (April 2001): 375–90.

Schlegel, Kip, and David Weisburd, eds. *White-Collar Crime Reconsidered.* Boston: Northeastern Universitiy Press, 1992.

School Construction Authority, Inspector General. Letter from Carl M. Bornstein, vice president and inspector general of the New York City School Construction Authority, to Lydia Segal, August 16, 2002.

"School Councils Can Meet More Often." *Chicago Tribune,* January 26, 1990, p. C3.

"School Phone Bill Lists Dial-a-porn Calls." *Washington Times,* October 27, 1989, p. D10.

Scott, W. Richard. *Organizations: Rational, Natural, and Open Systems.* 4th ed. Upper Saddle River, N.J.: Prentice-Hall, 1998.

Scott, W. Richard, and John W. Meyer. "Environmental Linkages and Organizational Complexity: Public and Private Schools." In *Comparing Public and Private Schools,* vol. 1, edited by Thomas James and Henry M. Levin, 128–60. New York: Falmer Press, 1988.

"Second School District 9 Board Member Pleads Guilty." United Press International, July 11, 1989.

Segal, Lydia. "Who Really Runs the Schools?" *City Journal* 5, no. 1 (winter 1995): 46–55.

———. "The Pitfalls of Political Decentralization and Proposals for Reform: The Case of the New York City Schools." *Public Administration Review* 57, no. 2 (March/April 1997): 141–49.

———. "Can We Fight the New Tammany Hall? Difficulties of Prosecuting Political Patronage and Suggestions for Reform." *Rutgers Law Review* 50, no. 2 (February 1998): 507–62.

———. "Corruption Moves to the Center: An Analysis of New York's 1996 School Governance Law." *Harvard Journal on Legislation* 36, no. 2 (summer 1999): 323–67.

———. "Roadblocks in Reforming Corrupt Agencies: The Case of the New York City School Custodians." *Public Administration Review* 62 (July/August 2002): 445–60.

Seigel, Max. "2 Are Indicted in Scheme to Get Pay for Teachers Who Had No-Show Jobs." *New York Times,* January 11, 1978, p. 35.

Sheridan, Chris. "It Matters How Schools Are Run." *The Plain Dealer,* March 9, 1997, p. 2E.

Sherman, W. Lawrence. *Scandal and Reform: Controlling Police Corruption.* Berkeley: University of California Press, 1978.

Shin, Paul. "U.S. Students Fail to Make the Grade." *Daily News,* December 6, 2000, p. 8.

Shover, N., and K. M. Bryant. "Theoretical Explanations of Corporate Crime." In *Understanding Corporate Criminality,* edited by M. B. Blankenship, 141–76. New York: Garland, 1993.

Simmons, Jeff. "In the Name of Cleanup, Ed Bd Sweeps Out Secretary." *New York Daily News,* July 18, 1996, p. 12.

Smith, Doug. "Judge Dismisses Charges against School Contractors." *Los Angeles Times,* May 12, 1994, p. B4.

———. "L.A. Schools' Fiscal Watchdog Faces Dismissal." *Los Angeles Times,* August 13, 1998, p. B1.

———. "Study of L.A. District Finds Widespread Weaknesses in Auditing." *Los Angeles Times,* October 16, 1998, p. B3.

———. "School District to Reinstate 5 Blamed in Belmont Fiasco; Education: L. A. Unified Works Out New Assignments, Saying They Were Not among Those 'Most Responsible' for Problems." *Los Angeles Times,* November 10, 2000, p. B2.

Smith, Doug, and Amy Pyle. "Zacarias Considering Defamation Lawsuit." *Los Angeles Times,* September 23, 1999, p. B1.

Smith, Greg. "He Wasn't True to His Schools." *New York Daily News,* January 22, 1994.

Smith, Kevin B., and Kenneth J. Meier. "Politics, Bureaucrats, and Schools." *Public Administration Review* 54, no. 6 (November/December 1994): 551.

Special Commissioner of Investigation for the New York City School District. "An Investigation into the Sex Crime Conviction of Former Personnel Administrator Jerry Olshaker and the Concealment of the Conviction by the Division of Personnel." October 1991.

———. "An Investigation into the Firing of Harmon J. Garvin by Alfredo Mathew, Jr." July 1992.

———. "A System Like No Other: Fraud and Misconduct by New York City School Custodians." November 1992.

———. "Power, Politics, and Patronage: Education in Community School District 12." April 1993.

———. "From Chaos to Corruption: An Investigation into the 1993 Community School Board Election." December 1993.

———. "Paper, Pencils and Planes to the Caribbean: Corruption in the Purchasing of School and Office Supplies." October 1994.

———. "Taking Their Time: An Investigation into BOE Custodial Employee Time Abuse." March 1996.

———. Case no. 97-0520 re Irwin Crespi. January 28, 1999.

———. "Cheating the Children: Educator Misconduct on Standardized Tests." December 1999.

———. "Educator Cheating." May 2000.

Spence, M., and R. Zeckhouser. "Insurance, Information, and Individual Action." *American Economic Review* 61, no. 2 (May 1971): 380–87.

Spencer, B. D., and D. E. Wiley. "The Sense and the Nonsense of School Effectiveness." *Journal of Policy Analysis and Management* 1 (1981): 43–52.

Spielman, Fran, and Rosalind Rossi. "Ex-Reporter Appointed Top School Investigator." *Chicago Sun-Times,* September 3, 1998, p. 18.

Stanbury, William, and Fred Thompson. "Toward a Political Economy of Government Waste: First Step, Definitions." *Public Administration Review* 55, no. 5 (September/October 1995): 418–27.

Stancik, Edward F. Guest lecture at John Jay College of Criminal Justice, City University of New York, March 8, 2001.

State of New York. "Report and Recommendations of the Joint Legislative Committee to Investigate the Affairs of the City of New York on the Board of Education." February 15, 1922.

State of New York Moreland Act Commission on New York City Schools. "Building Better Schools: A Critical Examination of How New York City Builds and Maintains Its Public Schools." Roslynn R. Mauskopf, chair, August 2002.

Steffins, Lincoln. *Shame of Cities*. New York: Peter Smith, 1948.

Steinberg, Jacques. "Crew Seeks to Overhaul New York City School Bureaucracy." *New York Times*, March 5, 1996, p. B2.

————. "School Board to Remove Its Secretary, a Bane to Chancellors." *New York Times*, July 17, 1996, p. B1.

Strahler, Steven R. "So Long, Pershing Road." *Crains Chicago Business*, August 7, 1995, p. 1.

Sullivan, John. "School Vendors Charged with Price Fixing." *New York Times*, June 2, 2000, p. B3.

Sullivan, Ronald. "Jury Convicts Ex-Principal in Drug Case." *New York Times*, January 27, 1990, p. A5.

Sutherland, Edwin. *White-Collar Crime*. New York: Dryden Press, 1949.

"Test Scores Show Dist. 29 Needs a Super." *New York Newsday*, October 25, 2001, p. A42.

Thompson, Dennis. *Political Ethics and Public Choice*. Cambridge, Mass.: Harvard University Press, 1987.

————. *Ethics in Congress*. Washington, D.C.: The Brookings Institution, 1995.

Thurow, Lester C. *Head to Head: The Coming Economic Battle among Japan, America, and Europe*. New York: William Morrow, 1992.

Tierney, John. "Money Per Pupil Is an Incomplete Response." *New York Times*, June 21, 2000, p. B4.

Tobier, Emanuel. "New York City's Public Schools: The Facts about Spending and Performance." *Civic Bulletin* 26 (May 2001): 1–4.

Traub, James. "In Theory: A School of Your Own." *New York Times*, April 4, 1999, sec. 4A, p. 30, col. 1.

Triant, William. "Autonomy and Innovation: How Do Massachusetts Charter Schools Principals Use Their Freedom?" Thomas B. Fordham Foundation, Washington, D.C., December 2001. Available at http://www.edexcellence.net/cgi-bin/search/search.cgi?terms=triant.

Trounson, Rebecca, and Melanie Markley. "Prosecutors Criticize Cost, Quality of HISD Theft Probe." *Houston Chronicle*, April 3, 1992, p. A1.

Tullock, Gordon. *The Politics of Bureaucracy*. Washington, D.C.: Public Affairs Press, 1965.

Tyack, David. *The One Best System: A History of American Urban Education*. Cambridge, Mass.: Harvard University Press, 1974.

Tyack, David, and Larry Cuban. *Tinkering toward Utopia: A Century of Public School Reform*. Cambridge, Mass.: Harvard University Press, 1995.

Tyack, David, and Elisabeth Hansot. *Managers of Virtue: Public School Leadership in America, 1820–1980*. New York: Basic Books, 1982.

Tyre, Peg. "Officials Indicted in Bribe Probe." *Newsday*, May 20, 1994, p. A7.

U.S. Department of Education. "The Third International Mathematics and Science Study (TIMSS) and Third International Mathematics and Science Study—Repeat (TIMSS-R)," by Cynthia A. Tananis, Steven J. Chrostowski, Nancy R. Bunt, Marcia M. Seeley, and Louis Tamler. Southwest Pennsylvania Regional Benchmarking Report, TIMSS, 1999; "Eighth Grade Mathematics and Science: Achievement for a Workforce Region in a National and International Context." International Study Center, Lynch School of Education, Boston College. Available at http://nces.ed.gov/timss.

U.S. Government Accounting Office. "Performance Budgeting: Initial Experiences under the Results Act in Linking Plans with Budgets." GAO/AIMD/GGD-99-67. April 12, 1999.

Van Meter, D. S., and C. E. Van Horn. "The Policy Implementation Process: A Conceptual Framework." *Administration and Society* 6, no. 4 (1975): 445–87.

Vander Weele, Maribeth. "Schools Feel OT Pinch: Private Custodial Pacts Studied." Schools in Ruins series. *Chicago Sun-Times,* April 29, 1991, p. 1.

———. "Overtime for Maintenance Staff at City Schools Tops $6 Million." *Chicago Sun-Times,* September 11, 1991, p. 35.

———. *Reclaiming Our Schools: The Struggle for Chicago School Reform.* Chicago: Loyola University Press, 1994.

Vander Weele, Maribeth, inspector general, Chicago Board of Trustees, Chicago Board of Education. Telephone interview by Lydia Segal. October 27, 2000.

Vaughan, Diane. *Controlling Unlawful Organizational Behavior: Social Structure and Corporate Misconduct.* Chicago: University of Chicago Press, 1983.

Viteritti, Joseph. *Across the River: Politics and Education in the City.* New York: Holmes and Meier, 1983.

Vold, George B., and Thomas J. Bernard. *Theoretical Criminology.* 3d ed. New York: Oxford University Press, 1986.

Wally, S., and J. R. Baum. "Personal and Structural Determinants of the Pace of Strategic Decision Making." *Academy of Management Journal* 37 (1994): 932–56.

Walton, Mary. *The Deming Management Methods.* New York: Perigee Books, 1986.

Weber, Max. "Bureaucracy." In *From Max Weber: Essays in Sociology,* edited by H. H. Gerth and C. W. Mills, 196–244. New York: Oxford University Press, 1946.

Weick, Karl E. "Educational Organizations as Loosely Coupled Systems." *Administrative Science Quarterly* 21 (1976): 1–19.

Weiss, Murray. "Ex-Queens School Boss Targeted in Kickback Probe." *New York Post,* September 28, 2000, p. 4.

———. "5 Rosedale Homes Focus of Probe." *New York Post,* September 28, 2000, p. 4.

"What's Up at the Docks?" (editorial). *New York Daily News,* December 13, 2001, p. 56.

Wheeler, Stanton, and Mitchell Rothman. "The Organization as Weapon in White-Collar Crime." *Michigan Law Review* 80 (1982): 1403–26.

White, John H., and Ana Mendieta. "Clemente 'Fraud' Found: Report: Poverty Funds Spent Unwisely." *Chicago Sun-Times,* November 23, 1998, p. 1.

Wildavsky, Aaron. *The Politics of the Budgetary Process.* Boston: Little, Brown and Co., 1974.

Willen, Liz. "Ultimatum on Principal." *New York Newsday,* July 29, 1994, p. A26.

———. "School Aide's Suite Deal: Crew's Former Spokesman Stayed Free at Swanky Hotel." *New York Newsday,* June 14, 1996, p. A2.

Williamson, Oliver. *Corporate Control and Business Behavior: An Inquiry into the Effects of Organization Form on Enterprise Behavior.* Englewood Cliffs, N.J.: Prentice-Hall, 1970.

———. *Markets and Hierarchy: Analysis and Antitrust Implications.* New York: Free Press, 1975.

———. "Transaction Cost Economics and Organization Theory." In *The Handbook of Economic Sociology,* edited by Neil J. Smelser and Richard Swedberg, 77–107. Princeton, N.J.: Princeton University Press and Russell Sage Foundation, 1994.

Wilson, James Q. "Corruption: The Shame of the States." *Public Interest* 2 (1966): 28–38.

———. *Thinking about Crime.* Rev. ed. New York: Vintage Books, 1983.

———. *Bureaucracy: What Government Agencies Do and Why They Do It.* New York: Basic Books, 1989.

Wohlstetter, Priscilla, and Karen McCurdy. "The Link between School Decentralization and School Politics." *Urban Education* 25, no. 4 (1991): 391–414.

Wolfinger, Raymond E. "Why Political Machines Have Not Withered Away and Other Revisionist Thoughts." *Journal of Politics* 34 (1972): 365.

Wraith, Ronald, and Edgar Simpkins. *Corruption in Developing Countries.* New York: W. W. Norton, 1963.

Wyatt, Edward. "Success of City School Pupils Isn't Simply a Money Matter." *New York Times,* June 14, 2000, p. A1.

———. "School Board to Turn to Outside Advisers." *New York Times,* September 26, 2000, p. B3.

Yukl, Gary. *Leadership in Organizations.* Upper Saddle River, N.J.: Prentice-Hall, 1998.

Zernike, Kate. "DeNucci Orders Audit of Schools in Lawrence." *Boston Globe,* January 7, 1997, p. A1.

Zook, Jim. "6 Ex-HISD Workers Fired in Theft Probe Sue District." *Houston Chronicle,* June 11, 1992, p. A34.